Make Over Your Man

Make Over Your Man

A Woman's Guide to Dressing Any Man in Her Life

LLOYD BOSTON

with Annmarie Dodd

Broadway Books New York

BROADWAY

MAKE OVER YOUR MAN
Copyright © 2002 by Lloyd Boston. All rights reserved.
No part of this book may be reproduced or transmitted in any form or by any means, electronic or
mechanical, including photocopying, recording, or by any information storage and retrieval system, without
written permission from the publisher. For information, address Broadway Books, a division of
Random House, Inc., 1540 Broadway, New York, NY 10036.

Broadway Books titles may be purchased for business or promotional use or for special sales.
For information, please write to: Special Markets Department, Random House, Inc.,
280 Park Avenue, New York, NY 10017.

PRINTED IN THE UNITED STATES OF AMERICA

BROADWAY BOOKS and its logo, a letter B bisected on the diagonal,
are trademarks of Broadway Books, a division of Random House, Inc.
Visit our website at www.broadwaybooks.com

First edition published December 2002

Designed by Terry Karydes, Ralph Fowler, and Lloyd Boston
Photography by Len Prince

Tommy Hilfiger U.S.A. is a proud supporter of MAKE OVER YOUR MAN.
TOMMY, TOMMY HILFIGER, TOMMY JEANS, TOMMY GIRL, HILFIGER ATHLETICS, tommy.com,
TH, Flag Logo, and Crest Design are trademarks of Tommy Hilfiger Licensing, Inc.

Library of Congress Cataloging-in-Publication Data
Boston, Lloyd.
Make over your man : the woman's guide to dressing any man in her life / Lloyd Boston ;
photographs by Len Prince ; foreword by Tommy Hilfiger.
p.   cm.
ISBN 0-7679-1036-2 (alk. paper)
1. Men's clothing.   2. Grooming for men.   I. Title
TT618.B67 2002
646'.32—dc21
2002026128

1 3 5 7 9 10 8 6 4 2

For Lynell Boston-Kollar, my mom and everything.

For Leonard Bridges, my "Budini Brown."

And for my Uncle Bob, I miss you.

Contents

Acknowledgments

TO GOD BE THE GLORY FOR THE SUCCESS OF THIS PROJECT! WHEN I WONDER IF I AM WORTHY OF your love, and others may say that I am not, you bring me blessings such as this (and the wonderful people involved), and I thank you first and foremost for this and all of your abundant blessings.

Thanks off the bat to Janet Hill, my editor par excellence—our "man" is finally made over! We did it through some very scary happenings in New York and the world around us, and I will always thank you for your extended patience, genuine warmth, and deep intellect and foresight. Right down to clasping the final cuff link, you remained by my side and saw that the book was smashing! And the amazing team at Doubleday Broadway: Stephen "Off the Cuff" Rubin, Michael Palgon, Gerry Howard, John Fontana, Jackie Everly, Suzanne Herz, Catherine Pollock, Brian Jones, Kim Cacho, Terry Karydes, Don Weisberg, Melanie Greco, Jennie Richie, Lori Zarahan, Emma Bolton. Thanks to Ralph Fowler for a stylish design! Last but certainly not least I'd like to extend a hearty thanks to Rebecca Holland for the amazing things you did to get this book out. Thanks to everyone for the warmest of welcomes to your phenomenal family of stellar authors and respected imprints. I am truly honored to finally be on Broadway!

Faith Childs, my visionary and incredible literary agent, we did it again! Your quiet elegance and style, stalwart work ethic, masterful communication acumen, and simple clarity continue to move me ahead with confidence and pride. Countless thanks.

Lynell Boston-Kollar, my mom and best friend, simple thanks will never express how indebted I am for your vision and sacrifice for me since day one—and especially while creating *Make Over Your Man*. And although I don't know all the details of your work and sacrifice in our early days, I do know that *we* are here in the light today because *you* would never accept anything less than the best for me. I love you, Mom.

Tommy Hilfiger, my industry "dad," friend, and supporter of both of my books, I owe so much to you, it's hard to mutter a common thank you. Before I could even recognize my place in fashion—you began carving it. And as I stumbled, experimented, and created over the years, you provided the first aid, the canvas, and the gallery. I am forever grateful to you for leveling the playing field and allowing me to run. *You* really are the best! Not to mention your right-hand, the cool, calm, and quietly stylish Joel Horowitz—so glad to have you in my corner all these years. Many, many thanks!

Peter Connolly, my friend, mentor, and president of worldwide marketing/communications at

Tommy Hilfiger. You are definitely one of the industry's most extraordinary marketing impresarios with an unmatched vision, which you articulate and execute as effortlessly as breathing. From the exposure to E! Networks, to backing both of my books, many heartfelt thanks for trusting and believing in my evolving style philosophy and budding lifestyle brand.

Len Prince, my friend and photographer extraordinaire, thanks so much for your incredible time, care, and patience with each and every original image that we created together for this book. Your artful skill is only exceeded by your spirit and gentility—bringing out the absolute best in anything from a superstar celebrity to an ordinary men's shoe. Now it's your turn, once again!

The entire NBC *Today Show* family, especially my extraordinary key producer Alicia Ybarbo and former executive producer Kim Bondy, who together opened the door and gave me a chance to speak style—you both rock! And the top-shelf personalities, Katie Couric, Matt Lauer, Al Roker, Ann Curry, Soledad O'Brien, David Bloom, and Janice Huff, you are a wellspring of inspiration and support; executive producers Jonathan Wald and Don Nash; senior producers Betsey Alexander, Kim Gerbasi, and Susan Dutcher; and segment producers Beth Decker, Jeremy Blacklowe, Pam Kawi, and Dee Dee Alexander, I thank you for honoring my style vision and seeing fit for America to do the same on a regular basis. A big thanks also to *Today Show* publicist Allison Gollust and Dan McCormack and Meredith Klein in NBC legal for your time and care as well.

Style Network, my new cable television home and west-coast family, I am so thrilled to be under your global media umbrella! The ultrastylish Style team led by Mark Sonnenberg, Mindy Herman, Ken Bettsteller, Stephen Croncota, and Danilla Koverman; as well as Jamie Glasson-Pergament, Jennifer Ferraro, Andrea Pilat, Maggie Lehan, Shannon Bernbeck, and the entire production staff—I'm beyond excited to be in your hands. A huge thanks also to the incredible Dan Gibson and Jeff Hobbs in casting, and Marta Tracy for simply giving me a chance to shine!

Craig Rose, my chosen brother for life and project director for both of my books, thank you for once again believing in my seedling vision and sacrificing a chunk of your own life to see it through on all fronts as my right hand—as if it were your very own. This, *our* second book, is the true testament of our unique and visceral connection. From securing the celebrity support to the seemingly effortless production behind each and every image, without you, there would be nothing on any of these pages. Keep on truckin'!

To my stellar cast of stylish celebrity friends, I sincerely thank you for trusting my vision and lending your time, support, and image to help any woman (or man) who picks up this book. Ginny and Tiki Barber, Lisa and Doug Ling, Patti LaBelle and Zuri Edwards, Cynthia Rowley and Alan Cumming, Elisabeth Filarski and Tim Hasselbeck, Elizabeth Parkinson and Scott Wise, Bobbi Brown and Steven Plofker, Kimora Lee Simmons, Tyra and Don Banks, Star Jones, Tamara Spinner and Brent Zachary.

Sharon Pendana, my kindred style sister and contributing stylist, they don't call you "Little Magic" for nothing! I remain spellbound by your innate sense of *authentic* style (not fashion), and all of its obscure nuances and references that you have so easily translated for me through simple pieces of clothing in this book. Your talent runs deep on the backs of everyone and on each page within this book—and I couldn't be more proud of our collaboration.

Annmarie Dodd, my right-hand and writing partner, thanks a million for burning the midnight oil right along with me—in an attempt to make my oftentimes bold and zany style philosophy make sense for real women. And this you did with ease and persistence—quietly adding your own spin, which was an education for *this* man of style as well. You are the best!

Leonard Bridges, my style impresario and primary fashion mentor. You are one of the fashion industries' brightest designers and a modern style icon. Thanks for being mine alone.

E. Lynn Harris, my big brother in life and literary pursuits, thanks for the love and late-night chats, which always hold me together, and for connecting me to Doubleday. You are a constant source of inspiration and a blessing in my life.

Westin Hill, my fellow Gemini and set designer of choice, much thanks for jumping city to city creating the clean, lean, minimal look that I always envisioned for this book—between your films and other more fabulous shoots. Your creative eye for nuance and verve is done so effortlessly, one wonders how to ever do it without you.

Naima "Nat" Turner, my protégé and flawless assistant, thanks again and again for keeping my life in check amidst the rigors of balancing my bicoastal television work, personal appearances, and writing. For this, and for your incredibly thorough and scholarly style research, this book is solid and truly successful—before the first copy ever leaves a bookstore.

Margarita Corporan, my new friend and photo research editor, "muchas gracias" for patiently dealing with me in "shifts" and unearthing historical photographic images that celebrate the book's mission with balance and a touch of whimsy. Your book is next!

Beth L. White, another new friend and illustrator of choice, I praise you for your beautiful work in illustrating the original necktie images for the book. You are so talented and skilled with your stroke, and I am honored to have your hand in my dream. Thanks!

Bethann Hardison, my industry "mom" and television agent supreme, I love that we connect as we do. Your rich and sage history within the world of global fashion and sharp savvy on matters of young, hip entertainment are a rare combination that leads and inspires me more than you'll ever know. Thanks for keeping me on the rise!

Jen Davidson and Beth Herbst of REACH, my brilliant television style coordinators and newfound friends, a sincere thanks for your extended support while writing this book—keeping me looking fresh and on-the-moment in millions of homes in TV land. You two are geniuses!

Daryl Pendana, my "brother-in-law" in style, and filmmaker, thank you for documenting each step of *Make Over Your Man* beautifully and with a technical knowledge and integrity that rivaled any big-budget motion picture. Your humor kept us all afloat, and I thank you.

To my talented team of male groomers, make-up artists, barbers, and hair stylists: Loretta Alston, Jake Bailey, Bobbi Brown, Johnny Gentry, Elena George, Oscar James, Jay Manuel, Brian Magallones, Matin Maulawizada, Christopher Michael, Terence "T-Nice" Payne, Gina Picone, Anthony Sorensen, Kim Weinstein, Barry White, Shanon Grey Williams. Without you, we'd be looking at the same ol' men in new clothes—and we know the power of being polished. You gave both my celebrity and "real" men the royal treatment from head to toe. I thank you all for completing each makeover with detailed care and beauty—as any woman would do for the man she loves.

Thanks to the male models who accepted style makeovers with grace: Brian Lee Allen, Click, Christina Ambers, Parts (for your perfect cover hands), Tre Bratt (TLG), Kevin Bulla (Click), Chris Comfort (Ford), Mike Dale (Click), Charles Deraczunas (TLG), Peter Hurley (Wilhelmina), Sean James (Ford), Will Lamay (NY Models), James Magee (Click), Rob O'Brien (TLG), Daryl Pendana, Todd Reigler (Ford), Damon Weeks (Next), Brian Wince (NY Models). And a big thanks as well to the savvy ladies of my round-table discussion: Diem Boyd, Ginger Brang, Catherine Fisher, Alice Flynn, Erica Kennedy, Lynell Boston-Kollar, Elena Romero, Bonnie Trompeter.

To all of my incredible research and style assistants: E. J. Akbar, Sean Allison, Lois Barrett, Anthony Q. Bell, Nicole Brewer, G. Boyd Caldwell, Capree Feliciano, Jennifer Griffin, Calvin Moore, Kwame Muhammed, Stephanie Scott, Danny Suggs, Naima Turner, and Caryl McGill for the speedy and precise transcriptions. Thanks also to Joan Moore and Jessica Dolan, The Everett Collection.

Much thanks to each and every designer, label, brand, publicist, and fashion public relations firm, particularly George Kolosa, Jack Rich, Caren Bell, Paula Rosado, Kristy Tatem, Trudy Bird, Carolyn Iglesias, Meredith Leiberman, Samantha Truedsson, Sheila Cox, and Keith Peterson of Tommy Hilfiger; Paul Wilmot and his team at Paul Wilmot Communications, especially Jill Gruetzmacher; Judith Agasim and Jason Grant of Judith Agasim and Associates; Mona Reilly and Huey Roberts at Paul Stuart; Martin Bradshaw and all of the wonderful folks at Canali; Emilio Fields at Andrew Marc. Thanks also to my expert voices: Stephen Amos, Kenneth Cole, Martin Cooper, Jeff Danzer, Ron Donovan, Jack Ferrari, Randy Heil, Dave Lackie, Joann Lee, Evelyn Meeks, Karen Murray, Jeffrey Savitch, Bari Seiden, Deborah A. Simmons, M.D., Audrey Smaltz, Matthew Jordan Smith, Gregory Sovell, Matt Teri, William H. L. Thomas, Gordon Thompson III, Barry White, John T. Yunis, Miriam Zoaui.

To my awesome family, the entire Mason-Johnson clan, Whitehead-Bostons, as well as my chosen family Cynde Watson, Sean Allison, Darian Trotter, Julia Chance, Gordon Chambers; and constant supporters Matthew Jordan Smith, Quincy Jones, Andy Hilfiger, Michelle Edwards, Jules Kollar, Angela Webb, Curtis Jeffrey, Angela Bolin, Tyrone Lewis, Emil Wilbekin, Stephen Barr, Charles Stephens,

Christopher Dyson, Christopher McDonald, Allen Harvey, Ludlow Beckett, Erica Kennedy, Jacqui Smith-Roye, Lolita Mitchell, Ann Marcus, Boris Kodjoe, Clayton and Toyin Hunter, Eugene and Clarise Lee, Jakki Taylor, Sam Jackson, LaTanya Richardson, Zöe Jackson, Jim De Yonker and Ché Graham at Lux Studios, Mavis Boston, Secunda Anderson, Gina Avery, Jashod Belcher, Dee Collins, Armstead Edwards, Lauren Kucerak, Holly Levee, Carolyn London, Beth Mann, Angela Niles, Michelle Perez, Pat Durkin, Sam Fine, Thelma Golden, Dr. Howard Schultz, Audrey Smaltz, Eleanor Watson, and Edward Wilkerson.

Last, but certainly not least, the greatest thanks to my budding fan base who tune into both the NBC *Today Show* and Style Network and log onto Lloydboston.com regularly. Like me, you look for style in simple terms—and I thank you for looking to me for solutions that actually work! Stay close.

Make Over Your Man

Foreword by Tommy Hilfiger

I'VE KNOWN LLOYD BOSTON SINCE HE WAS A STUDENT AT MOREHOUSE COLLEGE. WE MET briefly at a media appearance in Atlanta. After we talked a few minutes about his future in design, I gave him my card and told him that if he ever wanted to intern with my company, I would have a spot for him. The next day, I got a call from Lloyd and that was that—he worked for me for more than ten years.

So Lloyd began his career while still in college as my company's first intern. After he graduated, we hired him as a graphic designer to help develop the creative elements of our advertising. As our company grew, Lloyd worked his way up the ladder, honing skills that would serve him throughout his career. In his tenure with my company, he truly came to understand what I was trying to achieve, which was to communicate the power of classic clothes to people in a fresh, modern way. Lloyd became my vice president of art direction and wore many other hats, including organizing my fashion shows, casting models, and selecting and styling the clothes for our photo shoots.

I was very happy for Lloyd when he decided to forge his own career in fashion. I knew he would be successful. Not only did he publish his own book, *Men of Color: Fashion, History, Fundamentals,* which made the *Los Angeles Times* bestseller list, but he also made important contributions to broadcast media. He became a fashion contributor at NBC's *Today Show* and is a correspondent on the Style Network for E! Entertainment. His talents certainly have not gone unnoticed: New York's Fashion Group International nominated him for the very prestigious Rising Star In Fashion Communications Award.

His latest book is a natural progression in his passion for helping people understand and master the art of personal style. Not only is it an opportunity for a woman to understand what to look for in a quality suit for her man, but it is an education in understanding the distinct difference between shopping *with* him versus *for* him. With nearly $30 billion generated annually on men's clothing by way of purchases made by women, it is obvious that style and fashion play some part in all of our relationships. The power of style exists in all of us. Whether you use this book as your own secret style weapon or as a guide that you and the man in your life explore together, *Make Over Your Man* provides classic style information with a twist. How you use it is up to you.

Over the years Lloyd and I have developed a friendship, a sense of trust, and a great working relationship. We share an understanding of the importance of timeless fashion classics as the building blocks of a great wardrobe. Lloyd and I also have a common bond in our desire to sift through the trends and help people get back to the basics. This is something that Lloyd, as a fashion editor and a communicator, does so well. You will clearly see Lloyd's ability to make fashion accessible, to shed its pretensions, and to show that being stylish can be fun and easy. Good luck!　　　　　—Tommy Hilfiger

Do Try This at Home

LET'S FACE IT, LADIES, MOST OF YOU AT SOME POINT OR ANOTHER HAVE WANTED TO MAKE OVER your man, whether it was your husband, boyfriend, best friend, or even your dad, son, or favorite uncle. Not change him completely, but simply make him over. Come on, admit it. A new coat, a different shirt, or something other than a pair of khakis. It's pretty clear that most men don't think about their personal style—it's not their thing. And that's not going to change, despite whatever "men's lib" thinking may be in current fashion. What *can* change, however, with the help of this book—and you—is the way a man shops for clothes, organizes his wardrobe, and starts to imagine himself in a polished and stylish light. It's my hope that the term "getting dressed up" will have new meaning for you both once you're finished reading this book, and that you will understand what makes the well-dressed men you've always admired. How sweet it will be when you look over and realize that your man looks as good and as stylish as you always knew he could.

Most women understand how to imagine an outfit, select the clothes and accessories, and pull together a great ensemble. It's a practice many of you have nurtured throughout your lives. From that first special-occasion dress (I'm sure you remember just what dress and shoes you wore, and which lipstick) to the important events in your life, like your prom, wedding, or your first job, women's lives are punctuated by all kinds of style moments, fashion dos, and fashion faux pas.

Most men, on the other hand, have a very different relationship with clothing and style, and it usually boils down to three very essential points: (1) Comfort, (2) Shop only when necessary, and (3) Don't throw anything away, because you may need it later.

Make Over Your Man will not offer you those useless head-to-toe prescriptions for outfit "solutions" that end up looking good only on a model. Think of this book as a handy tool that will help you to decide, shape, and craft a new image for your favorite man—one that will match his budget and lifestyle and, most important, your life together. By simply embracing a few new essential pieces of clothing, possibly fine-tuning a grooming regimen, and improving or adjusting his dressing habits, your man will learn that style is just another form of self-expression.

Your guy's style isn't likely to change overnight, but this book will serve as a gentle helping hand that will get you results you'll both love.

Yes, he might remember the day he purchased his first suit as more of a burden than a blissful day at a boutique. The sooner he got back into his clothes in the dressing room, the better. We can assume that he followed his dad's path, because he had his own similar experiences—from renting a tuxedo for his prom to selecting the same sort of rented tux for the biggest day of his life, his wedding day. Resisting dapper dress has become a ritual for so many American men.

We've strayed such a long way in such a short amount of time. Today's men are so unlike the elegant men of the 1940s and '50s who wouldn't think of leaving the house without a suit, a tie, and a fedora. Today's men, unlike their fathers and grandfathers, are the products of the 1960s sportswear revolution and all of its lax rules—from the birth of the 1960s leisure suit to the dawn of the 1980s sport-jerseys-as-clothing craze. (Ironically, Michael Jordan, the man behind that craze, would never let himself be caught off court in his basketball jersey and baggy shorts.) Men have been given a license to dress "down." No apologies.

But there are exceptions to this assessment. Certainly, not all men hate getting dressed up. There are many men who still believe in the power of a quality well-tailored suit, custom dress shirts with French cuffs and cuff links, and a wonderful pair of dress shoes with leather soles. And these are probably the same men who know the difference between a Windsor knot and a four-in-hand—as well as how and when to tie them and with what collar. But this man is not your ordinary Joe—far from it. This man is evolved in matters sartorial, and most likely prides himself on being a cultural, business, or political leader in your community. He is the "leading-man" type that most women wish for and most average Joes secretly long to be.

Who doesn't want to walk into a room and be lauded for looking great? Getting to this kind of image takes work and practice; most people don't realize that style cannot be purchased with the swoosh of a credit card. It is a practice that must be adopted as a way of life. To be christened "stylish," your every detail must take on new life—from what you wear to the pen you write with and even your key chain. And more than a business card, a car, or a firm handshake—great style is the most important nonverbal cue you have. It speaks volumes about you and your aspirations before you open your mouth and utter a single word.

So in preparation for making over your man, as my book promises, I want to offer you a realistic point of view on the task at hand and your expectations. Know from the start that you may not end up with that "perfect" leading man on your arm, a man who dons the right clothing and accessories from head to toe just for you. And here's the reason: Change is good, but most men do not willingly welcome it.

He probably believes: "Hey, she's always loved me with these same clothes—what's so wrong with them now?" The answer is usually painfully clear to everyone but the style-challenged man. Poor guy. Most regular guys put equal value on dressing to be comfortable and impressing women. So try and help him understand that accepting your advice on what looks best really makes a huge amount of sense and eliminates the guesswork involved in appealing to you.

I hope that this book helps you develop an honest and open style dialogue with the man you choose to make over. I've recruited some of my celebrity friends—including makeup mogul Bobbi Brown, Patti LaBelle, NFL star Tiki Barber, *The View*'s Lisa Ling, and supermodel Tyra Banks—to help readers go through the makeover process with some faces and names that can be trusted. Aside from learning all the details about fabrics, colors, silhouettes, and clothing labels in this how-to guide, I'd like you to develop an effective and unfaltering eye for good style. If you do, you'll be able to fuse your newfound knowledge of menswear in other areas of fashion.

When I started this book, I realized that I would be able to provide an invaluable and hard-to-find service and resource to women who were brave enough to take matters of men's style into their own hands. Many of you may wonder: What makes me the person to offer this advice?

The answer is simple: I love clothes, and I love helping average people look and feel their best through clothing. I've been obsessed with clothes for as long as I can remember, fascinated by garments, accessories, and, most of all, what exactly inspires people to choose what they wear on any given day or occasion.

The idea for this book came from conversations I had with some of my female friends who said they wished their guy would dress a bit like me. I've always been honored by such comments and found that compliments, questions on designer or manufacturer origin, or simply noting that one owns something identical, or similar, to what someone else is wearing can turn a conversation to clothes. But I've always wanted to go a little deeper, and that's my goal for this book.

I feel that my calling in life—even though some find fashion and style to be trite—is to help average people understand high style and humanize its mystique. It's an intimidating world, and I like to think of myself as a "concierge" of sorts to the oftentimes insular, but wildly fascinating, world of fashion that I inhabit. Thanks to the success of my first book, *Men of Color: Fashion, History, Fundamentals,* I've had the wonderful opportunity in recent years to follow my calling and offer style advice to millions of people as a guest on national television shows like ABC's *The View,* as a contributor on NBC's *Today Show,* and currently as a host on the Style Network. I like to offer viewers the same knowledge and confidence that designers extend to their VIP clients.

One general tip before you begin: Take baby steps and validate each change that your man makes with lots of love. Remember that you're probably starting by undoing a lifetime of nonchalance and bad clothing and dressing habits. Think of yourself as style training wheels—so easy does it! And finally, remember that the road can get a little bumpy at times, so keep a vision of the way you want to ultimately see your man. Remember: The first makeover is always the hardest. I guarantee that you won't regret *this* trip.

Happy styling!

Lloyd Boston

Make Over Tips from Real Women...

All men are not built the same and cannot wear the same style clothes.   *—Nadja*

Look at your shoes, we do!   *—Nancy*

Some men have errors that I would eliminate altogether: 1) walking with an apelike gait; 2) wearing their trousers beneath their posteriors; 3) allowing loose hairs to grow out of visible orifices and brows; and 4) wearing toupees that look like teepees!   *—Janice*

I can't stand to see black pants and black shoes with white socks.   *—Laurie*

Pedicures. Pedicures. Pedicures. Why? Because women love men to wear sandals too! (And please wear them without socks.)   *—Ayanna*

I simply wish that men would lose those wool socks and find some nice men's hose to complement their outfits.   *—Debbie*

Three wrong moves: Ties that are too short. Socks that are too short. And dress shirts with short sleeves.   *—Audrey*

Men's clothes are either too loose, or too tight. Find a happy medium.   *—Dyanna*

Listen to women's suggestions, and for goodness sake match your socks to your pants, not your shirt.   *—Michelle*

I hate a raggedy belt, it's like a cheap handbag!   *—Cynde*

Men always pull out their comfortable shoes that they think go with everything— but they really don't.   *—Alice*

Most guys should just hand over the money and let the women in their lives do the shopping!   *—Rhoda*

Women have their eyes arched, nails done, and hair styled. So why shouldn't a man make every effort to groom his facial hair and keep his nails manicured?   *—Michelle*

Let him think that a new style is his idea.   *—Lawrine*

Women would love it if more men put more of an effort into their appearance. We do it, our men should too!   *—Yasmin*

The dreaded COMB OVER! Men need to realize that most women would prefer to see them completely bald. Just get over it—we love you as you are.   *—Lawrine*

Women's Roundtable

BEFORE THE MAKEOVER PROCEEDINGS BEGIN, LET'S EAVESDROP ON A CONVERSATION BETWEEN eight women (including my mother, Lynell Boston-Kollar!) and hear what women really think about men's style (or sometimes lack of style!). I gathered these ladies together because they have candid and sometimes funny views, and what they say should confirm this for you: You are not alone, and your guy is not the only one who needs a little style TLC. Women of all ages and walks of life step in and offer the men in their lives a little guidance with their appearance. And that's an experience shared by Ginger Brang, Erica Kennedy, and Elena Romero, who are in their twenties; Alice Flynn and Diem Boyd, who are in their thirties; Catherine Fisher, who is in her forties; and my mother and Bonnie Trompeter, who are fifty-something baby boomers.

To get the conversation started, I wrote down a handful of questions, dropped them into a glass bowl, and asked each of the women to take her pick. I plugged in a tape recorder and let the conversation take off. Here are the highlights . . .

Elena Romero, Lynell Boston-Kollar, Alice Flynn, Diem Boyd, Catherine Fisher, Ginger Brang, Erica Kennedy and Bonnie Trumpeter.

ALICE FLYNN, senior vice president of design for Tommy Hilfiger's children's collection, dips into the bowl and removes a question: What's the biggest mistake most men make when getting dressed?

BONNIE TROMPETER, model, Ford agency: The biggest mistake my husband makes is not asking me if he's dressed properly. [Laughter] I think men don't think enough about what they're going to wear. They just put everything together and say, "Oh, this is going to be okay." I can explain to him exactly what goes with what.

[Laughter]

LYNELL BOSTON-KOLLAR, president of a real-estate transactions firm, The Lynell Group: Well, I think men start with a piece [of clothing] that they're comfortable with and then try to build around it. Sometimes with that one piece, and the other pieces they throw together with it, men just don't get it.

ELENA ROMERO, associate editor of fashion trade publications *Women's Wear Daily* and *Daily News Record*: I think some men just don't give enough thought to the process of getting dressed. Where am I going today? What's the occasion? What's my mood? They don't think of the complete ensemble. Like Lynell said, men go after that one thing. Maybe he likes shoes a lot, so he'll then work himself up from there, instead of thinking, "Okay, I need everything from a hat to a watch to a belt."

GINGER BRANG, fashion market editor, *Glamour*: I also think that when accessorizing, men don't realize that black belts and black shoes must go together—they can't mix and match their browns and blacks. Dressy occasions also tend to be a problem. Men don't really know what should be worn at a particular time of day, and they need to get that straight.

ERICA KENNEDY, freelance writer: I agree. Many men don't know how to dress for a certain occasion, and they sometimes wear the same shoes they like or their favorite belt but they don't realize that belt does not go with his black-tie outfit. Or those work shoes don't go with black tie. Men get stuck with the one thing that they feel comfortable with.

ALICE: A man complained to me yesterday about his pants not being cuffed and said, "But you know, the outfit was laid out for me, so I went with it." I've never heard of a guy say that his outfit was "laid out." I think if men "laid out" their outfits a little bit more, then they would make less mistakes in getting dressed.

LYNELL: What's the first thing you notice on a man, and why?

DIEM BOYD, Casting Director: I look at his shoes. It's amazing what shoes tell about a person. That little extra step of buying a really nice pair of shoes says a lot about a man and how he thinks of himself.

CATHERINE FISHER, senior vice president, corporate communications, Revlon: I agree. I notice two things actually—shoes and watches. Those seem to tell a lot about a man, and men are somewhat limited by the types of accessories that they can wear. Women have jewelry, and men don't have a lot of the same options. The care that they take in picking out and caring for their shoes and their watches is something that I take notice of. It's usually indicative of their personalities.

GINGER: If a man takes the time to pick out a pair of shoes and will spend a little extra money, then the rest can follow. Also, men will have something dressy on and then they throw, like, a windbreaker over it. [Laughter] I like when they go out and purchase a nice raincoat, trenchcoat, or something more appropriate.

ELENA: An outfit has to have some sort of balance. It either accentuates your personality and where you're going, or it doesn't.

ERICA: The first thing I notice about a guy is how he's dressed. Not one particular thing, but more how he carries himself. I can see a guy in a suit and think that's cute, but I can see a guy in a Sean John sweat suit and think that's really cute, too. I think what a guy wears says a lot about who he is.

ALICE: The first thing I notice about a man is his hands and how well—or not well—they're kept. If a man has well-kept hands, then the rest of his being is well-kept. I think a man who bites his nails or has rough and callused nasty hands—well, probably a part of his life is not together. [Laughter] I don't want him to be overmanicured—just well-groomed, because I think the rest of him will be well-groomed too.

BONNIE: The first thing I notice about a guy—because I look at his face first—is his haircut. I also look to see if he's dressed cleanly, pressed and together. Like Erica said, I don't care if it's a suit or casual clothes, but if it's clean and pressed and goes together, I'm happy.

LYNELL: I check out the overall look. Is it casual? Is it professional? Is it mixed up? Did he lose the plan halfway through? Is he professional on the bottom and then screwed up at the top? And the only detail I notice immediately is the neck. Does he need an edge up? You know, it's the grooming factor. If he's dressed in a suit and his hair is raggedy, he missed the plan.

ELENA: You take thirty minutes to get dressed; your man takes almost sixty minutes. Is this a concern?

[Laughter]

DIEM: God. That might raise a red flag. [Laughter] That's never happened. I've never thought about that.

CATHERINE: It's more the mental flexibility. If a man's a five, but he wants to be a ten, I like that. I wouldn't want to discount somebody who maybe has a wonderful warm heart and a great mind because they're ill dressed. I know we're all guilty of that. You want to have that room for improvement and room for growth. So I'm giving the ideal answer.

GINGER: If a man doesn't care, or isn't into style, then he probably doesn't have the same interests as me. Like being put together and pampering yourself with nice things. After all the other things, like his look, his face, his hair, having everything all together is a great package.

ERICA: It's not even about the clothes. I think the clothes are a reflection of him and his interests and who he is. Upon first impression, if I see a guy wearing tight jeans and cowboy boots, I don't think it's going to work out. [Laughter] I just don't.

ALICE: Whether it's bad or good, every person has a specific style. And I like to understand that person's style. You can always take a style and make it a little bit more expensive version and it looks even that much better. I met someone the other night—it was a first date—and he explained to me over the course of the evening that he had a really hard time getting ready for our date, I think partly because he knew I was in fashion. I said, "You did—really?" And he was in a T-shirt and jeans. And he said, "I never wear jeans. I put on three different pair of pants and this is what I ended up in." It was nice because he had made the effort to try and fix himself up.

BONNIE: Now, who would you consider to be the best-dressed man in America? I love the way Matt Lauer dresses. Every morning I think, "Yes, Matt! You look fabulous!"

GINGER: My favorite is Hamish Bowles from *Vogue* magazine. Hamish is always the most adorable dresser.

ELENA: I'll speak for a distinguished man. I'll say Samuel L. Jackson.

DIEM: I just worship Benjamin Bratt. I love him, the perfect man in every way.

CATHERINE: The first person to pop into my mind is Robert Redford, because he looks wonderful and poised and pulled together when he's very elegantly dressed, like in *The Great Gatsby*, but he can also do cowboy boots and jeans and look kind of wonderful, too.

LYNELL: Although my husband, Jules, always looks great, I'll say Lloyd Boston, my son. [Laughter] My son is the best-dressed man in my life.

The Quiz
How Does His Style Rate?

IT MAY SOUND SIMPLE, BUT "MAKING OVER YOUR MAN" ISN'T ALWAYS AN EASY MISSION FOR A woman. The world isn't so traditional anymore, and modern men want a definite say in how they look—and some guys also want to express how they *feel* about style, and what they like in current fashion. With change comes challenge.

Setting a style transformation in motion begins with an honest look at the man you wish to fine-tune or reinvent. So you'll have to carefully assess his style, fashion habits, and overall tastes. The fifty-question quiz that follows below is the gentle nudge you both need to make him over. Simply answer yes or no to determine the road map you'll need to connect your man with his ideal personal style.

His suits

1. My man owns three or more quality-tailored, traditional business suits.
   ☐ Yes ☐ No
2. In his best-fitting suit, my man looks more like Pierce Brosnan as James Bond than John Goodman as Fred Flintstone.
   ☐ Yes ☐ No
3. My man would rather own one impeccably tailored suit bought at a higher price point than ten so-so suits purchased at a neighborhood discount store.
   ☐ Yes ☐ No
4. My guy wears a suit to more than just a wedding or a funeral.
   ☐ Yes ☐ No
5. My man pays the same care and attention to his suits as he does to the rest of his wardrobe.
   ☐ Yes ☐ No
6. My man's "cool" or "good" suits from the days before we were together are either in the hands of Goodwill or are buried deep in the local landfill.
   ☐ Yes ☐ No
7. When you say "tailor" to my man, he thinks of James, Chuck, or Liz.
   ☐ Yes ☐ No

8. At the last wedding we attended, my man looked as handsome in his suit, in my eyes, as the groom at the altar.

☐ Yes   ☐ No

His shirts

9. When selecting dress shirts, my guy usually prefers those that require cuff links.

☐ Yes   ☐ No

10. My man always sends his dress shirts to be professionally laundered.

☐ Yes   ☐ No

11. My man has a selection of dress shirts ranging from classic white to French blue to an assortment of subtle stripes and patterns.

☐ Yes   ☐ No

12. My man understands that "dress to impress" doesn't mean wearing an autographed team jersey out to dinner with friends.

☐ Yes   ☐ No

13. My man knows that quality dress shirts are not sized in small, medium, and large.

☐ Yes   ☐ No

14. My man is devoted to the shirt label or designer he likes. And when the collection's not available, he tries to find something similar in style.

☐ Yes   ☐ No

15. Leisure suits from the 1970s and 1950s bowling shirts are something my man wears only on Halloween.

☐ Yes   ☐ No

16. My man would never wear a matchy-matchy shirt/tie/handkerchief combination that's sold as a packaged set.

☐ Yes   ☐ No

His pants

17. My man knows the difference between tailored trousers and a regular pair of pants.

☐ Yes   ☐ No

18. My man has gotten rid of all of his favorite jeans from college—especially the ones with the holes and frayed bell-bottoms.

☐ Yes   ☐ No

19. My man will wear only sweatpants or a track suit when exercising—not for dinner.

☐ Yes   ☐ No

20. My man's closet contains more than just khakis. They are not his second skin.

☐ Yes   ☐ No

21. Regarding pant length, I see my man's ankles only when he's wearing shorts.

☐ Yes   ☐ No

22. My man understands that dress pants should have only two creases on each leg—one in the front and one in the back.

☐ Yes   ☐ No

23. Flat fronts or pleated? My man knows which best suits his frame.

☐ Yes   ☐ No

24. My man knows Dolce & Gabbana is not the name of the chocolate I like to receive on Valentine's Day.

☐ Yes   ☐ No

25. The only letters or logos on my man's pants are on the inside label.

☐ Yes   ☐ No

His shoes

26. My man always makes sure his shoes are polished and in good condition.

☐ Yes   ☐ No

27. My man never wears sneakers when he's not working out.

☐ Yes   ☐ No

28. In the summer, my man will often wear a sandal instead of a closed shoe.

☐ Yes   ☐ No

29. My man has no problem throwing out the trendy shoes that he thought made him look cool.

☐ Yes   ☐ No

30. When shopping for shoes, my man sticks to the classics.

☐ Yes   ☐ No

31. My man's shoe collection is not dusty, discolored, and cracked as if they were discovered in an archaeological dig.

☐ Yes   ☐ No

32. If you asked my man what a shoe tree is, he would never say "an exotic plant with leaves in the shape of a loafer."

☐ Yes   ☐ No

33. My man tosses out old shoes on a regular basis; he doesn't wait until the dog steers clear of them.

☐ Yes   ☐ No

34. I love my guy's taste in ties.

☐ Yes   ☐ No

35. My man knows what it means when a tie "has a dimple."

☐ Yes   ☐ No

36. My man knows how to tie more than one knot and which knot to tie with different dress collars.

☐ Yes   ☐ No

37. My man owns a belt made from a tasteful exotic skin.

☐ Yes   ☐ No

38. If a pair of pants were sold with a matching belt, my man wouldn't purchase them.

☐ Yes   ☐ No

39. The majority of my man's socks have the heel and toe areas intact. Socks with holes go in the trash bin, not back in his dresser drawer.

☐ Yes   ☐ No

40. My guy owns a selection of solid dress socks in black, navy blue, dark brown, and small classic patterns.

☐ Yes   ☐ No

41. Sunglasses are not something my man picks up while making a quick stop at the supermarket.

☐ Yes   ☐ No

42. My man owns leather-lined gloves that are in good condition. They don't look like he's been chopping wood in them.

☐ Yes   ☐ No

His outerwear

43. My man's varsity letter jacket is packed in mothballs awaiting his next school reunion or homecoming tailgate party.

☐ Yes   ☐ No

44. A trench coat is for rain, an overcoat is for cold days, and a down jacket is for the snow and the ski slopes. My man knows the difference.

☐ Yes   ☐ No

45. My guy would never wear his down parka over his business suit.

☐ Yes   ☐ No

46. I love how the right overcoat is always the finishing touch to my man's daily wardrobe.

☐ Yes   ☐ No

47. When traveling, my man will usually pack a stylish light jacket, not one that can transform itself into a fanny pack.

☐ Yes   ☐ No

48. If asked, my man would know that a Burberry trench is not some obscure New England farming technique.

☐ Yes   ☐ No

49. My man prefers a coat check over tossing his coat onto a nearby chair.

☐ Yes   ☐ No

50. My man would stash this book in his jacket when shopping for clothes.

☐ Yes   ☐ No

Congratulations! You've just completed the first step in making over your man.

It's probably clear to you after completing the quiz that style and substance do not always go hand in hand. Some of the world's most forward-thinking and successful men don't have the first clue about looking their best from head to toe. And, ladies, this is all right. Men, for the most part, don't have the disciplined sense of style that women have developed from years of experimenting with clothing, hair, and beauty regimens.

Even if you don't consider yourself to be truly stylish, you can still want the man in your life to look the part. Where do you begin? The answer is simple: by completely separating your own tastes and style sensibilities from those of your guy. Think about him, and what he likes and doesn't like. Make an effort to understand habits and clothing rituals. How can they be enhanced or upgraded? Your man has his own will and tastes, so also keep in mind that you will never be able to dress him as you would a young child. Your new sartorial role is to help provide your man with strong style cues and to gently guide him into a new and improved look. This should be a transformation infused with love, trust, and care.

Now let's grade the quiz. Tally up the number of times you answered yes and disregard the nos. The total number of yeses will fit your man into one of the following style classifications: the Dandy, the Sartorial Soldier, the Man with Promise, the Fashion Neophyte, and the Fashion Beginner. These categories will help you focus on where you really need to get to work and on which chapters of this book will serve you best.

0–10   The Fashion Beginner   The good news is that your man is like many (too many) American men—he's a real "guy's guy" who couldn't care less about the way he looks and has no interest in "fussing" about clothing every day. Sure he bathes daily and shaves, but he doesn't care about style.

Fashion Beginner sounds like a harsh description and you've got some rebuilding to do, but you *can* make over your man.

Much of this man's wardrobe centers on what I call "pastime paraphernalia"—meaning his favorite team's logo is emblazoned on everything, from game jerseys to T-shirts and sneakers. Comfort (and team spirit) is the key to his wardrobe and his life. Remember, ladies, that won't change—comfort is the underlying principle in most of what men wear. But with my help your man will be comfortable, presentable, and stylish. Please read every chapter carefully to achieve maximum results. Be sure to work slowly and gingerly with the Fashion Beginner. Maintain a sense of humor and try to make the process fun.

11–20 The Fashion Neophyte Hats off to you! If you have a Fashion Neophyte in your life, you certainly have a smoother ride than lots of other women. "Neo" men are concerned with their appearance, but they don't let it consume their lives. Best of all, a man in this category understands the power of looking "put together," yet doesn't always understand how other men achieve it, and sometimes he'll give up and pursue other pastimes and hobbies. Style is not always fun for him, but when he understands what works for him, and why, he'll get into it.

Neophytes take direction well, which for many women is half the battle. If you pay close attention, you'll find that your Fashion Neophyte has a few pieces of stylish clothing that have sentimental value, such as his first pair of expensive shoes that he purchased after his first big promotion, or a cashmere overcoat that was a gift from his father, or his infamous "lucky" tie.

The challenge when working with a Fashion Neophyte is to develop a fashion focus and expose him to clothing and style habits that work for men he admires. A great starting point is to deconstruct the favorite looks of a man whose style he likes and offer suggestions on how your man can make that look his own. Then your guy will be more than willing to embrace trends and handpick classic, gentlemanly styles he once thought were for "other men." Although you will find direction throughout the entire book, pay attention to the chapters on suits, shoes, accessories, and grooming.

21–30 The Man with Promise The Man with Promise is gifted and confident enough to select a great suit, shirt, and tie—but only if he saw it first on a store mannequin or in a magazine. He's a well-rounded man, knows his own mind, yet he just coasts along with enough style knowledge to get by. But sometimes this is where the real work begins. Ladies, you may need to use a backdoor approach with this man. The Man with Promise thinks he knows it all, and fine-tuning his sense of style may require all the charm you possess.

This man has taste, but he is most likely stuck in an era or a trend that worked at some point in his life and can't quite let it go. Think *Miami Vice* or *The Preppy Handbook*. The Man with Promise is a template shopper who hates to spend time shopping and trying on clothing, but with help and guidance he might change his tune.

Let holidays be your occasions for breaking his suit, shirt, and tie habits. Or buy a gift certificate to his favorite store and plan a trip there to select something together. This approach won't make him feel like you're forcing his hand. If yours is a Man with Promise, the chapters on shopping, underwear, and closets will assist you the most.

31–40   The Sartorial Soldier   I would venture to say that this is the goal most women want when they decide to make over their man. And aren't you lucky to start here! However, with every upside, there's a down. With a Sartorial Soldier, you are blessed yet have a separate set of challenges. This man of advanced tastes can be summed up in three words: clothes, clothes, and clothes. His closet is probably stocked with apparel he almost never wears or may not be the best silhouette for his body. The Sartorial Soldier is not afraid to try new things mixed with old classics, and he believes in the careful art of looking good. Your task is to edit his closet, and your primary focus should be on the chapters that discuss closets, shirts (of which the Sartorial Soldier has many), and pants.

41–50   The Dandy   "Honey, can you fasten my right cuff link, please?" Not a foreign request to you, I'm certain. This man knows style, he knows good fabrics, and he even knows how to wear color, a scary word for most men. Your man has his style all together, but he is in need of a lesson on a casual, or "relaxed," elegance. A sexy pair of jeans and the right T-shirt might actually be a nice change for the Dandy, but getting him to loosen up his Windsor knot will be a fight to the finish. Pay attention to the celebrity and "real men" makeovers at the end of each chapter, where I'll show you how to create a fantasy look for men with the most discriminating tastes. 🖋

How to Use This Book

Each chapter starts off with a brief style history and then segues into style basics (I call these sections "101s"). Next you'll find a range of particular items—for example, shirts in a variety of colors and styles or suits for your guy's every occasion. The makeover closes each chapter and includes before and after photos and an interview that you'll find helpful and fun. There's a resource section at the end of the book called "Style Clinic," and it's filled with lots of marvelous information, answers to the most frequently asked style questions, helpful hints about packing, a listing of stores, and much more.

FRANK SINATRA
DEAN MARTIN
SAMMY DAVIS JR.
PETER LAWFORD
JOEY BISHOP

IN THE LOUNGE

The Rat Pack: Frank Sinatra, Dean Martin, Sammy Davis, Jr., Peter Lawford, and Joey Bishop

His Suit
The Little Black Dress for Men

TRADITIONALLY SOBER. ALMOST ALWAYS AUTHORITATIVE. AND JUST PLAIN "MANLY." CLASSIC tailored clothing is the benchmark of the well-dressed gentleman as well as the cornerstone of an elegant wardrobe.

A suit guards a man's body in ways most other garments worn by men do not—unless, of course, he's working in a race car pit and has on a zip-front jumpsuit. Covering approximately 85 percent of a man's body, the suit is a uniform that signals confidence and power in both business and pleasure situations. If it is fitted properly—rather than baggy or boxy—a suit should create the illusion of a seamless body that's consistent and perfectly balanced in both silhouette and color. And what's better, a true gentleman in a suit never goes out of style.

Most women love a man in a seemingly expensive, well-fitted, coordinated suit, since it creates a "leading man" aura around him that is certain to turn female heads. This in no way means that women want the men in their lives to wear a tailored suit 24-7. It's just that a suit signals *effort,* and in the current climate of no-rules fashion that has men sporting everything from their favorite baseball jersey to jeans dating back to their teenage years, a suit can be a refreshing and unexpected choice illustrating the respect that a man has for himself—and for those around him.

A good suit simply says to the world, "I've arrived." And for most well-dressed men, the adage is true—from the boardroom to weddings, funerals, a job interview, essentially any environment in which you are judged first by your appearance. Now relaxed dress codes, however, have spurred a style disconnect. Once seen as a suit of armor, the suit is often regarded as an obligation that goes along with life's more stressful events.

The American suit takes its original cues from men's formal wear common in the royal courts of France and England, including the Victorian pairing of slim pants with long and sometimes ornate jackets in heavy wool and velvets that were designed to add girth to the figure. It wasn't until the early part of the twentieth century that we started to see the shape of tailored clothing resembling what we now call the "suit."

England's influence on the modern suit made its way to the States thanks to famous clothiers who traveled abroad for sporting competitions. John Brooks, of Brooks Brothers, was a leader in

Miami Vice's Don Johnson and Philip Michael Thomas.

defining the look of American suits in the early 1900s, and the company he helped found remains a top purveyor of fine, and still affordable, men's dress and casual clothing. Brooks Brothers's natural-shouldered and boxy sack suit—one of the hottest looks for men in the 1950s—has been the pattern from which most well-known American suit makers have crafted their styles.

Through the decades, the suit has been one of the more adaptable garments in fashion, welcoming everything from knee-length knickers in the 1930s to the extra-long-jacketed comical zoot suits of the 1940s, created by and popular with African-American and Latino men as an alternative to World War II wool fabric rations. Through whatever folly fashion may throw its way, the suit has remained the foundation of menswear.

Now, fast-forward to some well-suited icons whom all women know and love. First up, envision 1950s screen idol Cary Grant in the double-breasted wool sack suit that was clearly his signature silhouette. The glitzy "Rat Pack" in their sharp sharkskin Continental suits, which defined the JFK-era 1960s view of the nattily dressed gentleman, could make petite Sammy Davis Jr. look more imposing next to taller crooner Dean Martin.

And just when you thought it was safe to go back into the boardroom with a boring conservative suit, Richard Gere, in the 1980s hit *American Gigolo*, introduced a new, deconstructed suit by Giorgio Armani that spotlighted—rather than artificially puffed up—a man's own physique. The movie caused such a fashion sensation that nearly every suit company was sent scrambling to create its own knock-off version. A few years later, the look was validated and given a more casual, Hugo Boss stamp by Don Johnson and Philip Michael Thomas as Miami's most stylish, pastel-dipped cops on NBC's long-running hit series *Miami Vice*. Women could finally connect with a man's wardrobe with a better understanding of color and near-unisex shape, but the masculine mystique of a "man's man" in a suit was fading.

The 1990s fixed all that with the help of the red carpet. Celebrity icons embraced a steely, sexier way of dressing up in suits, still with the dark palette, strong cut, and stately details of traditional menswear—but this time with a twist. Brad Pitt, Samuel L. Jackson, Sean Connery, and even Regis Philbin became icons of style through their clever use of suits—either by going sans tie, embracing a longer jacket, or with a monochromatic shirt and tie. The suit again demonstrated that it had power and a sense of play.

Of course, those in the constant flashing of the paparazzi can bend the rules a bit. Is the father of two who works in finance going to go sockless and tieless with his suit to his Tuesday staff meeting as easily as Tom Cruise would for the opening of his next film? Probably not. But he could definitely benefit from the confidence that comes with the power to enjoy a suit and all of its possibilities.

Just as a woman can create a number of different variations to her classic "little black dress" by adding a string of pearls to conjure up the elegance and simplicity of Audrey Hepburn in *Breakfast at Tiffany's,* or by pairing it with her sexiest pumps and evening makeup to re-create the look and feel of Elizabeth Taylor in *Butterfield 8,* a suit can give a man many different looks.

Rising Hollywood leading man Benjamin Bratt creates sizzle when he dons his jet-black suit with matching slim tie and white or black shirt for added drama. Like Clark Gable and Frank Sinatra before him, George Clooney opened his collar and shirt cuffs and sealed his claim on being the rogue with a smile in the remake of *Ocean's 11.*

So from the look of the *Blues Brothers* to that of a Monte Carlo tycoon and everything in between, there are a vast number of suit options, but still the average man rarely exercises such options. The inspiration is limitless as well, and not just from pop culture. Think history. Think culture. Think Wilde, as in Oscar, with his flashes of unexpected colored pocket squares and scarves. (Okay, this may be pushing it.) But how about considering the contemporary, dapper sophistication of CBS's *60 Minutes* anchor Ed Bradley, who will often pair a black suit with a matching (or dark) turtleneck, creating a look that's as intellectual as it is mysterious.

The suit appears to be the one element of a man's wardrobe that promises never to fade, despite the complaints of long-suffering retailers and manufacturers that business casual has caused declining sales ever since the early 1990s, when California's Silicon Valley embraced khakis. Regardless of the suit's retail and commercial success, it is obvious that a man wearing a suit will remain alluring and attractive to women who appreciate a guy who possesses a well-thought-out, strong, and masculine appearance. Be still your heart if *that* look ever goes out of style.

The well-suited
Samuel L. Jackson

HIS SUIT 101

The Details

There is no one perfect suit for every man. This is why it's so very important that you understand the makings of a suit's foundation and all of its many and varied nuances. Shopping for a suit with these ideas in mind will help you find one that's a two-pronged investment—a garment that will both last and always make your guy look distinguished.

Stitching

Stitching is a sign of quality and the work of a real clothing artisan. Typically a mark of a luxury suit, good stitching can also be found in pieces that fit more modest budgets.

Keep the following attributes in mind when checking out the stitching on a suit:

- Stitching overall, whether done by machine or hand, should be neat and sturdy.

- Hand-stitching is always the best.

- Be sure that all stitching perfectly matches the color of the garment—unless contrast stitching is one of the suit's decorative details.

- Buttonholes are a good place to examine the stitching process. Check the inside for a slightly lumpy finish, which is usually considered a bad thing but ironically is the sign of the utmost in hand-tailored clothing. However, snug and uniform stitches made by a machine are totally acceptable.

Lining

A lined suit is best for wear and comfort. Understand that a "fully lined" suit is a bit of a misnomer—by today's standards, it means that ⅜ of the jacket and the pant legs are lined. Check the fabric content of the lining as well; most linings are made of rayon and should be finished properly, with a fold just short of the edge of the suit.

Perfectly lined pattern

Patterns

Whether it's a subtle pin-striped suit or a bold chalk-striped windowpane check, patterned sur-faced fabrics require that extra examination for what is commonly called "pattern consistency" in areas such as the back of the jacket where it joins the collar, the pockets, where the sleeve joins the shoulder, and the full horizontal breadth of the suit. To check this, it is best to have your guy slip the jacket on and stand a few feet away from you. Under those unforgiving dressing-room lights, also check to be sure that the pattern on the jacket and that on the pants match exactly.

Lapels and Collars

This is the part of the suit that designers and mak-ers of tailored clothing have modified the most. Remember how lapels got real wide in the 1970s and then shrunk when doused by the New Wave a decade later? That's just about as radical as men's fashion gets. Generally, lapel width should be some-where between 3" and 4" and should be kept in pro-portion with the rest of the jacket. A simple way to determine that a lapel is properly designed is to measure from the collar to the top of the sleeve. The end tip of the lapel should be positioned just short of halfway between these two points.

Pockets

Although pocket styles vary, the tailored suit looks best with the besom pocket (a pocket that can be used to hold a pocket square) on the chest and flap or slit pockets on the hip area. The besom pocket style is commonly found on classic men's suits and can be identified by its bandlike stitched

Proper lapel, collar, and pocket

fold on both the upper and lower side of the pocket opening. By contrast, a slit pocket, as you might expect, is a clean, finished slit on the fabric. On certain quality suits, what appears to be a flap pocket (with an extra flap of fabric covering the actual pocket opening) is actually a convertible pocket, which gives the wearer the option of placing the flap outside or inside the pocket.

Vents

Vents are vertical slits or open sections placed on the lower back of a suit jacket. This treatment, which has been in existence since the nineteenth century, was originally a military detail to provide width, fullness, and ease of movement for soldiers and horsemen.

Today, many men may not even be consciously aware of their "vent preference," but they subliminally know the freedom they feel—seated or walking—when they place their hands into their pants pockets with ease.

Classic suits are generally offered with one of three types of jacket vents. *Note:* If you happen to find a suit that has a vent placement that does not fit into one of the three aforementioned categories, be careful: You are most likely encountering a trendy or even experimental design that will not stand the test of time.

- The single vent placed at the center of the back of the jacket is one of the most recognizable details of an American suit. The vent gives your man access to his pants, belt, and pockets without rumpling the jacket's natural drape. The detail's one downside—unless the jacket is tailored to slim a man's torso,

The timeless single vent

The snappy double vent

25

The clean ventless

the vent can force the jacket into a somewhat boxy shape.

- Double vents are the mark of a classic Hollywood leading man, as this detail is by far the sharpest-looking finish on a suit jacket. The suit's two vents are placed in perfect symmetry on the side hips of the jacket, which allows ultimate access to your man's pants pockets and waist. The dual-vent design also offers additional shape to the suit by helping to better define the suit's overall silhouette. Jackets with double vents are also more comfortable to wear.

- Continental men have historically preferred a ventless jacket because it is the cleanest and most body-hugging silhouette for a suit jacket. Also, the ventless jacket does not disrupt the fabric's inherent drape. Although the shape of this suit design is considered modern, and flattering to slimmer men, the ventless suit's functionality has always been a challenge because it's restricting, and the simplest of arm or hand gestures create large gathers and rumples.

Suspender/Brace Buttons

Quality suits are equipped with six buttons positioned on the inside waist lining of the trousers—four of which are placed in pairs on either side of the pant's front closure, and the remaining two at the center on the back of the waistband to secure suspenders—or braces, as they are also known.

The modern single button

Buttons / Closures

Though seemingly a small detail, the buttons are an important part of a suit's construction—not only because of their fastening ability but also because of their high hand traffic and handling with each use. So make sure that you either purchase a suit with quality buttons or have a professional tailor replace buttons.

Take a moment and inspect the buttons. Notice if they are made of plastic, which should be avoided, or of natural horn. Higher-quality buttons are raised, or have a dome-shaped underside. Most suits sport horn buttons, with the exception of formal suits, which may have buttons ranging from mother-of-pearl to leather, metals, or ceramics.

Second, examine how the buttons are attached to the suit, and be certain that they are secure—a good old pull and tug never hurts, but you can also check the neck (the area between the button and the suit itself). The button should not be too tightly sewn to the suit; it needs to give a bit. Clean workmanship is important, and this is indicated by a generous amount of thread, with a ring of added thread for extra support. Pay close attention to the stitching pattern on the top of the button; the benchmark of a quality suit is as many hand-sewn operations as possible. And finally, the buttonholes should be just as meticulously rendered. Avoid loose threads, and check for perfectly finished stitching—when the suit is buttoned, your closures should be level and even with no pulling or straining, and so should the fabric around them.

The classic two button

The three button

27

The stalwart double breasted

The Suit's Fit

- Shoulders give a suit balance and proportion. The amount of shoulder padding in men's suits ebbs and flows with the fashion of the times, just as it does in womenswear. Be careful not to select a suit with ultrawide shoulders that do not flatter your man's frame. If your man has broad shoulders, he should avoid excess padding, and if he is a slope-shouldered man, then light padding may be in order to level him off a bit. In any case, light shoulder padding is incorporated in most quality suits for overall form and to help them keep their shape, so you cannot avoid it altogether (unless you are selecting a decidedly unconstructed suit that fits more like an unlined shirt). When observing a suit's shoulder treatment, take into consideration the size of your man's head, his waistline, his stomach girth, and his neck width. All of these factors contribute to a properly balanced look.

- Lapels should lie flat against the suit. They should not pucker when the jacket is closed and buttoned; this is an instant signal that a jacket is too tight.

- Armholes are the toughest areas for a novice eye to judge and are best evaluated by the suit's wearer. The most important thing to keep in mind is the height and cut of the armhole—the opening should be roomy enough so that the wearer can move freely. You will know that the armholes are high enough when he can move his arms easily without the entire jacket lifting up.

- The jacket should fit around the body but not hug—unless that's the intention. There should always be at least enough space between the jacket and your man's body for a dress shirt and maybe even a light sweater. When he is standing at a resting position with arms at his sides and his jacket buttoned, all sides of the jacket should lie smooth and flat. And there should be no visible pulling around buttonholes when the jacket is buttoned.

Taller men, obviously, need slightly longer jackets—but not a zoot suit!—whereas shorter men may select a slightly shorter cut to add length to the legs. In either case, the jacket should always cover his posterior.

- Men's suit sleeves are pretty standard. You rarely see a man in a cropped-sleeve suit jacket, or a ¾-length model, unless you are catching a rerun of *Miami Vice*. This tip is easy to remember, because the rule of thumb is exactly that. Regardless of the size of a gentleman's hand, his jacket sleeve should always end five inches from the tip of his thumb. If the jacket fits properly, about ¼ inch of his shirt cuff will be exposed. Be sure that his arms are at rest at his sides while he is being measured.

- Dress trousers should rest on the waist, not the hips. Emphasize the waistline. The drape of the trouser should flow along the natural lines of a man's legs, right down to his feet.

- One should also take note of the positioning of the crotch of the pants. This area should fit closely to the body—but within a level of comfort, of course. This is called a pant's rise.

- There are basically two options available in the hem of a man's trousers: cuffed and clean. Cuffs provide a bit of added volume and weight to the bottom of the trouser, creating a longer line to the pants, and added interest to the overall look.

  The cuff is the one part of a well-dressed man's attire where size does matter. Most traditional designers and style aficionados stipulate that suit trouser cuffs be no wider than 1¾ inches. Some men take cuffs up to 3 inches—especially big and tall men. Another sartorial note: Formal suits should never have a cuff. When deciding on the length of trousers, simply remember that you never want to see too much of a man's socks when he is walking. Always put this to the test when trying on off-the-rack suit trousers that are prehemmed, as well as when working with a tailor who is customizing the length of an unfinished trouser.

- For the best-fit analysis, turn your man around and look at the collar stance from the back. When he tries on a suit, make sure he's wearing a dress shirt so you can be sure the suit collar starts to fall around ½ inch beneath the rear of the shirt collar. Also, make sure that the jacket collar does not rest away from the neck and collar—ideally, it should lie completely flat.

THE PERFECT SUIT

When you see a guy who is "perfectly suited," what does that mean? Is it the suit itself? Or is it a combination of many elements, including his body, height, and posture? Let's deconstruct and demystify the well-suited man:

1. The Suit Jacket   Most important, a take-notice suit jacket such as this one always fits the body properly, as if it were either a custom-made or bespoke suit. For most average men it is an off-the-rack suit that has been altered at the hands of a professional tailor. The shoulders are softly defined and in proportion to his body, and the waist of the jacket hovers around his body without any visible pulls or tugs, so that even if your guy has a slight stomach, you would not know it.

2. The Suit Pants   Notice the knife-sharp creases on both suit-trouser legs. Pay close attention to the drape of the pants; it should float around the body, not flare or grab. The trouser cuffs should be at least 1¾ inches wide and be unbalanced against his overall size. Also, the break in the pant leg at the cuff should create just the right relief and ease to the line of the pant, adding just a wink of personal flare.

3. The Suit Pattern   The navy blue pinstripe suit is by far the strongest and most masculine pattern for a man who wants to make a statement of power. And although it may not be the most versatile choice in suits, it is the most authoritarian and is the pattern of choice in financial and legal circles because of its classic and sober tone.

4. The Button Closures   The well-dressed man never buttons the bottom button on his suit jacket. As a matter of personal taste, on a three-button jacket, he may elect to fasten his top button alone, middle button alone, or both. This rule applies to two-button and double-breasted jackets as well. For single-button jackets, the choice is totally up to the wearer; just be sure he always unbuttons when seated.

5. The Shirt Cuffs   The perfect amount of shirt exposure speaks volumes about your man's attention to detail and comfort level. If you witness the perfect ¼-inch rule in operation, look again: You may very well see a monogram on the cuff upon further inspection.

6. The Shoes   Most women agree that a beautifully shined pair of quality dress shoes are the true mark of a stylish man. This man dons a pair of ¾ boots that are a traditional plain-toe oxford style: an ideal choice, for they have a clean, nondescript surface that does not compete with the bold pattern of the suit—and won't highlight his socks when seated.

7. The Overcoat   The camel cashmere topcoat is outerwear par excellence for the man who believes his coat is as important as what is worn underneath. Some coats provide only warmth; this coat not only does just that, but does it with a luxurious hand and classic silhouette. The versatile caramel colors can be worn with just about every suit your man owns, from a bold dark classic to earthy browns and charcoal grays.

8. The Pocket Square   He wears just a hint of a white cotton, hand-rolled pocket square. By revealing just a bit less than ¼ inch in a perfectly aligned strip, he conjures up the clean and dapper men of the 1950s. And although there are varied "classics," his traditional treatment far exceeds the three point, the four point, and the peak as a truly timeless handkerchief-folding method.

9. The glasses   Whether it is his sunglasses or ophthalmic eyewear, he never allows you to see more than the arm when temporarily positioned in his pocket. Ideally, this man would keep his frames in their own crocodile clamshell case, but every once and again he will rest them on his outfit for a wink of confidence through haberdashery.

10. The dress shirt   He features a spread collar, which is traditionally considered more formal than a straight point and its button-down counterparts. This reveals that your man owns more than his share of dress shirts, as the spread collar is usually added to a man's closet after he's outgrown all its safe and boring counterparts.

11. The tie   Neckwear is usually tied in a bold Windsor knot for maximum thickness and impact to complement the width of his spread collar. Notice the handwork on the dimple, which adds perfect symmetry to the lines of the suit.

THE SEVEN ESSENTIAL SUITS FOR MEN

NOW THAT YOU HAVE A BETTER UNDERSTANDING OF WHAT TO LOOK FOR IN A QUALITY MEN'S SUIT, the next step is helping your man create a diverse and functional tailored clothing collection to suit his lifestyle. The seven highlighted here are timeless suits that outlast trends and are a great starting point for your man to build on once he becomes more comfortable purchasing, wearing, and accessorizing suits. You will find that these suit ideas are truly classics—yet aren't as stuffy in fit and shape as the versions his father may have donned. So embracing the practice of wearing a tailored suit today may not be as much of a leap for your man as you may think.

It is obviously a costly proposition to consider purchasing all of these suits at once. A suit

A. The solid navy suit   B. The gray flannel suit   C. The navy chalk-stripe suit   D. The khaki suit   E. The black suit

should be purchased carefully and considered an investment piece selected for the utmost quality that one can afford at the moment, and tailored specifically to one's present physique. To have a closet equipped with these seven time-honored favorites—virtually one for each day of the week—is something that can take even the most well-dressed men years to achieve.

It's smartest to begin by purchasing the suit that will be the most versatile, offering a number of outfit possibilities—from day to night, to semiformal, to even a snappy weekend look. Here are the basics to keep in mind, in order of importance. ➢

F. The plaid suit   G. The pinstripe suit

A. The Solid Navy Suit   Invest in a solid navy blue suit first, if only because your man can wear this almost three days out of a week with different shirt-and-tie combinations and not get a second look at the water cooler. From solid white dress shirts and small, subtly patterned ties to bold checked shirts and soft dressy knit polo shirts, the pairings here are broad. Be careful when switching to an evening look; first be sure your man's suit is a true midnight blue and pair it with either a solid dress shirt or turtleneck in the exact same color.

B. The Gray Flannel Suit   Flannel is such a rich, stately fabric in suitings. It emits power, but with a gentle hand and a wink of mystery. The main idea here is really about a classic medium-gray suit that works for him—the climate your man lives in and his profession. Keep

The Tux Commandments

The classic tuxedo will always be the pinnacle of formal dress for a man. Indeed, a legacy like that comes with its own set of conventions and enduring traditions, whether the tux be worn for a wedding day or a night at the opera. There are ten rules that can assure your man looks his absolute best in a tuxedo.

- *His tuxedo jacket should be single- or double-breasted with silk-faced, peaked lapels—even if he's got the height to make it in the NBA.*
- *Classic tuxedos come in either black or midnight blue, which registers as black to the night eye.*
- *His tuxedo pants should have silk taping down the side of each leg and never be cuffed.*
- *A white dress tuxedo shirt should have French cuffs and either a full spread collar or wing collar. For a touch of authenticity, look for a small honeycomb-weave piqué on the front bib area and cuffs.*
- *Cummerbund folds should face upward. At one time, men would conveniently stow theater tickets in these folds.*
- *Formal shoes should be a traditional lace-up, or a "pump" slip-on, in patent leather or a high-shined calfskin. Some men—like a natty Brad Pitt or Quincy Jones—can pull off a dress loafer sans socks.*
- *A "cravat," or a long necktie, is meant to be worn with morning coats. No bow ties before 5 P.M.*
- *Match cuff links with shirt studs. Silver or gold, either solid or combined with black, is always a winner at sophisticated black-tie events.*
- *Most "black-tie" events mean just that—wear a black tie. Terms like "creative black tie" and "festive black tie" mean that men have an option to drop the tie altogether. Remember that white bow ties are reserved for tails.*
- *If your man attends three or more black-tie events each year, he should take the plunge and purchase a tuxedo.*

shirt pairings either soft or bright and bold. A matching soft gray cashmere turtleneck brings to mind the gentlemen's club aesthetic of old. A bold gingham check shirt in soft pink with a contrasting tie is a dandified classic that works for the man who dares to be unique.

C. The Navy Chalk-Stripe Suit Once you have both light and dark solid suits in your man's wardrobe, move on to a classic chalk stripe, which will give him just a flash of sartorial confidence. There is nothing better than a crisp white, spread-collared dress shirt and a solid tie with a touch of sheen for ultimate male glamour. Or to cool it down Brit style, wear it with an eclectic mix of pattern and print by pairing contrasting shirts and ties—have fun, but don't go crazy with too much color.

D. The Khaki Suit Is he ready for the summer? The khaki suit is like a breath of fresh air, because while it's casual, the suit also possesses a gentlemanly tone of authority—and it's the one suit that is actually OK to be worn without socks! This is the perfect suit for a casual outdoor wedding, and the Great Gatsby–esque earth tone welcomes butter-soft pastel shirts in solids and stripes like no other on this list.

E. The Black Suit Well-dressed New York men have long embraced the power of the black suit for its mystery, formalness, and slimming capabilities. The perfect suit for a man who works in creative environments, a black suit should be selected in a year-round, middleweight fabric like worsted wool—so that he can do three weddings and a funeral with no sweat! Single-breasted is best, and its underpinnings should be chic and modern, ranging from the solid white or black V-neck sweater, to a rainbow of solid shirts in rich jewel tones or pastels—worn sans tie—to create a confident nighttime look.

F. The Plaid Suit The plaid suit has actually made quite a stylish comeback in recent years. Top options include the glen plaid or a small houndstooth in earthy tones of browns and tan grounds. Because of its texture and pattern, it's best to pair them with shirts in strong jewel-toned solids. Experiment with bold checks and stripes in blues and lavender tones in warmer months, and pumpkin, hunter green, and rust lightweight knit sweaters in the cooler months.

G. The Pinstripe Suit The pinstripe suit in a tone of navy blue or gray is a wise final investment because it has staying power. (Ladies: A beaded pinstripe is a term used by designers and suit makers for the broken spaces in the stitches of the stripe.) He'll nail that job interview, secure that mortgage, and ink the deal on that partnership in this baby! And he'll gussy it up with pale, solid dress shirts and power ties, or claim the high-powered-magnate vibe by simply donning his crispest, whitest dress shirt—unbuttoned, and with a matching pocket square.

Before

THE MAKEOVER

Tiki Barber and his wife, Ginny Barber

Tiki, an All-Pro running back for the New York Giants, and Ginny, a publicist for Ermenegildo Zegna, met while they were students at the University of Virginia. Since then, Tiki, who is also an up-and-coming sports broadcaster, has traded his UVA Cavaliers sweats and multicolored silk camp shirts for fine cashmere sweaters and designer suits. Giving loving credit and thanks to Ginny, Tiki says he's learned to see the sweet and sartorial things in life.

LLOYD: Ginny, you've known Tiki such a long time. How would you say his style has changed over the years?

GINNY: Try tenfold! Tiki now likes and appreciates quality in things, such as really well-made suits.

LLOYD: What's it like shopping with him?

GINNY: I honestly love it. He's like a big Barbie doll.

TIKI: Now, see, that's what I hate. I like being in and out of the store in about twenty minutes . . .

GINNY: He never tries anything on.

TIKI: . . . and she likes to be there for two hours.

GINNY: I love putting Tiki in clothes. I love shopping for him just as much as I love shopping for myself.

LLOYD: Are there any fit challenges because he's an athlete?

GINNY: Tiki has a diamond-shaped physique. He's bigger in the chest and smaller in his waist, so his drop is ill-proportioned. His pants are also hard to fit, so he gets a lot of his suits custom-made.

LLOYD: Now, a lot of guys look up to you, Tiki, because you're a pro athlete. For you to just say I trust my wife to pick out anything is remarkable. What is Ginny doing right?

TIKI: I trust my wife to tell me what looks good, and she knows my style. My suits are crisp, clean, and to the point, and they do what they are supposed to do—accentuate my good parts and hide my somewhat awkward shape.

I literally can't dress myself when I go out at night. It's "Ginny, I have to go to an event—pick out an outfit for me" or "I have to do *CBS This Morning*—pick out a suit."

LLOYD: Before Ginny, who influenced the way you dressed?

TIKI: My uncle gave me a few of the suits Ginny got rid of before we got married. We didn't have a lot of money growing up, so my twin brother, Ronde, and I wore hand-me-downs to church. They fit well enough and I didn't care. I didn't have a clue about that kind of stuff.

LLOYD: How many suits do you think you own now?

TIKI: I'd say somewhere between twelve to fifteen and a tux. I never, ever, thought I would own my own tux. I just got one, and it's great.

LLOYD: It's a good feeling, right? Now, why would you recommend that men purchase more suits?

TIKI: I think suits are the ultimate in sophistication. When you wear a suit, you feel good about yourself, and people look at you and say: "That guy, now he's got it together."

The Make Over Prescription: *Ginny took the English-inspired, natty route for Tiki, and draped him in a perfectly tailored, soft blue double-breasted pin-stripe suit to fit his full physique, pale blue windowpane, spread collar shirt, striped silk tie, and hand-rolled pocket square. She chose sterling silver knot cuff links and cognac brown wing tips for a detailed finish. The result: Timeless elegance, with an athletic twist!*

After

Harry Belafonte

His Shirt
The Unnoticed Power

PUTTING ON A CLEAN SHIRT IS THE UNIVERSAL THING MEN DO TO REFRESH AN OUTFIT, regardless of how they feel about style. While it's an easy and quick fix, the shirt is also the key piece each man needs to dress himself either up or down.

A new or freshly laundered dress shirt has always been a sartorial secret for men of style and taste. The crispness of its touch—or "hand," as they say in the fashion industry—the serious air of its appearance, and its soft yet sturdy construction make the dress shirt one of the clearest signals of a well-turned-out gentleman.

The modern-day dress shirt as we know it—fashioned in soft cotton with a full row of buttons down the center breast placket; a finished, fitted collar; and cuffs that fasten either with buttons or cuff links—took form near the end the nineteenth century at Brown, Davis & Co., a shirt company in Aldermanbury, England. The company was the first to register this fully buttoned shirt, thus making its pullover counterpart obsolete.

America's fascination with the dress shirt is nowhere close to matching that of British men, who have an established culture and commerce solely dedicated to the life, force, care, and breeding of Jermyn Street, a main shopping artery of custom shirts and tailored clothing, bespoke touches, and fine accessories. Jermyn Street is the sentimental center for the world's most savvy dandy set and their admirers, who know the difference between Turnbull & Asser, T.M. Lewin, and Thomas Pink.

At Turnbull & Asser, a minimum order of fine dress shirts is a half dozen and comes with a three-month waiting period. T.M. Lewin, one of the thoroughfare's oldest and most reputable stores, offers one of the largest selections of less-than-conservative stripes and bold print ties, which correspond to their prestigiously crafted, narrowly fitted dress shirts. And the "new jack" on the block is Thomas Pink, named after Britain's most revered tailor.

Pink's attention to detail and reputation for the finest craftsmanship led to the phrase "in the pink," which refers to the jubilant reaction one received in royal courts when wearing his clothes. Today, Turnbull & Asser and the store bearing Pink's name and following his design principles are two of Jermyn Street's neat cluster of insular tastemakers to reach beyond the Atlantic and open

v.v. British (very, very, as Bridget Jones would say) stores in the States, as well as offer a catalog and an online shopping service.

As a hallmark of fine dressing, the custom and fine-quality dress shirt certainly has a place in a man's wardrobe. But what about the day-to-day shirt? The shirt that gets laundered, layered, and relayered, rolled, cuffed, frayed, and pressed again and again? For a man, such a shirt serves as his second skin.

Paul Newman and Elizabeth Taylor in *Cat on a Hot Tin Roof.*

Many style analysts feel that America's penchant for the dress shirt begins and ends with the one that is pure, white, and has served men well for generations. Selecting a colored shirt is often the leveling device for men of all backgrounds, income levels, and careers. Today, the workhorse white shirt is vastly different from the one worn in the mid–nineteenth century, when a clean shirt was something only the privileged and fortunate could afford. Even then, hard labor was certainly not a function of a "white-collared" man— the origins of the term *white-collar professional*—since he'd find his shirt stained too often by his efforts. On the other hand, "blue collar" indicated that a man worked with his hands and likely wore a stain-hiding indigo uniform issued by his garage or factory.

The sexiness and allure of the men's dress shirt, especially the classic white version, has jumped in and out of pop-culture fashion—from author Tom Wolfe, whose white style statement extends beyond his shirt to his full-on signature, year-round commitment to an all-white ensemble of suit, hat, and soft leather buck shoes, to Calypso-belting vocalist Harry Belafonte, who pushed the envelope with his bright, barely buttoned, white flouncy shirts that revealed a bit more with each tallied banana. And then, who can forget Tom Cruise dancing around his parents' living room wearing his tighty-whitey underwear and white oxford shirt in the 1983 preppy fantasy film *Risky Business*? And speaking of sexy, one of the most memorable—and steamy—Hollywood movie scenes involved Paul Newman, Elizabeth Taylor, and a simple cotton shirt.

It's a steamy Mississippi night. Enter Newman as the broken-down Brick Pollitt and Taylor as his wife, whom he loves as much as he hates in the 1958 Tennessee Williams classic *Cat on a Hot Tin Roof*. While the scene may not have been essential to the plot, when Newman makes an on-camera costume change into a fresh white dress shirt fitting damply around his body, wet from running in a hot summer downpour, he leaves a powerful style impression. Especially with women.

In the 1940s, the advertising campaign for the classic Phillips–Van Heusen shirt asked this popular question: "Can you put the right shirt on the right man?" The answer, as well as the challenge for you ladies, still remains today.

HIS SHIRT 101

The Beauty Is in the Craftsmanship

At first glance, all dress shirts seem so ubiquitous, so alike, so homogenized in shape and form—two flat, nondescript sleeves, a familiar pointed collar, and a staid row of buttons down the center. The first mistake one can make when buying a dress shirt is to truly believe that they are all one and the same. Even the most knowledgeable shopper can be fooled, for the dress shirt really comes to life when it is worn—and particularly when it is considered as part of an outfitted ensemble of pattern, texture, and color.

A good shirt is a wardrobe anchor, it's the underpinning of a suit and the better half of a pair of weathered khakis, and still many men don't know what to look for in its details and what makes a good dress shirt. Here are the cues:

Stitching

You'll find that quality men's shirts come in either single- or double-needle stitching. The choice is yours, but know that single-needle shirts are the more costly of the two because, as the name implies, it takes more time to produce the shirt. Single-needle shirts are renowned for being stronger, cleaner, and better-fitting and are considered a mark of quality and luxury. The double-needle-stitched shirt is more common and more available; most of the packaged dress shirts you find at the store are of this type.

Collar

This is the focal point of a man of style. Be sure to check that the stitching is discreet in color and placed no more than about ¼ inch from the outer perimeter of the collar itself. Custom-made shirts may have slight irregularities on the collar, which are actually nice, subtle signatures of the craftsman's style.

The collar and stitching

Cuffs

There are two simple options here: the barrel cuff, the cuff that comes with buttons already attached; and French cuffs, a double-folded cuff that requires cuff links. French-cuff shirts are preferred for dressier and more formal suits and occasions. On better shirts you will also notice a series of two or three pleats where the shirt arm meets the cuff, which is considered a mark of elegance and craftsmanship.

The Tail

A pretty nonfunctional area of a man's dress shirt, the tail has become more popular in recent years as men have embraced casual dress in the workplace and on weekends. What used to remain tucked in is now exposed, so be sure that the tail is intact and has a smoothly finished stitch line. When wearing a shirt relaxed and untucked, consider your exposure; there is nothing worse than a large bottom barely covered by a small shirttail.

The Yoke

This is the piece of woven fabric, sewn behind the collar from shoulder to shoulder, connecting the shirt's front and back panels; the yoke is important in maintaining good shirt fit. Custom shirtmakers will split the yoke with a seam, which is said to increase mobility. Men who love bespoke details prefer their yokes split.

Pocket

Avoid buying too many shirts with a front chest pocket, as men have a tendency to use it as a stor-

The yoke and tail

age space for potentially dangerous shirt destroyers such as ink pens. If he does prefer this detail, keep the pocket simple and clean. Stay away from ornate details, like Western snap closures.

Placket

The placket is the band of fabric that keeps the shirt on. Buttons are sewn onto the placket—and most traditional shirts have even spacing between each. A quality single-needle-stitched placket not only joins the shirt, but also gives the shirt a smooth, balanced centerline down the front.

Buttons

Buttons are the most overlooked detail in a shirt. Be sure that the buttons are sewn on securely with a firm cross-stitch. The more expensive the shirt, the better the buttons. Many luxury and custom-made shirts have mother-of-pearl buttons, while most of those from off the rack or out of plastic packaging have inexpensive plastic ones.

The Gauntlet Button

As a little wink of classic English detail, many quality men's dress shirts have an additional button sewn toward the elbow end of the sleeve's placket, which not only helps to keep the cuffs closed but gives slight help in rolling up the cuff. This is usually the first button to get lost on a busy man.

Fit

No single attribute of a good dress shirt varies among manufacturers, shirt makers, and designer

The pocket and placket

Buttons, cuffs, and gauntlet button

brands more than fit. It's one of the few deliberate design marks of distinction among shirt brands, ranging from full and boxy to skin-skimming. Honor his preference first for maximum comfort and wear.

The Collar Fit

A quick study of overall dress shirt fit should always begin with the collar. A visibly snug collar is not always a bad thing; it's actually considered a mark of a dapper man who knows his details. By snug, It does not mean squeezing or choking—a collar should not cause physical strain. When measuring for collar length, allow the measuring tape to fit loosely around the neck and then ask your man to move his head and neck a bit. Can he move? Or do you see any gaps in the tape? Adjust and measure again to find the spot where the tape doesn't move but he still can.

Shirt Waist Fit

A slim man may want a bit more room in a dress shirt to give the illusion of a broader build, whereas a stocky man may gravitate toward a more tapered fit rather than a boxy shirt. The choice is purely his; comfort must come first, because a dress shirt is really a man's second skin.

Cuff and Sleeve Fit

As with the collar, shirt cuffs should fit closely but allow room to move. But not too much—a man should never be able to get a clenched fist through his cuff. Improper sleeve length is one of the biggest fashion mistakes men make—and it's so easy to avoid. Be sure your man gets his arms measured by a professional tailor or a trained sales associate, starting from the center of the shirt's back yoke, down his shoulder and arm, to right before the wrist. Armholes and sleeves should hover right below his armpit and allow just enough room for an undershirt.

Pairing Collars and Faces

The Big Matchup

Some men may simply throw the following tips to the wind in favor of personal style preference, but designers and taste makers have always agreed that a collar should complement the shape of the face. This small consideration can make all the difference between a man who looks like the cool, dashing Superman alter-ego Clark Kent and Seinfeld's hotheaded friend George Costanza.

Here are the basic collar-and-face partnerships that actually work well:

- The slender-faced dude should choose a spread collar or classic high-roll collar, which is often considered a fashion trend.

Tab collar shirt with French cuffs

Modified spread collar with French cuffs

"A" collar shirt with barrel cuffs

Button-down collar shirt with barrel cuffs

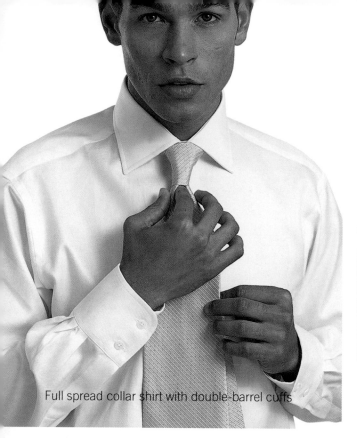

Full spread collar shirt with double-barrel cuffs

Straight-point collar shirt with barrel cuffs

- The wide-faced man should stick to lower-falling collars and avoid a spread collar. He should also steer clear of collars that are too small. A good rule: the fuller the face, the wider the collar; the slimmer the face, the straighter the collar.

- Most men of average weight look best in a standard straight-point collar. Luckily, this kind of guy also has the freedom to experiment with other collar types, like the spread, tab, and retro rounded collar. But wait first for that last one to come back in style!

- The short-necked fellow should own only shirts with collars that lie as flat as possible to the chest.

Fabrics

Regardless of the trend of the moment, dress shirts are the one area of a style-conscious man's wardrobe where synthetic fabrics are utterly unacceptable. Long live cotton! It's the shirt king and will always reign.

The basic cotton fabrications always work when paired with suits and ties. The quality, finishes, and softness of a cotton shirt often determine its price. Remember these kinds of cotton fabrics:

Poplin

This 100-percent-cotton fabric is faintly ribbed to the hand and is usually moderately priced. Generally speaking, Sea Island poplin shirts made from softer and slightly translucent imported cottons come with a higher price tag.

Pima

This fabric is very soft, holds color, and is a good value. While similar to Sea Island poplin, pima comes with a more affordable price tag.

Cotton Batiste

This shirting fabric is the finest weave and is very thin, appearing almost sheer when held against the skin. This shirt is worn with a formal suit for an occasion like a wedding or an elegant black-tie affair.

Oxford

This chunky, boldly woven pure cotton fabric is usually used for more rugged or casual shirts. The button-down-collar oxford in white and distinctive shades of pink, yellow, and blue is the most popular shirt made in this fabric. A sporty and durable fabric, oxford is generally lower in cost.

Chambray

This is a popular alternative for the man who loves a dress shirt but wants the comfort and ease of his favorite pair of jeans. Chambray is made in the same manner as denim but is lighter weight and treated with a softening finish.

Linen

The summer-shirt hero, linen was the only cottonlike shirt available in the late 1800s for well-dressed men in the United States and Europe. With its natural fibers and bumpy texture, linen can be crisp when pressed. Linen shirts are not considered a typical dress shirt and should be worn only casually.

THE PERFECT SHIRT—THE WHITE SHIRT

RELAXED ELEGANCE AT ITS BEST, THE CLASSIC WHITE DRESS SHIRT IS THE ULTIMATE expression of basic style. The beauty of the crisp white shirt is that it complements virtually any suit, pair of khakis, or jeans with the same amount of ease and elegance. And whether lightly starched and buttoned to a near close, or just out of the dryer with a little texture and rolled sleeves, this pure statement of comfort is a perfect primer for eye-opening style.

- Aesthetically, designers, celebrities, and stylists have always known the "lifting" power of wearing white near the face and chest. It is almost like having one's own personal lighting reflecting gently onto the face and neck.

- For the man who embraces the five o'clock shadow look no matter what time of day, or a beard—especially one that is "salt and pepper"—the white shirt should be a key element to balance out the scruff and rugged texture of his facial hair. The white shirt instantly complements any gray in his head hair as well, and, ironically, balances his look.

- White shirts should be somewhat "airy" in fit. A great partner to full-legged khakis—both with rolled cuffs. Or, a roomy pair of white jeans for a classic "good boy" look. Loose-fitting white oxfords are a legendary preppy favorite, especially the well-worn, washed-down versions that might even be frayed a bit around the collar, cuffs, and tails. The look speaks of comfort and a life built around high-quality clothing that only gets better with time—so why toss it?

- With the white shirt, your guy can relish in the power of not thinking about what he is going to wear. The white shirt looks great with just about any tie and suit and is the ideal partner (untucked, of course) to absolutely any pair of jeans or shorts.

- Remember to look for cotton fabrics that match his lifestyle when purchasing white shirts for your man. Some simple rules apply: the rugged man is best suited for oxford cloth because of its durability; the persnickety man will always love Egyptian or Sea Island cotton for its silky hand against the skin; the all-around "Joe" will certainly appreciate good old cotton poplin for it's versatile, nondescript surface that can be dressed up or down in an instant; and for the already well-dressed man, splurge on a silk or silk-cotton blend as the ultimate example of luxury and love.

HIS SHIRTS

TO THE STYLE-CONSCIOUS MAN, SHIRTS SERVE as a colorful and expressive thread that is woven through his wardrobe to a sartorial stitch. The shirt is the one piece of apparel that has the ability to revitalize a tired suit, change a look from day to night, or give a man an air of distinction. Owning a wide array of fine dress shirts is what separates truly well-dressed men from guys who just own loads of trendy clothes.

Creating a balanced collection of dress shirts begins, naturally, with basic solids—including French blue, yellow, and white, which should be at the very top of the shirt pile. Contrary to the advice of the sometimes pushy salespeople in men's clothing stores, it is not necessary to buy shirts and ties at the same time. It may seem like it makes sense, but buying a shirt-tie combo, in fact, creates a series of singular "looks" and can box some men into a corner when, say, one shirt is not clean or a tie seems to have a spot on it.

Who wants to be pigeonholed like that? Instead, encourage your man to select an array of dress shirts based on their quality and color. Then do the same with neckwear. Putting the two together allows your man to trust and reflect his own taste, mood, and lifestyle. Consider the elegant combination of a white shirt with a solid tie in matte silk, a modern spin on 1960s sartorial style. Here's a breakdown of the classic shirt standards: ➤

1. Linen   A summertime favorite that's best when worn casually without a tie or sport jacket. Wrinkles are inherent and add character to the shirt's ease and comfort.

2, 3. End-on-End   This fine and light fabric is recognized by the way its colored and white threads are woven to create a very faint mini-check pattern. Or sometimes it shows up as a light pinstripe. This is a businessman's basic—it's sturdy enough to be washed and ironed often and blends in nicely with neckwear and suits.

4, 5, 6. Twills   A heavy and rugged cotton shirting that is often worn casually with jeans and khakis. Twill is discernible by the diagonal wale on the fabric's surface.

7, 8. Herringbone   The pattern is identifiable by its short, slanting parallel lines adjacent to other rows that slant in reverse directions and create a V-shape pattern. The understated texture against a bold tie is for the man who embraces the subtle nuances of men's fashion.

9. Piqué   Instantly recognizable as the fabric typical of short-sleeve polo shirts, piqué is sporty and goes with anything from casual suits to kick-around pants. Think Lacoste or Tommy Hilfiger.

10, 11. Basket Weave   These are "baby plaid" shirts that come in solids for tone-on-tone texture, or in contrasting colors for a shirt with a slightly checkered effect. The basket weave can be quite natty when worn with tailored suits and chunky knit ties, and it looks fresh and rich when worn untucked with a distressed pair of jeans and loafers or sneakers.

Stripes and Patterns

12, 13. Fine Stripes on Broadcloth   The backbone fabric of better men's dress shirts, broadcloth is a medium-weight fabric that has very fine crosswire ribs. Executive types need an array of these shirts in microstripes and solids to serve as the background for "power" ties.

14–17. Pin and Mille-Raie Stripes   The time-honored partner to the business suit, pin-striped shirts were at one time reserved for spring and summer wear. The shirt is now a year-round essential that's stately and always manly. These shirts serve as great contrasts to ties with small, tasteful prints.

18. Two-Tone Chalk Stripes   This is a racy variation on the traditional pinstripe.

19, 20. Candy Stripes   Preppy to the core, especially when fashioned with a button-down collar, candy stripes have grown up a bit in recent years and are wearable with anything from flat-front dress shorts to a tailored suit with a tie.

21, 22. Variegated and Hairline Stripes   This is a breath of fresh air that's reminiscent of old-world men's haberdashery. These stripes beautifully incorporate pastels and look smashing under dark suits in cooler months, as well as tan or khaki suits in the spring and summer.

23–26. Awning and Two-Toned Stripes   These patterns are his bold, fun shirts that don't necessarily need to be starched to a crisp when worn casually. The dandy who is not afraid of color and pattern will be bold enough to pair this wide stripe with contrasting patterned ties.

27–29. Gingham Checks   An English favorite, and a southern gentleman's pride, ginghams in pale blues and lush pastels are serious "swooning" shirts that display a man's softer side. There is nothing better than owning a range that fit his suits and ties perfectly, and a few oversized versions for chinos and vacation days.

30–34. Tattersalls and Windowpanes   The height of snappy dress, this pattern is simply a classic bold grid done in color atop white or a soft color. Be careful when matching these shirts with patterned suits—it takes a sharp eye and an even more confident wearer.

Before

THE MAKEOVER

Elisabeth Filarski and husband Tim Hasselbeck

Elisabeth, a footwear designer, and host of The Look for Less *on Style Network, met Tim six years ago. Tim is a professional football player. Elisabeth's friendly, sweet exterior is deceiving. She endured thirty-nine days in the Australian outback and twelve* Survivor 2 *tribal councils, but outlasting her husband Tim's hold on his true-blue ways and getting him to see life's little rainbows is now one of Elisabeth's biggest struggles.*

LLOYD: What was the first thing you noticed about Tim's style when you met?

ELISABETH: I really liked the sportiness he had to him. He wore really clean, classic lines that had just a little funk to it. I liked that.

LLOYD: Anything you remember him wearing back then that stands out in your mind? Anything you remember wishing to change?

ELISABETH: In the early days, . . . gosh, this might come back to haunt me.

TIM: There is a shirt that I know of. It was a green mock-turtleneck thing. I liked it because I thought it was comfortable, and then one day Elisabeth got up enough nerve to say it was hideous, and I don't think I've ever worn it again.

ELISABETH: I think it might have been our second date, and when he came to pick me up I just looked at him and was thinking, "I hope he borrowed that."

LLOYD: And you took heed when she got up the nerve to tell you she hated it?

TIM: I did. I still wanted another date at that point. Is that bad?

LLOYD: Absolutely not. Now, getting beyond that first mock-neck, what's it like shopping for Tim?

ELISABETH: I love to shop for him, but he's picky when it comes to shirt collars. A shirt has to have a good neck. So when I'm shopping I'm just thinking, "Okay, I've got to find a good neck."

LLOYD: A good neck? Like a turtleneck? A secure, beefy neck on a T-shirt? What kind are we talking about?

ELISABETH: Yeah, a secure neck. If it's a crew neck it must be good and well-fitting around the neck, and if it's a turtleneck it can't be too high and choke him. To find all that and then start working with colors, it's a little tricky. Tim doesn't like shirts you have to tuck in, either.

LLOYD: Tim, Elisabeth is a designer and loves color. Do you have colors that you never, ever wear?

TIM: Definitely. It's not the colors you'd normally think would bother me. I'm not afraid to wear a pink or a purple shirt. I'm just not a yellow person. If you went in my closet, you would see just about every shade of blue.

ELISABETH: It's all blue. He may call something green, but it's not. It's blue.

LLOYD: So you really stay away only from yellow and gold tones.

TIM: Okay, okay, I admit it. If it's not blue, I won't buy it.

ELISABETH: How about this? We recently went out shopping and I found this great green shirt. Lime green. I said get that, it's great, and he's all "I don't know." Then he goes and reaches for the blue one . . .

TIM: I think it's almost a trained habit rather than an absolute preference. It's just that most of my stuff is that color, so I should just stick to it. I'll wear a light powder blue or a navy . . .

ELISABETH: He knows his colors, and he looks good in color.

TIM: I usually just stay away from yellows and oranges.

LLOYD: Would you be willing to try a new color if it pleased her?

TIM: I would, especially if she said it looked good. I trust her.

ELISABETH: His shirt collection, in terms of style and cut, is great. Tim just needs a little pizzazz. When he comes to the door and he's in color, I'm surprised, but I love it, because I'm attracted to color. Yeah, when I see he's put on color just for me, I go "oooh." I think color goes directly with confidence. If you can wear something that's a little edgy or a bold color, I think it says "I feel good about myself." I think that's one of the most attractive things about someone, when they feel good about themselves.

LLOYD: Well, Tim, you know what you've got to do from now on.

TIM: Exactly. You'll know when I'm in the doghouse. That's when I'll be breaking out a new shirt in a new color.

The Make Over Prescription: *Relaxed elegance with a burst of unexpected color was Elisabeth's shirt makeover goal for Tim. Her simple, yet colorful take on style comes to life in a baby pink check spread-collar dress shirt, worn super casually. And as a bonus that most women secretly wish for, she finally got him to don a classic pair of flat front (not pleated) sand chinos. The result: She proves that real men do, in fact, wear pink!*

After

Richard Roundtree as *Shaft* sporting plaid pants that epitomize cool.

His Pants
The Wardrobe Workhorse

MODERN PANTS WERE ONCE THE SINGLE ITEM OF CLOTHING THAT SEPARATED THE SEXES. She wore the dresses, and he wore the pants. Period. End of story. Menswear would sometimes complement or borrow the fabrics used for making dresses, but pants always remained male. While the traditional role of pants has changed, their shape and function have not.

American women have long understood the mystery, power, and practicality of pants even before it was acceptable for them to get into a pair of their own. In May 1943, Norman Rockwell's "Rosie the Riveter" graced the cover of our country's literary leisure bible, *The Saturday Evening Post*. It featured a then shocking, but now classic, American image, of a pretty but strong blue-collar woman who had biceps to rival those of Atlas. She was working hard and she was proud of it; her pants said it all. Rockwell chose the rugged, deep-indigo denim overall that was well-worn, cuffed, and adorned with patriotic pins and a wartime salute. The style changed for women and a whole new world opened up; traditional roles started to change. Yet the pant still remained the nucleus of a man's wardrobe; it didn't change his world.

Today most men prefer casual pants, but it wasn't until the late 1940s that American men ushered such casual fabrics like cotton into their regular wardrobes. Cotton chino twills—what we call khakis—were integrated into social dress after World War II when the military-issue uniform pants made their way into off-duty settings and more peaceful times. Corduroy also was once considered to be the tough and protective anchor of the blue-collar uniforms. And denim was the Navy's answer to offshore "play clothes"—stark white uniforms were saved for active duty.

Before the war, *Esquire* applauded the arrival of a new staple for men's dress trousers—alas, gabardine in all its splendor. The flowing look of the wool fabric became synonymous with dapperly dressed 1930s and '40s screen legends like the aloof Gary Cooper and the earnest Jimmy Stewart. Worn with a higher waist, a knife-sharp crease, and a billowing drape, gabardine lingered around the leg like a ring of smoke.

Here's an excerpt from the August 1935 *Esquire* article titled "Now Everybody's Going in for Gabardine":

We've been talking about gabardine for so long that the only expression we have left on the subject is a tendency to yawn now the season has arrived in which the whole country seems suddenly to have gone goofy over it with a wide-eyed air of discovery. Well, you'd better excuse or ignore our boredom, because it's very good although, like sex, it had been around for quite a while before everybody began taking it up . . .

Who would ever have guessed that we would actually miss the age of elegance in men's dress by mourning the exclusivity of pants? It certainly seems like racy stuff for 1935.

In *The Wild One* (1954), Marlon Brando toughened American men's psyches by encouraging men to follow his lead and wear "dungarees" without apology. A year later, in *East of Eden*, James Dean took up the antiestablishment cause by sporting obviously soiled flat-front cotton pants. The two images must have been a shock to buttoned-up 1950s men, who were not far removed from the clean and pressed military uniforms they wore in World War II. Where Tinseltown left off, America's counterculture youth picked up by bucking every rule they could, turning men's pants into a symbol of sexuality.

Most women remember the 1960s by the men who turned them on. Think of Sean Connery as James Bond in the 1964 hit *Goldfinger*. Remember his slim "cigarette" pants? The decade's flip side proved to be a sartorial split for men, which left Connery behind for more radical trouser trendsetters like Jimi Hendrix, whose hip-hugging denim, velvet, and leather pants set female fans ablaze as much as his prowess on the guitar. In the '60s, pants became a form of personal expression; rules were often left bent or broken. It was not uncommon to see heavyset men in flat-front "Italian-style" pants reminiscent of mod English kids on London's Carnaby Street, or slim men donning earthy and androgynous belly-skimming flares well into the *Soul Train* 1970s.

However, it was just a matter of time before pants sobered up; the obligatory return to a more "wearable" model was inevitable. Like history, fashion is cyclical; the masses wanted their simple pants back. The late 1980s brought men khakis that were economical, utilitarian, and, above all, comfortable.

Companies like Dockers, the Gap, and Tommy Hilfiger transformed khakis into the "new" blue jean for men. The same '60s Haight-Ashbury hippies who made blue jeans their love-in uniform were Silicon Valley CEOs by the mid-1990s, and they made one truth crystal clear: Khakis became their social equalizer, ready for the boardroom and a pizza dinner out with the family.

More than almost any other area of a man's wardrobe, the future of pants will always lie in its past. Those tried-and-true styles that have served as the sturdy building block of a man's wardrobe will always be the fittest style to survive. From faded denim jeans to khakis and a pair of flannel trousers, it is clear that the classics will always remain the hallmark of a man of taste and style.

James Dean in *East of Eden*

Marlon Brando in *The Wild One*

His Pants

HIS PANTS 101

From the Bottoms Up

Your man may wear the pants, but are they the right ones? Or does your man *think* he wears the pants in your house and has no idea what wearing the "right" ones could possibly mean? We're not talking run-of-the-mill pants here. Not khakis, jeans, or sweatpants, but dress trousers, which you really should consider to be the nucleus of your man's new and improved wardrobe.

Jack Ferrari, vice president of menswear for Zanella—an Italian trouser company whose wares are sold at classic men's stores, including Saks Fifth Avenue and Bergdorf Goodman Men—points out some of the nuances on a walking tour through good and bad britches.

On the importance of "good" pants:

Regardless of what happens with the suit today, either in the workplace or in a more formal setting, dress trousers are still important. A man might not wear a suit to work, but a man who works in an office environment will always have the need to wear a nice pair of wool dress trousers—they're becoming the cornerstone for the wardrobe of well-dressed men today.

On the "fold war":

Although women love a man in flat-front trousers, men still have a penchant for pleated dress trousers. Understand that it took men ten years to get out of flat fronts, like those of the '40s and '50s, and get into pleats. It may take another ten years for average guys to get back into flat-front trousers.

The relationship between flat fronts and pleats is cyclical. It's fashion. I do see, when you get into cotton-based fabrics, the moleskin, the corduroys, that men are much more receptive to some flat-front pants. It's becoming more of a lifestyle choice than an across-the-board change in men's attitudes. Despite how popular flat-front pants and trousers may seem, today flat fronts are only five percent of our business. So, sorry, ladies, we still sell a lot of pleated trousers here.

Pants—the great divide:

Most average guys don't know how to put "outfits" together; they don't have the eye for it. I think the women have a better understanding of knowing how to pick out the right jacket, the right shirt, and the right trouser because they've been doing it a lot longer. It's complicated for men, because this whole "dress-down" thing has happened almost overnight. It can be tough for a guy who wears a suit, because he doesn't always know how to go out and buy separates, like pants.

Britches and blunders:

The biggest mistake many men make when trying to spruce up their personal pant collection is jumping on hot new trends in trousers or trying to be too fashionable. Remember when yellow and red were popular tones in all areas of menswear? I mean, it was just too much in pants. Too much color is a no-no. My advice: When dressing up and updating his pant selection always remember: Less is more.

Taking him by the seat of his pants:

A lot of men are falling short today in not keeping up with the elegance of modern women. I see a lot of women on the street today, especially in the evening, very nicely dressed, and the men they are with are unfortunately not dressed to the same level. Every man should make every effort to own a nice blazer and tasteful trousers so they can respectfully be on the same level as their female counterpart.

Pants don't just stand alone:

Women need to also remember that a great pair of pants should go with a quality shirt. So balance your time, care, and eye in all areas of sportswear, especially his sport shirts and knits. I think that some men still may be a little bit leery to go out and buy a beautiful cashmere polo shirt for $500, but a woman is used to doing it, and I think that's where a man really needs help. As you focus on pants, keep one eye on putting together his "better sportswear" wardrobe.

The switched britch:

I wish that men would just throw away all those plain, old khakis. It's such a boring uniform. If your man is a die-hard khaki type, you can satisfy his love for casual cotton pants by choosing Italian-made cotton chinos or even corduroys that have a familiar cut to them and a beautiful imported cotton fabric. For the price, it's a worthwhile investment, because they last longer and look much more elegant—relaxed elegance, that is.

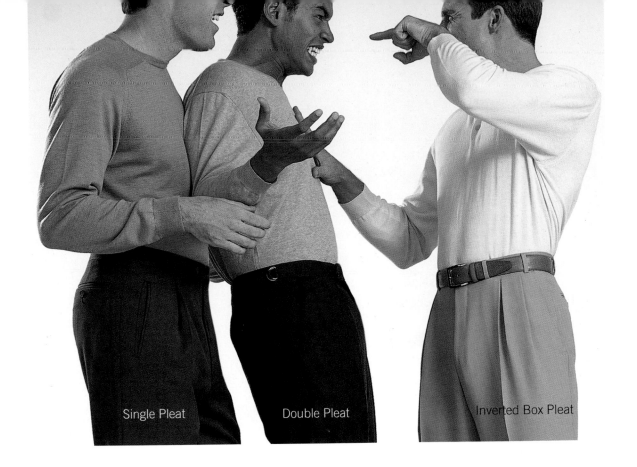

Single Pleat

Double Pleat

Inverted Box Pleat

The checkpoints:

For high-end men's dress pants, the fit is the first thing to keep in mind, followed by versatility. He needs to determine if he can wear them with a sports jacket, a solid blazer, and casually with a polo, sweater, or his favorite relaxed knit shirt.

From a quality standpoint, you should be aware of the inside as well as the outside. Ladies should be sure to check for an inside lining that extends down to the knee of the trouser. Quality is always immediately evident in the closure on a pant—we don't use traditional metal clasps on our trousers, we use double button, and it's considered a trademark of Zanella workmanship. We also incorporate a beautiful lining inside the waistband of our trousers and tape all the seams inside the garment, which is a mark of excellence for any label and simply helps with the comfort of the trousers.

The bottom line:

The bottom line is that when a man gets dressed up in a beautiful pair of well-made navy blue or charcoal gray pants, with a white dress shirt and a beautiful tie, nothing looks better.

THE FIT DETAILS

MOST OF THE SAME FIT PRINCIPLES THAT APPLY TO MEN'S SUIT PANTS APPLY TO SELECTING trousers (see the suit chapter). The one main difference is determining where the pant fits around his waist and backside, as this area is obviously more visible when a man wears just a shirt and trousers than when he's wearing a suit jacket. Your man should pay close attention to his own body flaws to make sure that he doesn't inadvertently highlight them with an ill-fitting trouser. Here are a few easy watchpoints:

- Pleated pants create a smooth drape on the trouser leg, and this can help a slimmer man appear a touch fuller. Contrary to popular belief, flat-front trousers are rather slimming—even for some heavier men. Pleats actually add additional fabric around his waist, which sometimes creates the illusion of an even larger midsection if he has a pear-shaped body and slight "love handles."

- Stick to zippers for well-endowed men, and avoid button-fly dress trousers because of the trousers' tendency to bunch and pucker around the crotch area.

- Cuffs help to add a slight bit of weight at the bottom of his trousers, creating a smoother line from waist to toe.

- Pants without cuffs usually look best if they are hemmed with a slight angle, allowing a touch more fabric near the heel.

- Pant length should always allow the shoe to be exposed from about the middle of his instep on a low dress shoe. Remember that about a quarter of the top of his shoe should be covered.

- Skintight pants really look appropriate only on rock stars. The leg shape on a pant should be moderate and somewhat trim, not overly blousy or ultraslim. These looks will come in and out of fashion, and on the wrong-shaped man will visually shift his frame in the wrong direction. Examples are a big-bellied man in trim pants (an "egg on legs"), and a pear-shaped man in blousy pants that add volume.

- And, for the last time, never allow him to wear a belt and braces with pants at the same time. It's amazing how many men still do this! Imagine wearing a pair of thigh-high stockings with panty hose—this is the same look and idea, and is a true style faux pas.

THE PERFECT PANTS: MOLESKIN

LET'S FACE IT, LADIES, MEN LOVE KHAKIS. SO LAY DOWN YOUR SWORD AND SHIELD, AND embrace the comfort and kinship that most men feel about this American classic, chinos. His second skin was once the college trouser of choice—especially for the preppy set—or the weekend decompression pant for the professional man who wore dress pants for forty or more hours during his workweek. For lots of men, chinos are now the preferred work pants, but there are options.

Upon first glance, you'll both be singing the praises of the moleskin pant, its duality of fit and wear. The moleskin pant is an easy yet gently enhancing addition to any man's wardrobe—especially for those men who need to learn the difference between dressing down and dressing down-and-out with the same old khakis over and over again. The benefits are clear:

- Traditionally used for sportswear and for work clothes, moleskin is wearable from the fall to late spring. Pure cotton moleskin fabric is extremely soft and warm, yet modish, and it has been a long-standing favorite for casual pants in England, where the cool, damp weather has never stopped natty men from looking comfortably chic.

- Durability is one of the main reasons that, next to his dog, khakis are truly a man's best friend. The beauty of the moleskin pant is that it machine-washes just at easily as any chino, and it gets more comfortable over time. This pant rarely loses its hand, and it embodies a well-worn charm that rivals that of his favorite pair of jeans.

- Although the most versatile colors are traditional khaki, sand, or British khaki, moleskins hold color very well. For a fashion-forward man who is not afraid of color, choose a classic fire-engine-red pair for the holidays, which looks great with a tweed blazer. Navy blue moleskin pants transition easily from day to night with a matching cashmere sweater and high-shined black dress shoes or boots.

- With or without cuffs, these pants look snappy, and he can pair them super-casually with his favorite sneakers by just rolling up the cuffs or add a sharp, finished hem and create the yacht club mood by pairing them with a crisp white dress shirt and a pair of driving moccasins.

- While pleated styles are fine, choose flat fronts for the most modern take on this comfortable, slightly dressy upgrade to khakis. Plain fronts create a cleaner line and convert easily between the workplace and sportier, casual looks.

THE SEVEN ESSENTIAL PANTS FOR MEN

IT CAN BE PAINFULLY OBVIOUS THAT MANY MEN DON'T NEED MUCH ASSISTANCE WHEN IT comes to collecting casual pants they can kick back in—from khakis to jeans and the occasional pair of track pants—since these pants are all about comfort and familiarity. Collecting dress trousers, however, is a very different matter.

Investing in well-made trousers can be an unwelcome task for a man, because most men do prefer comfort to style. This is especially so of trousers he's expected to incorporate within his

A. Wool or Cotton Gabardine

B. Worsted Wool

C. Crepe

day-to-day wardrobe. The truth is this: Less is far beyond more when it comes to selecting trousers. Typically, men need their trousers to sit nicely on the body, not constrict, and wear well. That's it. And that's easy enough.

There are seven standard dress pants out there that can give polish to your guy's wardrobe. This list starts with versatile, year-round pants that fit almost every lifestyle, continues on to the more relaxed, and then to tweedy masculine favorites that create a season-specific look. ➤

D. Cavalry Twill   E. Flannels   F. Linen   G. Tweeds

A. Wool or Cotton Gabardine

Some think of wool gabardine as the big brother to khakis because of its tendency to be colored in neutrals and because its twill is woven in the same way as cotton khaki. However, gabardine is decidedly more elegant in its drape and still durable in its smooth, almost firm finish. While the fabric's weight fluctuates from designer to designer, most men living north of the Mason-Dixon line can wear these trousers year-round. They are an almost perfect match to almost any blazer or sports jacket. Start with British khaki to take a step up from cotton khakis, then add a pair of navy and charcoal to give your man's wardrobe a sophisticated touch.

B. Worsted Wool

These trousers are probably the easiest to recognize because of their smooth, clear fabric finish and lightweight hand. This is *the* fabric for most men's tailored clothing, because worsted wool is never itchy and keeps an even, fuzz-free surface that drapes beautifully and holds a sharp crease. Worsted wool trousers in pleated or flat front are probably the smartest place for a guy to start building or expanding upon his dress pant wardrobe.

C. Crepe

A member of the worsted wool family, wool crepe can be a plain flat weave or slightly ribbed twill similar to gabardine. You will recognize this matte, dry fabric because it's so prevalent in womenswear. Pants in crepe are ideal for the traveling man because, in a pinch, wrinkles steam out easily in a humid bathroom. Crepe trousers pair nicely with other rich textures, like cashmere and merino wool sweaters. If your man has invested in the basic colors and still wants other options, try a chalk- or pinstripe that looks sharp on the pebbly surface of crepe.

D. Cavalry Twill

Some men love this rugged yet dressy fabric for its wide use in military uniforms. When woven in a "beefier" twill, sometimes labeled as "Tricotine," it looks similar to cotton chinos—but with a softer and more elegant finish. Most men can easily slip into cavalry twill without feeling stuffily dressed or constricted. Add a denim shirt and cool dress boots for a casual take, or pair them with a tweed blazer for the look of a country gentleman. Since these pants are an easy upgrade to khakis, start with light neutrals and then move to darker tones of tobacco, olive, navy, and black.

E. Flannels

Known for their nappy, soft finish and gentlemanly aura, flannels connote elegance and maturity. This pant, when lined, is a great cold-weather dress-pant essential. Soft pinstripes and chalk stripes work extremely well on flannel trousers, and cuffed models provide just the right amount of natty verve, harkening to the elegant silver-screen stars of the 1940s. Timeless outfit combinations would include pairing charcoal gray flannels with a matching wool turtleneck, chalk stripe navy blue flannels with a French blue dress shirt, or the quintessential black flannel pants sported with a camel sweater or blazer.

F. Linen

To be linen means to wrinkle, but this is the beauty of the cool, breathable cottonlike fabric that is the summer pant for men who are well put together. Linen pants have an air of wealth and nonchalance that is confident and sexy when worn casually cuffed with a sandal or as a part of a tailored suit with a tie and white bucks. Since these pants have a rotation time of about three months, help your man play into the fun of the season and wear colors that are as fun as his favorite vacation spot. If he's a mountain man, go for pale neutrals and washed cognacs. Or maybe he's an island guy and can appreciate crisp white for evenings, butter for sunset, and sky blue for walks along the beach. The fit should be just as loose and carefree.

G. Tweeds

Tweed is rough to the touch and tough enough to stand the damp temperatures near the Tweed River, which separates Britain from Scotland. Tweed's nubby nature is great for autumn and winter months and comes in a variety of solids, checks, plaids, and—for the trendy—a combination of all three. Although solids are acceptable, the best bet is to lean toward Donegals, made up of tiny multicolored woolen knobs; houndstooth; and tartans, which look great around the holidays.

Before

THE MAKEOVER

Cynthia Rowley and her best friend and muse, Alan Cumming

Cynthia and Alan are not the kind of people who fit themselves into one easy box. Alan is an actor/director/writer/fashion darling with more than thirty-five film roles under his belt and a 1998 Tony Award for his breakthrough and role-redefining performance as Cabaret's *Emcee. Rowley is a designer/mother/financial guru/coauthor. With Ilene Rosenzweig, she wrote* Swell: A Girl's Guide to the Good Life, *and is the head of a youthful and spirited collection that's earned praise from the Council of Fashion Designers of America. While Cynthia and Alan are two real trendsetters in every sense of the word, who wears the pants?*

LLOYD: But what's so cool about you, Alan, is that you have no problem switching from a great pair of pin-striped pants one day to a kilt the next. You just like to have fun and some guys won't wear linen or drawstring pants. Who taught you how to dress? Who has been your biggest style inspiration?

ALAN: I think it was more like a combination of a series of bad fashion times I've lived through, like the '80s. And then, when I was in my late twenties I discovered my own style. I think the way you feel about clothes is a sort of expression of how you feel about yourself. If you're comfortable, you wear a certain type, and if you feel you can flit in and out of different things, you're more adventurous. I think that was the way I progressed as a person; I made my sense of style.

LLOYD: What would you like to see men do in this new millennium?

CYNTHIA: Wow. I think men should experiment a little bit and get rid of . . . what are those called, Dockers?

ALAN: I think every man who irons his jeans should be killed. I really think that's a capital offense.

CYNTHIA: I like a guy who can iron other things for me, though.

ALAN: Like money.

LLOYD: Money's good. Why do you think khakis are such a bad thing?

CYNTHIA: They're just so safe. I think we shouldn't want to have anything too safe. Just experiment with fabric, velveteen, and leather and wool, and then experiment with color, too.

LLOYD: Overall, Cynthia, does it make women happy to see a guy experiment with pants?

CYNTHIA: Yeah. Well, it can certainly be the start of some very weird conversations. It's almost as though it should take place over a martini, or a margarita.

ALAN: I did wear a kilt to a fund-raiser in New York at the Metropolitan Museum of Art. I wanted to do a Scottish warrior, a modern take on it. I had on a big fluffy thing and a hat with a feather in it, and the kilt had a big slash up it. But it was a girl's kilt from Cynthia's girls' collection, and there was a thing in the newspaper in Scotland, it said, "Alan, if you can't wear the kilt properly, don't wear it at all."

CYNTHIA: In general, I think, men are more interested in fashion now. It seems like there's a lot more out there and they can be expressive with their clothes. They just need a little encouragement.

LLOYD: Not that Alan does! What do you love about his style?

CYNTHIA: It's very eccentric and very Alan in every way. Even if I would say here's a suit, plain black suit, it would never just look like a plain black suit. It would always look very expressive in a very Alan way.

LLOYD: Has he been a muse for you and your menswear collection?

CYNTHIA: Definitely.

LLOYD: Do you have one pearl of wisdom that people should keep in mind when it comes to fashion?

CYNTHIA: I'm not very good at dictating to people and saying "This is you" or "This is what you should do." Maybe try leaving new stuff around and make it seem inviting. If he likes Budweiser, then give him new stuff in a Budweiser box. Or maybe you just empty out the guy's closet and fill it with cool stuff. Put the old stuff in a Hefty bag and put it in the trunk of your car and get rid of it. Then he's left with no choice.

ALAN: I think men should remember it's their sense of style, but listen to other people's advice. Sometimes men wear something so not them and its obvious someone's tried to change them, and all of a sudden they're like those fridge magnets that you stick clothes on.

The Make Over Prescription: *Cynthia got her best friend Alan to jump into pencil thin, flat-front white cotton trousers that hold a knife-sharp crease, and three-inch cuffs—for an edgy take on dress pants. She chose to camp it up in her usual "swell" way by topping his fresh pants with a slick brown silk striped jacket, and layered a yellow and white bias striped shirt and a white knit vest beneath. The result: The high-octane, made-over man!*

After

The Perpetually Polished Fred Astaire

His Shoe
The Daily Judgment

FOR SOME WOMEN, THERE'S NOTHING MORE IMPORTANT ON A MAN THAN HIS SHOES. IS this passion an extension of her own penchant for footwear? Or is it just part of sizing a guy up and giving him the once-over? The average man thinks footwear is simply a necessity, not a nicety. Shoes protect his feet from the elements. Men believe that their shoes are "body vehicles," of sorts, that power them from point A to point B.

For a woman, shoes can capture a range of emotions—even just for an evening. A sexy strappy sandal makes her feel as smolderingly beautiful as Elizabeth Hurley. Put on the good pair of sneakers and suddenly she's Venus Williams; or a pair of thigh-high boots and she's Jennifer Lopez.

Shoes just don't do the same thing for men. Some guys may have seen movies starring well-heeled style icons like Fred Astaire and Gene Kelly, but a man doesn't put on a pair of high-shined oxfords and think he's suddenly a dancing romantic. Or in the 1970s, some men may have watched New York Knicks star Walt "Clyde" Frazier strut off-court in custom-made crocodile boots, but they didn't catch every last detail about Clyde's boots in the same way a woman would.

Fashion in men's footwear is found in the nuances, the color, or shape of the toe. Unlike the vast array of shoes available to women, men have several basic styles to choose from: wing tips, oxfords, loafers, sneakers, and boots. Sometimes it takes nothing short of a pop-culture revolution to really inspire changes in men's footwear. For instance, the popular 1960s boot referred to as the "Beatle boot" was inspired by the Fab Four from Liverpool. The boot had been a part of British culture since the mid-1800s and resurfaced as the must-have shoe once John, Paul, George, and Ringo paired it with their slim Carnaby Row suits.

It is clear that shoe trends come and go very quickly. Today's hottest shoes can easily become Fido's next chew toy. Also remember that the most finely tuned style arbiter always measures from the ground up, so getting your man in the right shoe is the best foundation to building his style.

HIS SHOES 101

ALTHOUGH MEN'S SHOE STORES AND SHOE DEPARTMENTS PALE IN COMPARISON TO WOMEN'S, the process of recognizing and selecting a quality pair of shoes is the same at both places. The privilege of purchasing custom shoes is one that's afforded to a very elite few. There are still many Europeans and some Americans who believe in the time-honored craft of "commissioning" a shoe style: the exact style, color, material, and most of all, a fit custom-tailored to the foot.

New York City–based custom men's and women's shoe maker Ron Donovan is best known for his strong lines, signature stitching, and distinctive shapes that grace the feet of a clientele of professional athletes, Wall Street barons, and many of the models you see on New York City fashion runways. An engineer by trade, Donovan switched career paths to train at the elbow of old-world shoe craftsmen in Italy and France. He offers some simple tips for finding a shoe that looks good and is well made:

The first thing to look for:

Before looking at the shoe, look at your man. Think about his lifestyle. His career path. What would you and he want? Then look at shoes that are consistent with that image.

On quality:

When examining your shoe of choice, look at the quality of the material. When choosing leather, I always recommend looking from the inside out, because shoes are built from the inside out. The sturdier the components on the inside, the longer the shoe will last on the outside. For example, many shoes, even very expensive shoes, are made with compressed board for insoles, instead of leather. By industry standards this compressed cardboard lasts for a long time, but it's not as durable as leather. A leather insole allows the shoe to maintain its shape on the bottom, and it can be resoled, unlike the compressed-cardboard versions.

On lining:

You want to make sure that a high-quality leather is used for the lining. As with clothing, you want to look at the stitching to see if it's straight and consistent and finished.

On the outside:

On a leather shoe, make sure the leather is supple to the touch. Firm or less firm leather is used for shoes depending on its style; firm is used for wing tips, and softer leather is used for moccasins. Look for calf, soft calf, or kid leathers.

A common leather of good quality used to make men's dress shoes is napa, a type of calfskin, which is very soft and is typically used to make slip-on shoes. The softest leather is typically used to make dressier shoes. Kid leather is a little softer than napa and is typically used for men's casual shoes.

If you're considering a shoe's details—like wing tips, which traditionally have bold perforations and stitching—you want to make sure the perforation and stitching are consistent and uniform. Keep in mind that for custom-made shoes, there is usually some variation, since the work's all done by hand. Craftsmanship has its own signature. You'll never have one custom-made shoe that is exactly like the other.

Searching the sole:

You should invest in leather soles whenever possible. The best dress shoes have leather soles. As with clothing, natural fibers are better because they breathe. Synthetic fibers such as pressboard in the insole, don't allow the foot to breathe. A rubber sole causes the foot to perspire; the shoe retains moisture and, as a result, deteriorates.

On cost:

I've seen some pretty high-quality products that are affordable, and I've seen some very expensive designer shoes that aren't the best quality. I believe in that old retail adage that "the educated consumer is the best customer."

Simply put, there are quality shoes in pretty much everyone's price range. People say, "I can't afford good shoes," and I respond that you should look for the best shoes you can find in your price range and buy only what you can afford. Good shoes should be a combination of comfort and style. When making over your man, if you place emphasis on style and not comfort, trust me, he'll never wear the shoes—and that's no bargain.

Why choose custom:

My custom men's shoes average about $1,200 a pair, which, believe it or not, is pretty low in comparison to more traditional European and Madison Avenue shoe stores, which start at $2,800 and soar up to $19,000 a pair. There are several advantages to custom-made shoes: First, the shoes will fit perfectly. Two people who wear the same size shoe will not have the same shape foot and will need different types of shoes. Custom shoes are made from a mold of a person's foot, which allows them to reorder new shoes easily.

Men's biggest shoe mistake:

Most men neglect their shoes. They don't spend the time and effort to get them polished—and that's part of the preservation process, it's not just aesthetic. I've heard men say, "It's raining. Why should I get my shoes shined?" The answer: Polish is a layer of wax that coats and protects shoes from being damaged by the rain.

The eight classic shoes
every well-dressed man should own

The Loafer, Slip-On

This is not a formal shoe; hence the name loafer. The slip-on shoe is designed for ease and casual wearing and goes best with clothes that do the same. Preppy guys may prefer the penny loafer. However, the slip-on shoe is more versatile because it has fewer design details and surface decorations. The formal evening slipper will be described a little later. When in doubt, pick black. (For more about the loafer, see page 93.) ➤

The Oxford

Simple, elegant, and sturdy, the oxford is the shoe that can take a man from a business suit to a tuxedo if needed. This shoe is for business and dressy affairs that require a strong, sophisticated, and formal statement. Oxfords—first made in 1640 in Oxford, England—were the first lace-up shoes for men. First they were popular among Oxford University students; today they are still considered the bestselling style of men's shoe.

The Cap-Toe Oxford

This shoe, a slightly more casual cousin of the oxford, was created more than a hundred years ago by English shoe maker John Lobb. The cap-toe with tiny holes or perforations along the seam of the shoe are commonly known as "brogues" and have more of an ornate dandy tone, yet in rich browns and black are more classic than trendy.

The Wing Tip

The wing tip is another popular classic dress shoe that can swing more casual when needed, yet is still the perfect match for business suits and sport coats. The traditionally thick leather sole makes the shoe look both authoritative and fancy. Wing tips come in lots of different colors, but brown-based earth tones always look best. Pants worn with ornate wing tips should be no bolder than a tonal chalk stripe or fine pinstripe.

The Boot

Once reserved for colder months, boots are now the new casual and dressy shoe for smart, stylish men almost year-round. Bad boys look to the motorcycle boot for a macho edge of mystery, whereas good guys embrace the lace-up, ¾-ankle boot for a polished professional look that is just a small departure from oxfords. The happy medium for all men is the classic English jodhpur boot, which is great to wear with casual dress pants, khakis, or a pair of boot-cut jeans.

The Monk Strap

Named for their similarity in design to the sandals that monks traditionally wore, this is a versatile dress shoe that can actually carry both narrow-legged suits and casual dress trousers. Look for versions that are clean in design, without pronounced stitching or crimped edges, since the asymmetrical, buckled closure is the focus of the shoe. Monks are equally powerful in both suede and leather, and work best in black and rich browns.

The Casual Shoe

For some modern men of style, the sandal is one of summer's many pleasures. Many men are even becoming more comfortable wearing a backless version of a classic slip-on or loafer known as "men's mules." Another sockless solution for the man wanting comfort but who is a little shy about exposing his toes to the world is the classic driving moccasin, which is a look that definitely bespeaks a man of leisure and taste and can even be paired with a summer suit. Authentic driving moccasins have a series of rubber knobs along the sole.

Basic Men's Shoe Care

- *Keep a cedar shoe tree in each shoe to absorb moisture and retain the shoe's shape.*

- *Limit wearing new shoes to a maximum of three hours at a time to allow the material, especially leather and suede, to get accustomed to the foot.*

- *Forget shoe boxes. Store shoes made of any natural material—leather, suede, and canvas—in open closet space on shoe racks to allow them to breathe.*

- *Avoid wearing the same pair of shoes every day—instead, wear them a day on, a day off. Rotate your shoes and give them at least twenty-four hours' recovery time. Your feet will thank you.*

- *Avoid smashing your foot into the back of the shoe, because this can damage the shoe's heel. Take an extra minute and use a shoe horn.*

- *Buy soft fabric shoe bags for travel. Many high-end shoe designers include them with the shoes at the time of purchase. Shoe bags protect shoes from scuffing inside luggage.*

- *Loosen your shoes and take them off slowly. Try not to force one shoe off with the help of the toe of the other foot, as many people do out of habit. This repeated practice damages the shoe.*

- *Always untie lace-up shoes after wearing them to allow the shoe to "decompress" after being tied for hours. This action also allows the laces some relief.*

The Formal Shoe

Many well-dressed men simply add a high shine to their existing clean-toed black oxford shoes, but for the man who wants that complete, head-to-toe statement of luxury and taste, formal shoes are in order. Sometimes referred to as the opera pump, the black calf—and sometimes patent leather—evening slipper is the pinnacle of dress footwear and evening elegance. However, don't let your man make one of the cardinal mistakes of style and wear his formal shoes with his everyday suits. The evening shoe is strictly for black-tie occasions.

THE PERFECT SHOE—THE LOAFER

THE PERFECT LOAFER THAT WILL TAKE YOUR MAN FROM DAY TO NIGHT, WEEKEND TO WORK-place, should have the following elements:

- Select a clean-lined, nondescript loafer that does not play into any trends of the moment. Choose a toe shape that is neither too pointed nor too square. Notice that there's no signature beef roll detail, or severed cross strap to hold change, placing the loafer in an overly casual category. Instead, the perfect loafer has one simple stitch around the toe and is as sleek as an aerodynamic stealth bomber—not a bump on the surface. That's style.

- Black leather is the smartest choice because it's so flexible. Unlike earth colors, black is never mistaken as informal when worn with dress clothes, yet can easily be "dumbed down" to go with casual clothes. Add a high shine for days in the boardroom or a first interview. Or let 'em go a bit for his favorite khakis or jeans; this way it doesn't look as if he's mistakenly wearing his "good" shoes on his day off.

- Help your man to embrace the pleasures of going sockless. For you ladies, this is like the joy of going barelegged in the spring after months wearing opaque tights or stockings. Tell him James Dean and Michael Jordan have gone sockless and it looked effortlessly chic yet very masculine. Omitting the socks gives the shoe a different look and offers a natural match to all of his casual pants—and definitely his shorts.

- Study craftsmanship. If your man thinks of his black leather loafer as his "everything" shoe, it will need to be of the best quality he can afford. Avoid rubber soles and choose leather soles, the essential detail that allows the shoe to be appropriate in both casual and near-formal circles. Look for supple quality leather that not only gives a little when wearing but will also last for years.

Before

THE MAKEOVER

Elizabeth Parkinson and Scott Wise

Dancers have to do more than just think fast on their feet. A husband and wife who are both on Broadway, Elizabeth and Scott know how to keep up with each other step for step. Scott, a choreographer, has starred in the show Damn Yankees *and earned a Tony Award for his performance in* Jerome Robbins' Broadway, *and he's alongside Catherine Zeta-Jones and Renee Zellweiger in the silverscreen version of* Chicago. *Scott and Elizabeth, formerly of the Joffrey Ballet, appeared in the original cast production of* Fosse, *and their careers reunite again in Billy Joel and Twyla Tharp's Broadway musical* Movin' Out. *Scott dances in the production and serves as assistant director and choreographer to the legendary Twyla Tharp, and Elizabeth costars.*

LLOYD: Elizabeth, what is the first thing you notice about the way a man dresses?

ELIZABETH: His shoes.

LLOYD: Why?

ELIZABETH: I don't know. It's not like I have a foot fetish, but for me there's nothing worse than a guy in a terrible pair of shoes. Have I ever told you that before?

SCOTT: Only when I wear my favorite shoes that it took you years to warm up to.

ELIZABETH: No, that's not true. Those shoes are neat.

SCOTT: I think they make a statement.

ELIZABETH: They're unique to you. I've never seen anyone else in those shoes.

SCOTT: No?

LLOYD: What kind are they?

ELIZABETH: Nike water moccasins.

LLOYD: What about dressy shoes? Do you look at those as well?

ELIZABETH: I like pretty simple shoes—nothing too fancy or outrageous.

SCOTT: It's unfortunate, but when I go out shopping for shoes, I always tend to gravitate toward the ones that cost, like, $5,000. I guess it's because I like a clean-cut shoe with simple design lines, and usually those are the ones that are so expensive. I like light and streamlined; I don't like a thick, heavy sole.

ELIZABETH: That probably has to do with being a dancer, because the shoes you have to wear are clean and simple.

SCOTT: Exactly. I like to have a thin and flexible sole so I can feel the floor beneath me when I'm moving around.

LLOYD: Elizabeth, have you ever bought Scott shoes? Would you dare?

ELIZABETH: Yes. In fact, I bought him that pair of crazy Nike water moccasins.

SCOTT: Now that I think of it, I only have one pair of dressy shoes. That's pathetic. I have about six pairs of sneakers, two pairs of regular shoes—and one pair kills my feet—and then I have boots. I used to wear cowboy boots all the time. It used to be that anytime I would get into a Broadway show, I'd treat myself to a very nice pair of cowboy boots . . .

LLOYD: And they're not cheap.

SCOTT: . . . and I'd get the good ones. I mean, we're talking about $500 to $1,000. Oh, they were beautiful. I'd wear them with my tuxedo to show openings. I always wore them, but I'm older now and my legs are tired. They're too dressy for the country, and I can't wear them around the city because they wreak havoc with my legs and knees and back because they have such a thin sole. I need a little more cushioning; I've been dancing for thirty-nine years.

LLOYD: You look great!

SCOTT: Yeah, I've been dancing for thirty-nine years. Now I'm looking for comfort. Do you know of something in a nice orthopedic?

The Make Over Prescription: *Elizabeth took up the battle for all women and got her man, Scott, to finally embrace a well-made, quality dress shoe—that he actually loves! Her choice is a honey tan, cap-toe Oxford with chocolate brown piping and traditional English topstitching. And this brilliant shoe commands a stellar outfit to boot. Elizabeth went "cozy chic" and draped Scott in a camel shawl-collar cardigan, ecru silk twill camp collar shirt, flowy classic tan "Hollywood" trousers (for his dancing feet), and just the right natural ribbed cotton lisle socks. The result: His best foot was finally put forward, making the rest of him stand at attention.*

After

His Outerwear
The First Façade

"THERE IS NO GOOD IN ARGUING WITH THE INEVITABLE. THE ONLY ARGUMENT AVAILABLE with an east wind is to put on your overcoat," said American poet James Russell Lowell in an 1884 address in Birmingham, England. Like a good guardian, outerwear is meant to serve and protect. It saves you from harsh conditions and wraps you safely warm. A really good piece of outerwear is like a trusted friend, because it's reliable and dependable. Most men have a soft spot for their favorite coat.

Coats and jackets are pieces of clothing that the world notices first. Sometimes, outerwear is a hallmark of a man's personality and his ambitions.

Think of rush hour in cities like New York and Chicago and the legions of men hustling and bustling around in sweeping cashmere overcoats. There's a business world out there to conquer, and these men are ready to grasp the brass ring. Or think of a BMOC—Big Man on Campus— ruling what's cool in his school in his varsity letter jacket.

Most outerwear trends have followed what's popular in current culture and the men who made them famous—from Napoleon in his sweeping wool coat to Sean Combs earning the nickname "Puffy" from the oversized down jackets he wore.

One of the most iconic coats in modern fashion is the belted Burberry trench coat. Thomas Burberry debuted his first gabardine raincoat in the 1890s. Due to its popularity, and with the help of a royal commission, he was asked to produce a version of waterproof coats for British army officers. The classic trench as we know it—with strong shoulders and epaulets, a D-ring belt, and a removable cashmere lining—was first worn during World War I.

The Burberry trench coat creates an imposing silhouette, and it has been worn by kings and presidents, captains of industry, and legends of the silver screen. Humphrey Bogart turned the Burberry trench into an integral part of his *Casablanca* legacy. Warren Beatty, too, donned a Burberry for his portrayal of Dick Tracy. Most recently, Ben Affleck carried the trench coat with the trademark check lining while pursuing his love interest in *Pearl Harbor*.

Sean "P-Diddy" Combs

Humphrey Bogart

Omar Sharif

Michael Jackson

The military spawned two other outerwear classics, one of which was the peacoat. This thick wool coat, woven in either black or midnight navy and designed to keep out the chill, was part of the U.S. Navy's uniform for more than a hundred years. Men couldn't live without this coat during World War II, and later hipsters flooded army/navy surplus stores in search of it. The peacoat's collar was worn coolly flipped up and the pockets were just deep enough to jam hands in and strike a perfect slouch. Utilitarian in the 1940s, a symbol of arty rebellion in the '50s, '60s, and '70s, the peacoat is considered an American classic today. Hollywood helped this craze along by dressing leading man Omar Sharif in *Dr. Zhivago;* making the peacoat a big screen icon.

What Bogart did for the trench, former President Dwight D. Eisenhower did for the golf jacket. The short, cut-to-the-waist jacket he preferred on the battlefields of Europe was modified to suit the passionate golfer. Eisenhower was photographed so frequently in this cropped jacket during World War II, and later while playing golf during his presidency, that any jacket cut to the waist with a banded bottom is now affectionately referred to in men's fashion as an "Eisenhower."

Around the time Eisenhower was creating his fashion legacy, on-screen rebels Marlon Brando and James Dean were doing the same thing. Who can think of Brando slumped over his motorcycle without his studded leather jacket in *The Wild One,* or Dean's brooding posture in his red windbreaker as he smokes a cigarette? In *The Catcher in the Rye,* Holden Caufield ran away from prep school to New York City wearing only a windbreaker.

A well-worn barn coat may be as tough and reliable as its wearer: President George W. Bush puts one on as soon as he gets to his Crawford, Texas, ranch. The man who likes the latest technical piece of extreme-conditions outerwear from companies like Timberland and North Face most likely owns a whole cache of gadgets as well. Oftentimes, a cashmere overcoat can be as smooth as the big-money negotiator it warms. A leather jacket can give a guy a distracting edge of toughness—even Michael Jackson has tried to use the leather jacket to best advantage. It's simple, the right coat can reflect a man's position, ambitions, and personality traits.

HIS OUTERWEAR 101

BEYOND ITS PRACTICAL PURPOSES, OUTERWEAR IS THE ONE CATEGORY OF CLOTHING THAT must also mix and commingle with the rest of a wardrobe. Outerwear projects one's street self, or the "look" the whole world is allowed to see.

Have you ever seen a man slip on his favorite "team" jacket and wear it with everything he owns—from khakis and jeans to a suit? Yikes, doesn't he realize that the Buffalo Bills and Brooks Brothers have never been in the same league? One of the biggest style faux pas a man can commit is to wear a jacket—like a team jacket, or a leather bomber—with a much longer suit jacket. In most cases, a coat is not just a coat, or a jacket just a jacket. Some men don't understand, and are confused about the levels of dressy, sporty, and endurance outerwear (jackets with lots of pockets and gadget-friendly zip-offs) available to them and which jacket or coat should serve as a final layer to their ensemble.

From my experience, a man either owns very few jackets—maybe no more than three, which he wears in and out for several seasons—or he owns a closet stuffed with a dozen or so items— hoodies, bombers, trenches, parkas, and overcoats—that for the most part go unused. For both scenarios, your man will probably have to come to terms with the sort of outerwear pieces he really needs that will withstand his hometown climate, his travels, and his activities.

For nearly a decade, Jeffrey Savitch, a top sales associate at Saks Fifth Avenue's New York City flagship store, has been helping men—from "average Joes," as he calls them, to CEOs and Wall Street tycoons—match themselves with the right outerwear piece. A common thread, Savitch says, among many of these men is that they consider their outerwear to be an afterthought and, therefore, an apparel "stepchild." Savitch's views on coats and jackets come from the perspective of a salesman who interacts directly with customers, not that of a fashionista hailing the "look of the moment." Here Savitch offers some advice on selecting outerwear:

The final frontier:

For most men, outerwear is just an afterthought and they throw on the most comfortable coat or jacket that's within reach before they leave the house, not realizing that good outerwear says so much about a man because it's the first thing that people see. So many times a man will come through the doors at Saks wearing a suit that costs thousands, beautiful shoes, gorgeous cuff links, and then a beat-up old raincoat. Instantly his look is ruined.

The classic coat for him:

Men should invest in a quality raincoat. Regardless of how casual we've become as a society, a good raincoat is a versatile and fashionable classic. An important tip for men who have sloping or broad shoulders: Pick a raglan sleeve that extends diagonally from the neckline. It will give an impressive silhouette.

The other coats he'll want and need:

Invest in a ¾-length cashmere or soft wool coat in camel that layers wonderfully over a suit. Second, your guy should consider a timeless barn jacket, like the one that Barbour and L.L. Bean made famous. Barn jackets are great foul-weather jackets that look better as they age. Shearling coats, lastly, provide maximum warmth and a touch of luxe. Shearlings are now great for fall and winter, because designers are creating them in lighter-weight versions and they can be worn over suits, unlike the bulky 1970s Marlboro Man versions.

The long and the short of length:

Men who are 5'10" or shorter should select a standard ¾-length coat and stay away from floor-length coats. Some coat manufacturers are offering slightly longer ¾-length coats for men who are taller than 5'10". It's important to keep a man's height in mind when selecting an overcoat; he'll look misfitted and awkward if the coat does not fall to the middle of his thigh.

Care and storage:

There are two myths about caring for outerwear. First is that coats and jackets should be dry-cleaned often; instead, do it maybe once a year. Dry cleaning can sometimes ruin natural fibers like wool and cashmere. Another common mistake many men make is that they store their "good coat" in a garment bag in the off-season. It's terrible to store natural fiber coats in a plastic garment bag. They need to breathe, so select a bag made out of mesh nylon or canvas.

The look of love:

Ladies, your guy should keep his outerwear subtle. Be conservative by avoiding bright reds, oranges, and bold patterns, and select classic shades of navy, black, camel, or olive. Also, don't let your guy buy a jacket with a gathered waist. That's a no-no. It looks so awful on most men.

The Details

It's important to scrutinize every detail of a coat or jacket, since outerwear lasts longer than most other clothing. On the flip side, before your guy decides he needs a new piece of outerwear, have him take another look in his closet. Since most outerwear is built to last, it could be that the coat or jacket just needs a quick fix at the tailor's, or a trip to the dry cleaners. The following are some of the details to examine:

Construction and Stitching

The garment should have stitches that are taut and uniform and created from a thick, sturdy thread. Some men can be pretty rough on their coats, so solid stitching is important for durability.

Linings

A coat has either a permanent or removable lining, or is unlined:

Permanent linings are sewn into the coat or jacket and should be positioned smoothly inside. To test its quality, turn the jacket inside out and look at its workmanship and construction. The finishing should be well stitched and sturdy enough that the jacket would do its duty even if it were worn inside out.

Removable linings are mostly found zipped into fall/winter coats and assorted foul-weather gear. The removable lining should be as well made as the jacket itself. Be sure your man tests the zippers or buttons to make sure the lining is easily removable and/or replaceable.

In unlined jackets, make sure the surface and its shape are smooth and the stitches are flat and do not pucker. Examine the interior to make sure the coat or jacket is properly finished and doesn't look like a mess of unfinished hems. The highest-quality unlined jackets have interior seams finished with tape.

Patterns

If your guy selects a patterned or plaid coat, have him be sure that the color and fabric are uniform throughout the garment (unless that's what the jacket is *supposed* to look like). If the fabric does not match perfectly, it could mean the coat was fashioned from two different bolts of material—a factory imperfection.

Collar

An outerwear collar is very important since it frames a man's face. As with dress shirts, stockier men should select wider and thicker collars and men with thinner faces should pick collars that

Lining

are thin and straight. A fastened collar should fit a man's neck. Examine the collar's underside to make sure it has no rough edges. Also, be sure that the collar is thick enough to withstand a cold wind. Don't have your guy wait for a blustery day to see if his upturned collar helps keep out the cold.

Pockets

A woman has her handbag, a man his coat pockets. On outerwear, pockets must be functional and sturdy enough to carry a number of things, including keys, a wallet, and a cell phone. In better outerwear, pockets are stitched beneath the lining. Pockets should be double-stitched and have a gusset, or an extra fold of fabric, to allow a full pocket some give.

Fasteners: Buttons, Clasps, Snaps, and Zippers

The fastener is the most critical outerwear detail and should be tested for quality.

Buttons should open and close easily. Stitching should be sturdy and even on buttons and buttonholes. The button should also be anchored to the outerwear by a small knot beneath the button—considered a mark of quality—or be reinforced by a plastic disc on the underside of the coat.

Zippers should be sewn flat and should open and close evenly and easily. Have your man check to see if the zipper moves smoothly up the zipper track. There's nothing more frustrating than having to fumble with a zipper on a cold day.

Snaps should be tested to see if they stick or

Pockets

do not match up properly. Any problems your guy encounters with snaps in the store are sure to worsen later on. Look for veneered snaps that protect metal snaps from rust.

Fit

No matter what kind of outerwear your man is selecting—be it a trench coat or leather bomber or jean jacket—it should fit comfortably with a little room to accommodate layers of clothing. If it doesn't, then when the weather turns, he'll look like stuffed sausage in his new coat. Leave at least enough room for another sweater under his outerwear. To be safe, your guy may want to bring an extra sweater to the store to wear when trying on cool-weather coats. Have your guy take off his bulky sweaters when trying on a golf or spring jacket.

Fasteners

Shoulders

The shoulder line is essential when fitting outerwear because the garment drapes from this point. Shoulder fit must be secure, but allow room for movement. To check for movement, have your guy test his golf swing or pretend that he's hitting a baseball. He should be able to do one or both.

Sleeve Length

Outerwear follows the same rules as those for suits and casual wear, and coat sleeves should be a tad bit longer than shirtsleeves. A good rule of measure for a man with average-size hands is to take a credit card and place it lengthwise on his thumb. With his arms resting alongside his body, the credit card should be completely visible and not reach into the sleeve.

Length

Full-length overcoats and trench coats should fall past a man's knees to protect his trousers from the elements. A ¾-length jacket, also called a car coat, should reach midthigh, allowing plenty of room to cover a suit or a blazer.

THE PERFECT COAT

The Burberry Trench—From Officer to Gentleman

It was once considered boring. Then it became the indispensable uniform of the weary businessman. Now the trench coat is regarded as the must-have classic for every well-dressed man. Its military rank-and-file lines are benchmarks of its design, and protecting a wearer from the elements is its main function. Versatility and style, however, claim most of the trench coat's reputation, since legends like Humphrey Bogart, Warren Beatty, and even Inspector Gadget have made them cool, fun, and sophisticated.

Martin Cooper, vice president of design for Burberry USA, expertly pinpoints time-honored details as the reason why the Burberry trench continues to carry on a tradition that's equal parts function and fashion:

"Thomas Burberry was a sportsman and outdoorsman who produced garments for English sporting events like fly-fishing, hunting, and other outdoor sports. So when the company was originally founded in 1856, it was as a performance-wear company—like we know Nike to be today—not the luxury goods company which it has evolved into.

"Thomas Burberry, around 1900, was also the first to chemically treat yarns for water repellency, and there was a big demand for his fabrics. He actually invented the weave that we call gabardine, a basic cloth that's found in literally every collection in the world today.

"The trench has actually had various forms over the years, but during World War I, the British War Office contacted Burberry to develop a garment in which the officers could maneuver through the trenches—the cloth was breathable and replaced a more traditional garment called the macintosh. They were losing more soldiers to pneumonia than warfare."

To identify a stylish and historically correct trench coat, Martin recommends these main features:

1. The best trench coats are double-breasted.

2. A true trench coat has a front rain shield that buttons down so that water cannot get inside your man's garment. (Not visible: the back rain shield, another detail that directs water away from the garment.)

3. The original trench had a one-piece raglan sleeve, meaning that there was no overarm seam, so water could not penetrate the seams, and therefore the garment.

4. The throatlatch beneath the collar is a triangle-shaped removable piece that prevents wind and rain from getting down inside the chest area.

5. Signature epaulets on the shoulders, which were originally used for rifle straps and to hold shoulder bags in place, remain a key identifier of a true Burberry trench.

6. The camel's-hair warmer is a wonderful removable layer that helps this coat travel well and adjust to many climates, perfect for the man on the go. World War I officers removed the warmer and wore it as a bathrobe at night.

7. The belt with D-rings is a mark of authenticity, function, and quality.

8. Notice the traditional check inner lining, which has been around since the 1900s. Americans call it a plaid. It is a unique mark recognized around the globe as the mark of the Burberry brand.

THE FIVE OUTERWEAR ESSENTIALS FOR MEN

TYPICALLY, MEN TURN TO THEIR OLD FAVORITES WHEN TEMPERATURES START TO DIP. BUT, as with automobiles and stereo equipment, outerwear has been upgraded within the last decade and men's favorites have been modernized to combat foul weather in style.

The most significant improvement in outerwear is that it's not so heavy anymore. Upgrades have been made to fabrics so that jackets are lighter yet warmer than ever before. Outerwear is

A. The Trench   B. The Anorak   C. The Spring Jacket

not an area a man should scrimp on: A well-made, classically styled coat or jacket can virtually last a lifetime, and dime for dime there's no better wardrobe investment a man can make. Outerwear basics, however, don't change that much. For the most part, men still stick to the styles they've been wearing since they were boys. Here's a rundown of the six standards: ➢

D. The Leather Blazer   E. The Overcoat

A. The Trench

Gone are the days of the pedestrian look of Inspector Clouseau—worn-looking, off-kilter, and weather-beaten. Today, trench coats are a wardrobe cornerstone for the man who needs a coat that travels well, has layers without much bulk, and offers versatility. The trench can be worn with jeans and a sport shirt as well as with an expensive suit and tie. Plus, there's some variety out there, since the trench is a standard style in almost every big-name menswear collection.

Remember not to get too trendy. Shades of classic tan and cement tones are timeless. In fabric, look for gabardine that is weatherproofed. A trench coat should come with a raglan sleeve—a diagonal seam treatment on the shoulder—that allows for movement and permits the trench coat to be layered easily over a suit.

B. The Anorak

A casual yet traditional cold-weather favorite. The hooded anorak is a midlength jacket that ends just below a man's hip. Typically made from nylon or other water-repellant material and equipped with a fur-trimmed hood, the jacket looks like it belongs to a guy who is ready to run his dogs in the Iditarod. Modern versions have shed the fun and support an average man's sporty lifestyle.

C. The Spring Jacket

As we all know, spring can be "in like a lion and out like a lamb." This jacket is for the lion part of the season that's in that gray area between snow and sunshine. The spring jacket is versatile, lightweight, and can be worn by most men.

One version of the spring jacket is the time-honored golf jacket, in light microfiber or brushed cotton that stops at the waist. Remember that golf jackets are designed for on-course play and so may have additional snaps and pockets. This jacket may not be appropriate for your man's workplace; it pairs best with chinos or jeans and should be considered a key component of a casual wardrobe.

D. The Leather Blazer

Urban cowboys have always known the bravado of leather. A great investment piece that can last for years, the leather blazer is one of the fastest ways to add a dash of flash to a flat ensemble for a night out with friends. Leather blazers should be kept simple and worn with something like a T-shirt during the daytime.

A leather blazer should be of medium weight, suitable for indoor or outdoor wear in warmer months, and lined like a suit jacket. Avoid heavy quilted linings that can make the jacket appear bulky. Stick to chocolate brown or black, the perfect pick-me-up for jeans and a T-shirt, trousers and a cashmere turtleneck.

E. The Overcoat

The overcoat is English in sensibility and origin, yet so wearable for the average American man who needs a dress coat that won't constrict him. The single-breasted, three-quarter cashmere coat is the quintessential and versatile winter classic. Have your guy choose a dark-toned color like black, navy, or charcoal to expand his formal vs. casual options. Some overcoats have details to aid in this, like a detachable faux or genuine fur collar, that reference the reefer coats of the feel-good and fun 1920s.

The Barbour Coat

The barn jacket began here

"Barbour's oiled cotton jackets are uncompromising when it comes to being a waterproof jacket. For the last fifty years or so, the Barbour Beaufort jacket is the one look most associated with Barbour. It's worn by gentlemen in the English countryside and is one of our bestselling jackets worldwide. It can take years for a Barbour jacket to get to a 'worn-in' point that a man wants; some even believe that the more patches and tears on the jacket, the better the jacket is. A Barbour jacket never really goes out of style. It can be put in a bag and pulled out thirty years later, and it is still truly recognizable and looks as good as the ones in stores today."

—Stephen Amos,
  *vice president of Barbour's
  U.S. operations*

Before

THE MAKEOVER

Lisa Ling and her dad, Doug Ling

As one of five spirited women on ABC's daytime talk show The View, *Lisa Ling is used to giving a no-holds-barred opinion about what she likes and thinks on just about every topic—and her dad Doug's unadventurous sense of style is no exception. He's a man who likes his shirts flannel, his baseball hats shaped just right, and his blazers blue. Shopping is not his thing; he prefers the outdoors of northern California. Doug, a retired aviation supervisor, is a passionate fisherman, and according to Lisa works his schedule and his wardrobe around his "reel" love. True to her* View *role, Lisa had a rock-solid idea of how to make over her dad, with just the dose of downtown she thinks he needs for his visits with her in New York City.*

LLOYD: You talk about fishing as being your favorite pastime—a full-time pastime now, I guess. Outerwear is a big part of a fisherman's attire.

LISA: My dad likes to incorporate being a fisherman into every aspect of his life, even into his attire. One thing that's annoying is that my father has an absolutely enormous closet and mine is minuscule. The things that I could do with that closet . . . and he doesn't take advantage of the space he has. His racks are full of flannel shirts and fishing jackets.

LLOYD: Do you have a favorite fishing jacket?

DOUG: Yes, I do, as a matter of fact. I have a quilted khaki-color jacket with lots of pockets.

LLOYD: What do they hold? As a nonfisherman, I would assume that they would hold lures and such.

DOUG: No, I don't use my jacket pockets to hold lures. In my pockets I'll carry a handkerchief, maybe a lighter for a cigar, a pair of gloves, my glasses, and polarized clip-ons .

LISA: He has the whole thing down, you know.

DOUG: It's a routine.

LLOYD: I'd say. And style has a lot to do with it, though, because it seems function comes before the form itself. Lisa, what kind of jackets do you like?

LISA: I love a guy who looks great in jeans, a black leather jacket, and a pair of Pumas and a Kangol hat, just casual and kind of funky.

LLOYD: Do you like men to have a downtown edge?

LISA: Yeah.

LLOYD: What about dressy coats?

LISA: I say whatever keeps him warm that isn't too much of an eyesore.

LLOYD: What should a man keep in mind if he is the target of a loving makeover?

LISA: I don't want to say that a man's style is *so* important to me. I like the men in my life to be well-groomed to the best extent possible. My dad is just such a handsome man that when you dress him up a little bit, he really looks great. And I don't understand why he doesn't want to look that way all the time. But he really is more comfortable in his jeans and his flannel shirts. So I live with it.

LLOYD: So, Doug, you have a little smirk on your face. Do you think that comfort comes before style?

DOUG: Yes. And I have my Lisa and my girlfriend after me now. Lisa really wants me to dress a little different, and she's the one that's been buying me shirts, jackets, and so on.

LISA: My dad has gone without a girlfriend for a long time, so as soon as he started dating this woman—who my sister and I both love—we both hit the stores and we just bought him a whole new wardrobe. But it's a struggle to get him in those nice clothes.

DOUG: I can't match things, and being a bachelor all these years, I stay more or less with standards I can go to over and over again without asking for advice from other people.

LISA: I love my dad in whatever he desires to wear, but I really love when he dresses up. I've gone shopping with him on many occasions, and it's difficult. He never goes in the store. He stands outside and tells us to go in and get whatever we want for him, and he never tries anything on.

DOUG: Hey, I take whatever they suggest, as long as it's not too outlandish. I'm kind of a conservative person. I like a blue blazer, great slacks, and a blue or white shirt with a striped tie. I guess you could say I'm old-fashioned.

The Make Over Prescription: *Lisa decided to replace her dad's old leisure duds with layers of similar, more stylish items that were just as comfortable and functional. A classic white parka, zip-front sweater, tattersall dress shirt, flat-front cotton trousers, a herringbone driving cap, leather gloves, and sand desert boots. The result: a seasoned fisherman becomes a prime catch!*

After

Clark Gable

His Accessories
The Final Details

WHEN WE LOOK AT THE FUTURE OF MENSWEAR, IT IS CLEAR THAT DESIGNERS AND REAL men have very different ideas about where things are heading. Is a man's style the sum of the details? Or does it mean a makeover every six months in the name of fashion?

Every six months? It's hard enough to coerce a man into subtle changes; to do it every season could turn into a constant battle of wills. Most men are looking for clothes that speak to their whims, comfort, and budget—not necessarily the color and the pants cut du jour. Fashion is becoming one of the world's spectator sports, but to be honest, the seasonal whim of high fashion appeals to a very small sampling of the male population. It requires too much time, too much money—and what comes down the runway can be just *too much*.

One area of men's clothing that has never really faltered in the fashion equation is accessories. Ah, the beauty of the details. The finishing touches that make a suit sing and a man look truly suave. We're not talking Mr. T excess here, but the elegant message of a pocket square that peeked out of Fred Astaire's suit, the belt that secured Harry Belafonte's flat-front pants as he wiggled and belted out "The Banana Boat Song," or the perfectly formed dimple in Matt Lauer's silk tie each morning on NBC's *Today Show*. This is what can happen with the art of nuance and the power of accessories.

At the other extreme, writer Mike Walsh chronicled the late king of accessory excess, pianist extraordinaire Liberace, in his book *The Weird, Wild, Wonderful Liberace*. Speaking of just *too much*:

> At another point he pranced around in a pink glass suit embroidered with silver beads, which lit up during the encore. He was all gooey smiles in dimples, wavy hair, and outlandish rings.
>
> "Well, look me over," he said with a devilish grin. "I don't wear these to go unnoticed." The audience roared with delight. It was a real lovefest. I was stunned by the gleeful absurdity of it all. . . .

Rings, bracelets, necklaces, watches, glitzy suits, and fully coiffed hair gave Liberace the moniker Mr. Showmanship, but it was obvious to all who saw his flamboyant stage presence that this was not a showbiz icon whose style other men chose to evoke. "Less is more" is not a phrase he understood.

Liberace aside, most men do subliminally take style cues from male luminaries whom they respect. They may not admit it, but it's true. American men who flip through the style pages of traditional men's magazines, like *GQ* and *Esquire*, are greatly outnumbered by those who get their style guidance from television.

A man who lets nothing go unnoticed is the man who appreciates the details. The Crane brothers in NBC's *Frasier* are two such men.

FRASIER: Have you any idea of appropriate baseball-watching attire?
NILES: Obviously, you failed to detect the subtle diamond pattern in my tie.

And then there's Regis Philbin, who resurrected the monochromatic shirt-and-tie combination and made it a cool look at the height of business-casual dressing. Designers clamor to dress TV sports broadcasters, who transmit a style message to more men over TV than over any other medium. Bob Costas hosted NBC's Olympics coverage dressed in Joseph Abboud suits and ties. Because of the power of television, companies like Burberry, Polo Ralph Lauren, Ermenegildo Zegna, and Donna Karan have all taken turns tying ties for sportscasters within the last decade.

And why do the right accessories place the gloss on an otherwise simple look? Can a simple belt, designed to hold up a pair of trousers, actually be a pivotal element of a man's wardrobe? Let's give your guy credit. He does understand that, like the finer points of a Bang & Olufsen stereo, or a BMW roadster, the sum of the details can make him look truly great. And rich. And sexy.

Accessories send a clear message. They float in and out of fashion's favor, but there are always people who notice a powerful watch, cuff links, tie, and hats. When your man pays attention to the details, he can look as suave as James Bond—of any era, but mostly a Sean Connery Bond.

Mr. T

HIS ACCESSORIES 101

SHOES MATCH BELT MATCH HANDBAG, RIGHT? MAYBE IN YOUR WORLD, BUT THE JOYS OF nurturing a personal collection of artful bags, cute shoes, and belts that fit and flatter means absolutely nothing to men.

It's important that you know this: It's possible to like simplicity, quality, and fine details all at the same time. *Less is more* is a long-standing style credo for both well-dressed men and women— so the fewer accessories of good value you wear, the better. Reed Krakoff knows these principles better than virtually anyone else in American fashion. As president and executive creative director for Coach, Krakoff is responsible for driving the design, look, and feel of the collection of modern yet classically inspired accessories. He's turned the brand around from fading to fashion forward— and in 2001 was acknowledged for doing so by his peers and the fashion press when he received the Council of Fashion Designers of America's coveted American Fashion Award for Accessories Designer of the Year. There is as much to understand about men's accessories as there is about women's. Krakoff gives us his prescription for "the details" and his take on the accents that a well-balanced, functional wardrobe needs:

On leather quality:

> *From wallets to belts and overnight bags, carefully examining leather quality is an important step in selecting the finest accessories for men and women. A simple assessment can be done by lightly scraping your fingernail across the surface of the piece. On good leather, you should be able to rub out the mark with your thumb. If you can't, it's usually because the quality of the pigment isn't good, and the piece will not wear well over time.*

On wallets:

> *First, be sure that a wallet is made out of a great-quality skin that is rich in color, supple, and has depth. And equally important, wallets should always be durable and functional. They're not just decorative but an item that gets a lot of use, so craftsmanship is key. If he carries a ton of credit cards, there must be ample space. Men are carrying fewer these days because they can do everything on one card, from buying groceries to banking. Maybe he carries just a few things and the wallet should be compact so as not to create a huge bulge in his back pocket.*

Classic Silk Knots

Stately Braces

On cuff links:

Cuff links are a classic men's accessory that are definitely seeing a resurgence in popularity with men who want to dress up more. Everyone needs a great pair of everyday cuff links. Silk knots are a perfect basic cuff link for every guy. These cuff links travel well, and he can own a bunch in different colors for different occasions and they're not expensive. They usually cost no more than about $10–$15 a pair.

Just remember: The simpler the cuff links, the better. Tiffany & Co. and other jewelry companies also translate silk knots into silver. I have a pair of gold knot cuff links, and I find them perfect for any occasion, even black-tie events. They will never go out of style.

On braces:

Braces and suspenders are a cyclical trend, and traditionally work best with pleated pants. That look is a classic pairing that's sophisticated. Today, however, well-dressed men are wearing flat-front trousers that are usually cut much slimmer. So the need for braces is definitely not out there right now. Men are looking for simpler, cleaner ways to dress these days—and to simplify their wardrobe—and braces are not something a guy really needs.

On belts:

Well-dressed men should own a minimum of three belts. First, a classic dress belt, which is usually slimmer than the average belt, cut in calfskin and with a lighter-weight buckle. Dress belts are easy to recognize in that they are made of shinier polished leather. I would say a black belt with silver or nickel buckle is best. Stay away from chunky buckles that rest clumsily on tailored dress pants.

With the casualization of the workplace, my second belt recommendation is what we at Coach call a "khaki belt," which is usually slightly wider and comes with a little more detailing on it. A stitch detail, for instance, or it's made from distressed leather. Here, the buckle has two prongs instead of one and a leather strap or metal keeper to secure the strap. Belts like these are for your man to wear with khakis or any casual pants. This is not the time for a black belt; lighter tones like browns, tans, and brandy colors are great

And don't forget adding what I call the "fun" jeans belt. A wider, bolder, and more artful leather belt, often with ornate and authentic vintage buckles that have a little bit of a western or rock 'n' roll feel. For jeans worn with sneakers or a pair of motorcycle boots, this wider, expressive belt works.

On pocket squares:

I just love a clean white linen pocket square folded straight like those from the 1950s. It's nice when it picks up the white of a man's dress shirt, and it dresses up any suit when you are not wearing a tie. A pocket square gives a man a little more finish, and people will know that he's not missing the tie but has given it thought and decided to be daring and go without the tie on purpose. Fancy pocket squares in colored silks and textured poplins are considered too dressy for the office.

On ties:

If your man loves wearing ties, it's great to make a statement with a tie in color or pattern—but a simple statement looks the most stylish. Beware of "novelty" ties—like cartoonish prints, bold characters, or colorful icons—even around the holidays, because these are hard ties to pull off, and they wind up looking a little clownlike. Some men are drawn to such ties around occasions like Father's Day, so just know that a sophisticated "conversational" tie can be great if it's a small-scale abstract pattern.

I wear solid ties because they are easier. Interestingly enough, I probably have twenty navy ties, which are slightly different in texture and fabric, because they go with everything—a gray suit, a navy suit, or even khakis. When I am traveling, for me it's easy to bring just two or three of them along—and it's a shortcut, but I know I have what I need.

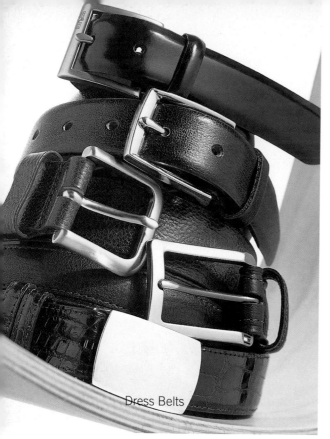

Dress Belts

On money clips:

Money clips are for a very specific man, usually older men who dislike carrying anything other than bills and very few credit cards. Or they're for the gentleman who prefers to have his cash in one place and his credit cards in another. A money clip can also be great for elegant events, like a black tie dinner, when your man does not want to carry a whole wallet and feel weighted down. In a way, money clips are a vestige of another time.

On pens:

I truly think that a pen is a great way for a man to express his style in a casual, unobtrusive way. It certainly varies by profession, but if your man writes a lot and deals with contracts and frequent meetings, a pen becomes his visual signature and is a great way to add subtle style to a man's wardrobe.

On driving gloves:

For men who are investing in that midlife-crisis car, driving gloves take on a style-forward, ritualistic approach to driving. This man may get his car washed every weekend, and driving gloves are one more thing he can buy to accent his fantastically stylish car. Stick to black gloves, and those in warm tones of brown, for a classic look that's also not too flashy.

On watches:

My motto is: "You have got to be comfortable about what you're saying to people with your choice of watches." Watches are clearly the most demonstrative detail a man can wear, because many onlookers know watches. To make his choice in a timepiece stylish and appropriate, it's best to try and match the watch to his personality. If he is low-key, he'll do better with a subtle watch. You can certainly find amazing watches that are quite expensive but more subtle, like those along the design lines of a Patek Philippe, which displays less ostentatious confidence and more of an innate sense of style, instead of saying "Look. I can afford this watch" to the world. He has to be extra careful and not look like he just took his first bonus and bought the most expensive watch he could afford!

On socks:

You can never go wrong with black, navy, camel, and heather gray dress socks. Choose ribbed, 100 percent wool or wool/Lycra© blends, and any man will look stylish and together. As with ties, patterned and conversational socks fall in the category of being either cartoonish or too casual. Pick a subtle menswear pattern such as tattersall or check. Socks are one category that a man shouldn't get too casual about—it reminds me of bad fashion from the 1980s. And on the age-old debate of whether to match his socks to his pants or to his shoes, go with the pants.

The big mistake:

The overstuffed wallet! Does a man really need his library card from college? I see the things guys keep in their wallets, and trust me, less is more. I've also seen wallets held together with a rubber band after they've fallen apart. Can't a guy buy a new wallet? It seems that most men buy wallets only when they absolutely have to, and as a result carry around an overstuffed wallet that creates a huge, unsightly bulge in their back pocket. This is a definite "don't."

The Money Clip

Dress Socks

127

THE PERFECTLY POLISHED MAN

A SELF-DEFINED MAN IS "PUT TOGETHER" BUT NEVER FUSSY. HE'S THE GUY WHOSE LOOK IS never flashy yet always seems to get noticed in a room full of dapper dressers and those who get dressed robotically every morning. For him, accessories are about fine details gracefully meeting function.

But why is it that the perfectly accessorized man gets noticed when his details are no more conspicuous than those of his better-heeled counterparts? While *they* clearly have on a belt, a tie, and a watch, the difference is that the Perfectly Polished Man consciously chooses high-quality and iconic accessories over both practicality and frivolity. His accessories can withstand the test of time.

Be encouraged and heartened because no matter what your guy's budget, the formula for being successfully accessorized is the same: Concept is more important than cost. Surprisingly, an expensive belt from a Rodeo Drive boutique may actually be less classic than a leather belt from a second-hand store.

Let's pick apart the finer points of the guy who has his *i*'s dotted and *t*'s crossed, and define the message in each of his letter-perfect accessories.

1. The Tie

A proper and artful knot is a surefire way to boost a tie's value. Yes, the expensive Charvet tie will make your man's suit look richer and well-made, but so will taking two extra minutes each morning to help him perfect the dimple in the center of a less expensive tie fashioned in a Windsor knot. That one small detail can leave a lasting impression.

Another accessory that can make a difference in your guy's appearance are brass or mother-of-pearl collar stays that will slightly lift his collar and provide a strong frame for the tie.

2. The Eyeglass Frames

The options in frames today are virtually limitless, and your man can select a different pair for every day of the week if he so desires. The tastefully accessorized man, however, typically owns one or two pairs of quality eyeglasses with fine wire or tortoise frames, and a pair of classic sunglasses, like aviators or Ray-Ban Wayfarers that properly fit his face. His glasses are simple without overly ornate details. Instead of owning a dresser drawer full of glasses, he's consulted with an eyewear professional to determine what frames best suit the shape of his face.

3. The Handkerchief

Bravo to the men who wear a pocket square in an age when casual dress has almost taken over the business world. Two easy tips can make a pocket square less serious and subtly stylish. First, the right color choice is always white—or a pocket square with almost no color at all. Think solid pale tones, with hand-rolled, hand-stitched details for a wink of old-world haberdashery. Second, the manner in which the pocket square is folded is critical to the message that it sends. The most classic, understated fold is what is commonly called the "TV" fold, which is slim, crisp, and peeks out of the pocket, so as not to compete with the shirt and tie. It takes a certain kind of confident gentleman to pull off the more festive folds, like the "peek," "three point," or the "flop." Most men can certainly serve up the elegant TV fold with no reservation.

4. The Watch

A man's watch says something about him before he ever utters a word. The well-accessorized man is smart enough to own several watches, but reserves his best-quality timepiece for the important business meetings and special occasions. For example, when he's going to "seal the deal" he wears a simple, clean face watch, in silver or platinum, to give him a strong yet discreet boost of confidence—and elegance! A round or rectangular tank watch always outlasts the trends. When this man is ready to get sporty, he slips on his second watch with a rugged and strong leather band.

5. The Writing Instrument

Most people, let alone men, care very little about what they write with in today's casually dressed world. The nearest ballpoint pen is usually all most men need. There was a time, however, when a man's writing instrument said as much about who he was as did his suit and accessories. Some men still care about the fine points and keep a well-made, distinctive pen with them at all times. This accessory is not about spending a ton of money; it's about having a great-looking and reliable pen accessible at all times.

6. The Driving Glove

No man really needs these gloves, but they are a fun bonus. Plus, they appeal to most guys' hidden desires to be James Bond or Shaft for a day.

7. The Cuff Link

Men often switch between cuff links like the traditional silk knot, a pair of which rarely cost more than $10–$15, and more grown-up cuff links in sterling silver and jewels. Either way, the cuff links are always simple, refined, and designed with a wink. Vintage stores are a great resource for unique cuff links with individual character and details that give a nod to decades past. While neckties used to be the canvas for self-expression in the bold and brazen 1970s and '80s, today a man's choice of cuff links offers a more subtle, offbeat peek into his personality.

8. The Belt

Dress belts literally take a beating because of their position on a man's body. Too many power lunches and heavy dinners, and the occasional extra buckle hole added without the help of a leather maker, can add stress and wear to a belt. It is vital for your guy to watch the condition of his current belt collection carefully. The polished professional in a calfskin belt, the sharp, casually dressed man in his Tommy Jeans belt, and the slick downtown guy sporting a black alligator belt with a military buckle usually all look great when the details are in place and are in good condition. A classic square buckle in silver or gold will always be stylish and versatile and can be paired with several pant styles and suits. The square, solid metal military buckle is a great sporty option.

ESSENTIAL TIES

AS WITH ANY OTHER AREA OF A TASTEFUL WARDROBE, REMEMBER THAT YOUR GUY'S TIES should stress quality first and then style. His neckwear should reflect his many varied moods and styles. Eliminating old ties from his closet is very important, but before he does, make note of the gaps he'll create. Here are eight categories that he can build his tie collection around.

A. WOOLENS Woolens are fall/winter ties for casual and dress shirts. In stripes, plaids, and nubby tweeds, woolen ties bring the country gentleman to mind, but they look just as great in the city.

B. KNITS Still trying to live down a bad rap from being the "it" tie of the 1980s, knits are super-functional and versatile, and they travel better than any other tie. He can dress them up or down, and he can have a wink of fun with bold stripes or small woven patterns for an updated look that is anything but '80s redux.

C. SOLIDS Solids are the favorites of men who prefer a spare, minimal approach to dressing up. The solid tie is also a great addition for the man who frustrates easily when trying to figure out which shirt goes best with which tie. Don't think that just because a tie is solid it's flat and boring. Look for texture and sheen when choosing solid ties to add flair to solid shirts of the exact color or complementary tones.

D. STRIPES Originally an English academic staple, traditional diagonal rep stripe ties indicated a man's schooling, tastes, and pedigree. Today, reps are the American prep standard, and have a broader range than just thick-lined primary colors. These ties are a cool fashion statement that

can be worn with their classic partner, the navy blue blazer. Brighter stripes look dignified yet fun when paired with conservative suits. For an authentic prep look, a tie can be worn as a belt with chinos. However, be warned: When a tie is worn as a belt, its insides get twisted and it can never go back to its neckwear function.

E. PRINTS and CLUBS A man's personality should shine through when he wears ties with prints—so choose wisely, or leave it to him. Either way, keep the prints subtle, and never too comical. Flexible, sophisticated, and acceptable in any formal business situation, printed ties are a sure thing for nine to five, but they are not the ideal look for evening affairs.

F. PAISLEYS, DOTS, and PLAIDS The rule "less is more" applies here. Artful paisleys, whimsical polka-dots, and noble plaids are perfect for the man who wants to add just a wink of fancifulness to an otherwise sober suited look. Keep the patterns understated so the tie isn't a clownish contrast to the rest of his ensemble.

G. FOULARDS Crafted in lightweight silk in a fine twill weave, foulard ties are printed with small designs. These ties have a natty and refined air similar to that of a fine, delicate women's silk scarf, and they coordinate well with both summer seersuckers and warm winter gray flannel suits.

H. WOVENS For those moments under the fashion microscope, when discerning eyes are measuring your man for taste and style, a woven tie is a good choice. The woven tie's weave creates beautiful color combinations, textures, and patterns.

Before

THE MAKEOVER

Tyra Banks and her dad, Don Banks

When it comes to the details of style, it's Tyra, not necessarily Daddy, who knows what's best. Breaking Don away from his favorites is always a challenge, even for Tyra. Despite his past fashion faux pas and his now steely conservative style, don't be fooled. If rules are made to be broken, Don says, the right accessory is the secret to tempting a man away from his usual ways.

LLOYD: Tyra, what are your earliest memories of the way your dad dressed? Remember anything that caught your young eye?

TYRA: Honest?

DON: Okay, be honest.

TYRA: I was probably five or six years old. I remember my dad wearing those white athletic socks with red stripes, and with dress shoes, shorts, and a pololike shirt. On a trip to Disneyland he wore dress shoes. Daddy, why did you do that?

DON: You remember that?

TYRA: Yeah! And then, when he used to dress me, he would do the same thing to me. There's a picture of me on a bridge, and I have on cute little yellow shorts and I think I'm wearing athletic socks with the stripes.

DON: Parents are allowed to do things like that. . . . And I think I still have the red-striped socks.

TYRA: Do you still wear them with the dress shoes, Daddy?

DON: It wasn't a style statement, but no, I don't wear 'em anymore . . .

LLOYD: Aside from the striped socks, Tyra, how has your father's style changed over the years?

TYRA: I think my dad's a lot more conservative now. Apparently he's retired the dress-shoes-and-sweat-socks thing. Thank God! He really is more casual now. He always wears simple slacks and a shirt. If he goes to work he has on a dress shirt and tie, and for church it's the same thing.

LLOYD: What about accessories? Don, were you ever really into the details?

TYRA: I do remember him having a dressing table area, and seeing some cuff links and some bracelets.

DON: I do have a couple of gold bracelets that I wear occasionally.

LLOYD: But you're also a watch man? Are these your essential accessories?

DON: That's about it.

TYRA: A watch and a bracelet.

LLOYD: Okay. Now, is there one accessory faux pas you regularly disagree on? For me, when I see the men in my family, it's "take that cell phone off your belt, please, and put it in your pocket."

TYRA: My dad has something like that. He has the really big wallet, so his butt looks like one of his buns is way bigger than the other. It's a big, thick wallet; it probably has *everything* in there.

DON: Oh, no. Now, if I pull out my wallet and she's wrong, will she have to take that back? Here you go . . .

TYRA: Oh, it *is* smaller now.

DON: Actually, this is my travel wallet. It's lighter and holds the essentials.

TYRA: You know what I'd also want to change on my dad? I'd like to change his shoes. They're pretty old-fashioned; I'd love to see him in some really hip, cool shoes.

LLOYD: If a woman wants to pick out an essential accessory for a well-dressed man, what should she focus on? What do you like?

TYRA: I'll go with my dad on the bracelet. I'm not really into a lot of necklaces, but I like a nice, really chunky bracelet on a man, and maybe an earring in the left ear.

DON: I'll break down and do just one piercing. I have no problem with that.

LLOYD: Hoops? A small stud?

TYRA: I'd like hoops, actually. Yeah, one little tiny little hoop

The Make Over Prescription: *Tyra's seasoned eye for luxe took her dad, Don, to new heights in a gray velvet pinstriped three-button suit and white dress shirt. But she also chose to take the time to properly focus on the details and make him shine even brighter! A silver/gray basket weave tie, magenta silk pocket square, sterling silver-tipped walking stick, pure silk socks, and highly shined lace-ups are the winning combination. Topped off by a classic Fedora in pearl gray and ebony leather driving gloves for a total* Cotton Club–*inspired look. The Result: From a diva daughter to a Don, Papa's got more than a brand new bag.*

After

Robert Redford in *The Natural*

His Casual Clothes
The Sins of His Second Skin

TAKE A LONG, HARD LOOK AT THE MAN YOU LOVE. STUDY HIS SHAPE. EXAMINE HIS WALK and his gestures. He may be a natty, well-groomed businessman who enjoys fine wine and golfing abroad, or perhaps he's a guy who revels in the simpler side of life. Maybe he prefers a job just to pay the bills over a flashy career that absorbs his quality time with family. The point is this: Your guy likes to be comfortable no matter what kind of lifestyle he leads, and you should focus on these ideals as you assess his sportswear. This is the part of his wardrobe that's closest to his heart and his real self.

Impressions of a classic American and British sporting life are the starting point for what we know to be "dressing down" today, like a quilted vest used for fly-fishing and a cashmere sweater worn on the golf course. The original purpose of sportswear was to provide a gentleman an escape from his shirt and tie, but still, it was far a cry from a T-shirt. In fact, it wasn't until the 1920s that the polo shirt, now a menswear standard, was worn for something other than sports. It took college kids wearing the shirts as "country-club" fashion to create a trend strong enough to allow polos to be considered as appropriate attire beyond a club locker room or athletic field.

Many style-challenged guys view their sportswear as the luck of the draw. Kind of like *Survivor*. The one piece of clothing that outplays and outlasts the others, the item that "survives," claims status as his favorite shirt. It's comfortable and sentimental, but it may not necessarily be the shirt that makes him look his most handsome. Ditto his favorite khakis, casual shirt, and blue jeans. Dick Clark has a better chance of retiring than any of these oldies do.

Your guy's casual clothes may also have a sentimental aspect and involve one or more of the following: his favorite sports team, his alma mater, and something he believes makes him "look cool." Ladies, you know what I'm talking about—jeans he swears make him look like a "Born to Run"–era Bruce Springsteen. Even the Boss doesn't boast that style anymore.

There is a solution to bridging the gap in his dress habits: gift-giving. When you think about it, who doesn't like a gift? Employ a method I call "present and praise." And who can't stand a little praise every now and again? This technique is a one-two punch that will serve you both if you offer up a certain amount of healthy praise: Your man gets to stay in the type of clothing and accessories that he enjoys and feels safe in, and you get a hand in improving his style.

Remember the relaxed elegance of Robert Redford in *The Natural* or *The Way We Were*, with his rolled sleeves and soft sweater vests that were preppy and relaxed? On the more contemporary side, how can anyone forget the cool duds Denzel Washington wore in *Devil in a Blue Dress*? A simple white tank top paired with some elegant trousers. While these films are, in fact, period pieces, the clothing is timeless. More important, Redford and Washington are respected actors and icons for being "guys' guys." When you two watch movies or television, ask his opinion of what other male stars are wearing and you may well get a style conversation—or a makeover—going.

It's a simple road map, but it works. Keep on choosing trusted iconic actors, musicians, and television personalities. Work in your gold seal of approval when you see fit. He'll soon become more confident and his personal style will grow. His tried-and-true favorites may not go away entirely, but just watch—they'll eventually move farther and farther back into his closet.

The praise part of the equation doesn't have to be prescribed or forced; just be well prepared for the rippling effect it causes. Remember, ladies, kind words of praise are welcome rewards. Before you know it, your man who thought all jeans were created equal will ask when he emerges from a store's dressing room, "Don't these jeans look like the ones that Tom Cruise had on in *Mission: Impossible*?" Inside you'll be screaming, "Mission accomplished!"

Tom Cruise in *Mission Impossible*

HIS CASUAL CLOTHES 101

A MAN HAS TO CONNECT WITH HIS CASUAL CLOTHING. HE'S GOT TO HAVE STYLES AND colors that he understands and feels comfortable wearing. When seeking to upgrade your man's style, remember what he loves about his current casual clothes and the role they play in his every-day life.

Helping him to kick it up a notch, however, doesn't come without a cost. As with anything else in life—no pain, no gain.

In a world of countless casual clothing options, let's highlight some of the time-honored basics that—regardless of brand or price level—appeal to most men and remain forever stylish.

The Khaki

The first and last word in relaxed elegance, flat-front khakis are the best basic pant for men who rely on a sturdy foundation for their casual wardrobe. Sand and tan are the most versatile colors, but khakis—a term for classic and casual pants that's become virtually interchangeable with chi-nos—are available in shades from butter yellow to crimson to black. You really can't go wrong.

The Jean

Styles may come and go, but denim is forever and it's considered one of the key pieces of nearly every man's wardrobe. Jeans are classic, and are at their best in a medium indigo wash with five-pocket styling, whether your guy favors Levi's 501s, Tommy Hilfiger's Freedom Fit, or a well-worn pair of vintage Wranglers.

The Solid Oxford Shirt

The traditional oxford shirt can dress up with a casual tie, or it can be as easy as a T-shirt with khaki shorts. The look rarely goes wrong. Your guy should start with white and then add on his favorite shades of blue, yellow, or pink.

The Polo

This is *the* casual shirt. Start with solid-color cotton piqué polos for the weekend. Then dress up the style in fine-knit sweaters in cotton, silks, Merino wool, and cashmere that can be paired with

Ribbon, Canvas, and Braided Belts

both khakis and dress trousers. Black, navy, camel, and heather gray are perfect shades to start off a new look.

The Cargo Short

There's nothing better than a pair of cargo shorts for the man who needs all his modern conveniences within his reach—his ATM card, cell phone, and BlackBerry pager. Leave it to the military to create a look that's functional and wearable and keeps true to its roots in shades of khaki and olive green.

The T-shirt

A classic that wears well both day and night. The basic T-shirt has evolved since the 1950s, when James Dean made it popular, and now comes in stretch-cotton blends in styles that slim through the waist and give more room in the arms. A man's wardrobe should start with bright white. Some guys may want to branch into shades of heather gray, olive, or black.

The V-Neck T-shirt

A trendier T-shirt choice than the boyish crew neck, this shirt is slightly sexier since it shows a bit more of a man's chest. V-necks are very versatile, and the solid dark colors can be worn on slightly dressy occasions with a casual blazer or with denim. Stick with bright white, black, and gray for a totally modern look.

The Classic Sneaker

The "classic" sneaker means different things to men of different ages and tastes. To wear them

Polos and Cargo Shorts

with weekend sportswear, sneakers should be cleanly and simply designed. It may sound plain nerdy, but it's best to leave the high-tech high-tops for the basketball court, not the family barbecue.

The Sandal

Most men don't want to show their toes in public, but in the summer nothing beats the freedom of wearing a sandal. A sandal that's a good starting point for some men is the relaxed flip-flop—a favorite in the backyard, on the boardwalk, and on the beach.

The Ribbon or Canvas Belt

A preppy favorite, the military-inspired ribbon or canvas belt is a cool and inexpensive addition to any casual wardrobe. Colors vary from khaki and black to whimsical pastels and regimental stripes for summer that hold up perfectly next to denim, chinos, and pale linens.

The Braided Belt

This is a rugged, simple, and masculine accessory. It's a time-honored classic that's recently been updated with a thicker and bolder braid in rich oxblood, cognac brown, and black. But buyer beware: Canvas and other fabric closures can make the belt seem stodgy and even out of date— stick to all-leather versions.

The Casual Dress Trouser

One of the best building blocks for a business-casual wardrobe is a flat-front, wool gabardine trouser with a touch of Lycra© (stretch) in gray, tan, navy, or black. Gabardine is versatile and

Sandals and Classic Sneakers

An Unconstructed Blazer

His Casual Clothes

145

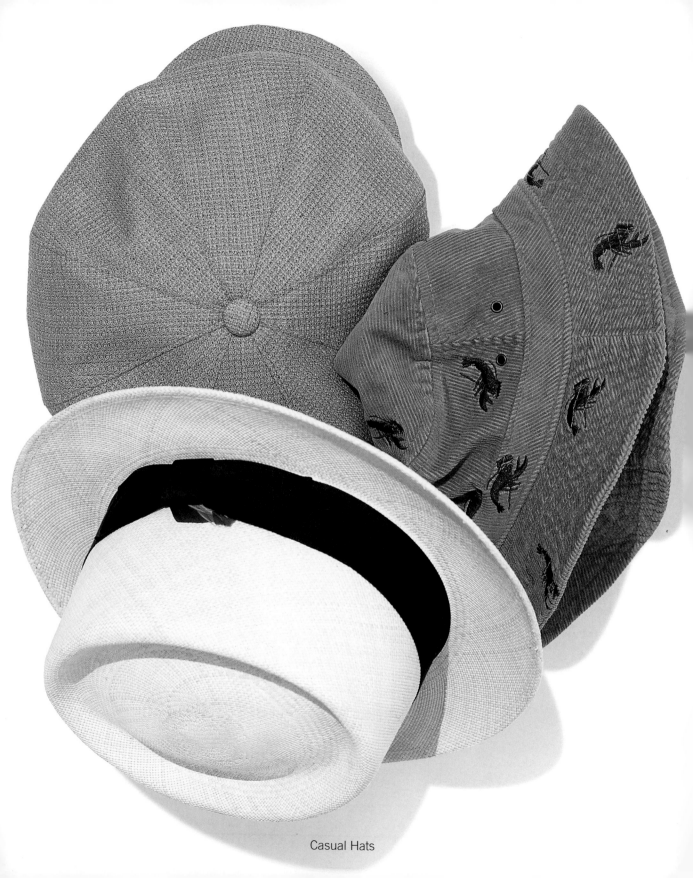

Casual Hats

lightweight for warmer months and can be worn well into the fall. Trousers made in a fabric with a touch of stretch or Lycra™ wear better and won't wrinkle as much.

The Leather Jacket

An instant outfit booster, the leather jacket adds shine and sex appeal. The simpler the jacket, the more it can be worn. Keep buckles, tassles, and snaps for your man's shoes. A three-button jacket is one that will serve him well.

The Unconstructed Blazer

Characterized by soft shoulders with little or no padding and loosely constructed lapels, the casual unconstructed blazer is relaxed enough to wear with khakis and jeans. To be considered a casual blazer, it must be in navy or black and must be ready to pair only with gray flannel trousers, khakis, and jeans. Nothing more, nothing less.

The Casual Hat

Seasons change, and so does the need to wear a hat. Not since before President John F. Kennedy's 1961 inauguration have American men been required to wear a hat to feel proper. (Kennedy went hatless on his inauguration day and hat sales immediately plummeted.) Today, hats are a fun and sometimes inexpensive way for men to play around with their personal style.

Hats are still one of the best ways to stay warm in cooler months, keeping one's body up to 10 percent warmer overall. While some men may select a corduroy bucket hat, others will reach for a knit skullcap to keep covered.

The driving cap is a time-honored classic that flatters almost any face shape and gets better with every crush and wear. Lightweight and simple, the solid khaki or flannel baseball cap is a no-fail way to solve a bad-hair day. Finally, a Panama, reminiscent of when men reveled in head-to-toe dressing, is still the coolest straw hat for the summer.

THE PERFECT
DRESS-CASUAL LOOK

STYLE AND ITS RULES DON'T ALWAYS GO HAND IN HAND. WHEN DRESSING CASUALLY, AND with a hint of sophistication, rules are made to be bent and tweaked. For a little more than a decade, ever since the words "business casual" came into the lexicon, men have been learning to take liberties with their wardrobe. What was meant as a Friday workplace perk has turned into a dress code for the whole week—and for some men, a new way of thinking about what to wear to work.

Karen Murray, president, Claiborne Menswear Brands, has watched the casualization of the American workplace unfold right before her eyes. Murray and her design team have positioned Claiborne as an essential resource men can turn to when they don't know if they should wear a suit, weekend wear, or something else entirely.

As a wife, mother of a preteenage son, and a menswear veteran, Karen has some well-seasoned advice for women to keep in mind before they start making over their men, which boils down to this: Be careful, and don't leave his comfort zone. Says Karen:

"Try not to make your guy into something he isn't. Men are sometimes afraid of looking too fashionable or too sophisticated. They don't want to walk into a room and make a fashion statement. Unlike women, who like this kind of attention, it's not cool to look like you tried too hard to get dressed."

Karen believes that the perfect dress-casual look can be achieved as long as your guy pays attention to "three easy pieces":

Piece One—The Sweater

Choose a fitted, fine-gauge sweater in black or a safe shade of brown, navy, or gray that can be easily paired with dress slacks and a sport coat. The simpler the sweater, the better.

"A sweater that's refined, a little softer, a little drapier, a bit more fluid, and lighter weight will look good under a jacket. I see guys who will put on a halfway decent sweater, but it's one of those bulky sweaters with the banded bottom, and then they put a blazer over it and they think they're dressed. That just doesn't work." ➤

Piece Two—The Casual Sport Coat

Combine the familiarity of a suit jacket and the comfort of a shirt with an unconstructed sport coat or "shirt jacket." Your guy should remember to choose a tone darker than that of the sweater or shirt he is wearing, and also to wear the coat relaxed and unbuttoned at the neck.

"Don't take your guy too far off his usual track," Karen says. "If he always wears black and grays, don't go and put him in a soft, melon-colored shirt. He won't feel comfortable. Let him slowly change his closet, and above all, make sure what he wears fits well. Nothing makes a person feel good like wearing something that fits them well."

Piece Three—The Flat-Front Pant

For the man who's wearing pleats 24/7, what is he waiting for? First of all, he needs to understand that flat fronts can be flattering—for example, if he finds a khaki with a fit closer to that of a pair of dress pants than jeans. To "ground" the outfit, pants should always be a few shades deeper than whatever he is wearing on top.

"How come guys can't buy the proper-size pants?" says Karen. "They always have to go with a pant that's too tight in the waist so that the waistband rolls over, and that makes them look so much heavier than they actually are."

Footwear

"Shoes are the biggest mistake most men make when they get dressed," says Karen. "They have no clue! If a guy's wearing a pair of rumpled khakis and a disgusting polo shirt, then he makes the situation worse by putting on the same pair of shoes he wears with a suit. It looks horrible! Instead, he should be wearing a ¾ boot that's a bit more rugged."

A Casual Mention

"To make over your man, you and your guy should look for clothes that aren't going to break the bank," Karen advised. "They should fit him well and not be too much of a stretch from his current style. Most men need to go through the shopping process slowly, and sometimes they need to just look, but eventually they'll come back and buy when they're ready."

The Power of Black

Johnny Cash has sworn by it. Rock star Lenny Kravitz likes his shiny, hugging his body, and unbuttoned to his navel. Still, the black shirt has not been seen as it was when John Travolta's wing-collared black dress shirt peeked out from beneath his crisp, white three-piece bell-bottomed disco suit in 1977's Saturday Night Fever. *The heat, sexiness, modernity, and air of mystery that's wrapped up in the power of a casual black dress shirt makes it the style equivalent of a lady's miniskirt.*

Style experts like to think of the black shirt as the new urban classic that can take a man from day to night, partying to mourning without pretension or remorse. In urban cities like New York, black is the primary color, some snidely say, because it hides city dirt. Jokes aside, the real reason is that garments like a black shirt not only have many uses but possess a sophisticated air and timeless sensibility.

The casual black shirt, like the classic black suit, is absolutely as versatile as the little black dress is for women, and it's a sound investment for your guy even if he never hits the Big Apple hot spots. The shirt can quickly, and mindlessly, create a cool look with celeb intrigue when it is paired with matching black pants and black boots. Or, pair the shirt with a gray business suit at 5 P.M. and skip the tie for an instant transition from day to night. As well as a black shirt dresses up, it also dresses down cool. Encourage your guy to pair an untucked black shirt with dark-rinse denim pants and his favorite sneaks for a fuss-free, comfortable look that is as easy to get into as his favorite sweat suit, and just as comfortable for brunch with friends.

Despite all these great qualities, the black shirt does have a few drawbacks:

- *The black shirt can be addictive. If he wears one too frequently, your guy will start to look like an extra from Michael Jackson's* Thriller *video. Make sure he mixes the shirt with different kinds of outfits—like black jeans, casual pants, or a suit. He shouldn't make the shirt his "uniform."*

- *Frequent washing, or professional laundering, can take the punch out of the crisp ink-black finish of a new shirt; dry cleaning holds color and is a great option. Your guy may reserve the first few wearings of the black shirt for special occasions when a style statement is mandatory, like a class reunion or dinner out with your parents. Once faded, he can rotate it into the casual side of his wardrobe.*

And finally, for those occasions when a tux is in order: Show him how to pair a solid black suit with a new and similarly toned black shirt, a black solid silk or cashmere tie, and black high-shined shoes. The look is straight from Hollywood's red-carpet events.

Before

THE MAKEOVER

Bobbi Brown and her husband, Steven Plofker

Bobbi Brown's heart still goes aflutter when her husband Steven wears good ol' American blue jeans. As an attorney and a real estate developer, Steven has a style that ranges from a formal suit for the office to sturdy shoes and a hard hat.

Theirs is a true-blue love. The couple works hard at keeping life real by juggling their jobs in New York City with serious downtime and fun at their suburban New Jersey home with their three sons. Being a woman who knows what she likes—and after fourteen years of marriage, motherhood, high-powered careers as a makeup artist and CEO of her own company, Bobbi Brown Cosmetics, and beauty editor of NBC's Today Show*—Bobbi still prefers the laid-back look and loves to see Steven dress casually.*

LLOYD: I'm fascinated by how some couples relate to each other through style. Do you remember the first thing that you noticed about Steven?

BOBBI: Absolutely. I thought he was handsome, but he just seemed too preppy for me at first.

BOBBI: And then, as soon as we started dating, I loved his style instantly. It was just really classic and comfortable. You know, I love the way he dresses. I think he could wear better shoes, but he's in construction sites a lot, so his shoes get destroyed. The night I met him I knew I was going to marry him. He had on blue jeans and a blue jean jacket that didn't really go together.

LLOYD: Now you two have been together for fourteen years. Bobbi, what have you contributed to Steven's style in that time?

BOBBI: I've added a couple of good items to his wardrobe that have made a huge difference. I gave him a Rolex watch when we got married. And then I've given him items like an alligator skin belt that's so versatile, he wears it nearly every day and it can really dress up a pair of inexpensive khakis. And I've given him some fun things, like a Burberry check button-down shirt.

STEVEN: We don't spend a lot of time shopping. But when we shop, it's in pent-up demand, like if we're going on vacation, or find ourselves in a mall without the kids. We can get a lot of shopping done in twenty minutes.

BOBBI: That's because we essentially keep it to five stores.

LLOYD: It seems like you both like to mix things up, and you're not the typical customers who purchase lots of designer clothing.

BOBBI: I hate when someone must have everything they're wearing be from a certain designer. That's why today I'm dressing Steven in a pair of simple blue jeans and a white T-shirt. That's my favorite look on him. I can feel my heart pound when I think of him wearing something like that, and it's something that's just *so* simple. I just like the way he looks in his blue jeans. And Steven doesn't wear the dark hip ones. He just wears worn-out Levis.

LLOYD: You can't get any more classic American than that.

BOBBI: Well, part of Steven's style is that he's really confident. He'll show up in shorts at a board meeting.

LLOYD: Really, why is that? Bobbi, do you think Steven cares too much about his appearance? Or too little?

BOBBI: No, no, he cares just the right amount. Women always want to change everything: their hair, their makeup, their dog, their men, and their home. I'm happy to say there are not many things I want to change about Steven or myself.

STEVEN: Men are accessories. Really, we are. And sometimes, women want to accessorize their accessory.

BOBBI: People, in general, are really having trouble these days accepting who they are. I think the media is constantly telling us to be like this or be like that. People have to stop and say: "Enough. This is who I am. And it's okay."

The Make Over Prescription: *Bobbi helped Steven to loosen up and make an easy return to the sexy jean-clad man who stole her heart. It may sound easy to dress your man down in denim, but is he sporting the coolest fit, wash, and look of the moment? For Bobbi, the look of the moment is embracing the classic five-pocket jean in an American blue, worn with a bleach white, crew neck T-shirt. She adds a touch of bad boy by slipping him into a buttery-to-the-touch, chocolate leather blazer, and cools it down with black driving moccasins—sockless, of course. The Result: If wearing only jeans and a T-shirt could nab every man a beauty queen!*

After

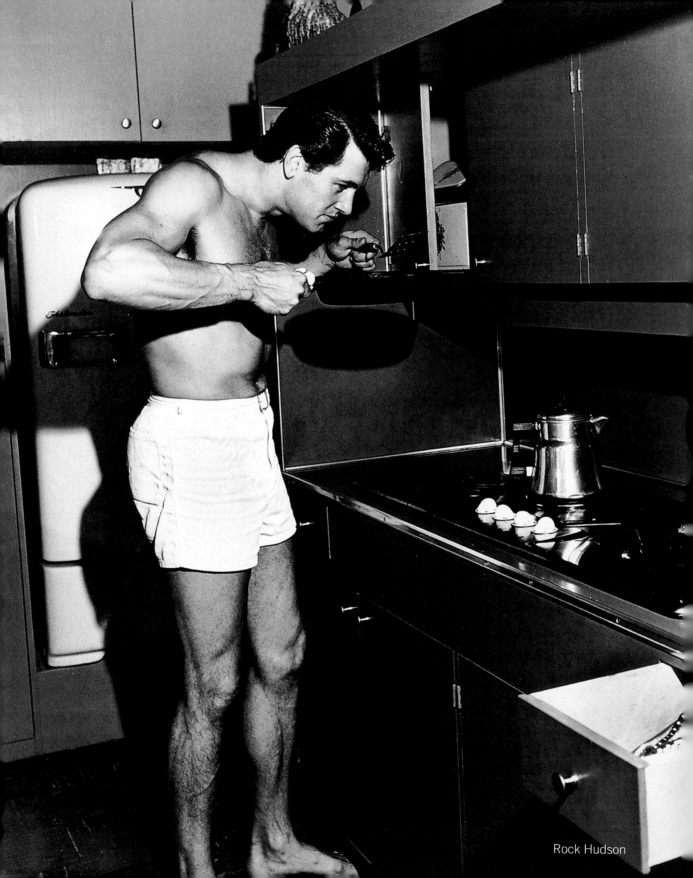

Rock Hudson

His Underwear
The Undercover Act

THERE'S AN UNFORGETTABLE SCENE IN THE FILM THE FULL MONTY WHEN THE GROUP OF down-and-out blokes on the dole, in full rehearsal mode, face their first moment of truth: They must strip down to their skivvies in front of one another. If a guy's desperate for cash and as motivated as he claims to be and makes it to this point, then there's a good chance he has what it takes to truly go all the way.

Six men drop their pants and stand around awkwardly in six different kinds of underwear: colored and striped, baggy boxers, and barely-there briefs. It's a true picture. Pick six men off the street—and get them to, first of all, agree to show their goods—and the story would be the same. There is virtually no "right" or "wrong" pair of new underwear, really; this remains the most personal apparel choice a man can make.

Seeking control of a man's underwear decisions is not easy, because, let's face it, it is the piece of apparel he's closest to. American women may be the biggest men's underwear buyers, but not one purchase is done without the guidance, or the opinion, or the wrath, of your man. Comfort, form, and function have long defined this niche market, but it no longer rides leisurely beneath fashion's radar. Since the early 1990s, underwear has come out from underneath and is finally considered an element of personal style. Big designer names and even bigger and glossier marketing campaigns are responsible for ushering in the enlightened era of underwear—men have come a long way, baby, from the sketch advertisements of the early 1900s, which was all that was permitted.

For most of modern history, men's underwear was something that was never, ever discussed. It was britches and a chemise, or something similar to a union suit, that covered as much skin as possible. It was bulky and it was hot. Its discomfort was considered a condition men simply had to live with. It wasn't until World War I that underwear ceased to be a full-body affair. Soldiers were issued lightweight boxers and singlet T-shirts for the summer months and never went back. In the 1920s, stores like Brooks Brothers and Saks Fifth Avenue modeled new underwear styles after the shorts worn by boxers like Jack Dempsey. A decade later, Arthur Kneibler, an executive at Jockey, promoted a new and utilitarian style of underwear modeled after the short, low-waisted swimsuit,

Tom Cruise in *Risky Business*

or brief—and it's been a bestseller ever since. A famous example is Tom Cruise's character dancing around his parents' house in *Risky Business* when they go out of town.

There's something inherently funny about underwear. It's beloved and bemusing, possessing more nicknames than any other piece of apparel: among them tighty whities, skivvies, britches, and gitch. Picturing an audience in their underwear is a folk remedy to cure stage fright. Dancing around in white briefs and lip-synching to Bob Seger illustrated the freedom and frivolity Cruise's Joel was about to experience for the first time. Men dressed as fruit in Fruit of the Loom commercials hawked underwear on and off throughout the latter half of the twentieth century. In the late 1980s, Nick Graham's Joe Boxer turned boxer shorts covered with smiley faces—some of which could be bought in vending machines—into a fashion statement meant to create a giggle when revealed.

Clark Gable was the first to transform underwear from a vaudeville cliché to sex-symbol status when he undressed in the Oscar-winning 1934 movie *It Happened One Night*, revealing his bare chest. Undershirt sales plummeted for nearly twenty years, until the silver screen redeemed itself with Marlon Brando screaming out to his wife, Stella, on a steamy New Orleans night in the film adaption of Tennessee Williams's play *A Streetcar Named Desire*. And let's not forget the famous image of Elvis Presley in his briefs as he measured up for Uncle Sam.

Sex and strength has sold underwear ever since—from Jim Palmer modeling for Jockey to Michael Jordan doing the same for Hanes. Calvin Klein used his erotic and arty print advertisements to make his underwear a must-have for men—launching careers for his washboard ab models Antonio Sabato, Jr., and Mark Wahlberg. The formula continues to thrive to this day, from Tommy Hilfiger's recent underwear campaign starring supermodel Jason Shaw, to New York Giant Jason Sehorn lending his sculpted quads, lats, and fair face to help 2(x)ist reach the platform it needs to earn the distinction of being the first designer brand to start out as an underwear company—instead of the other way around.

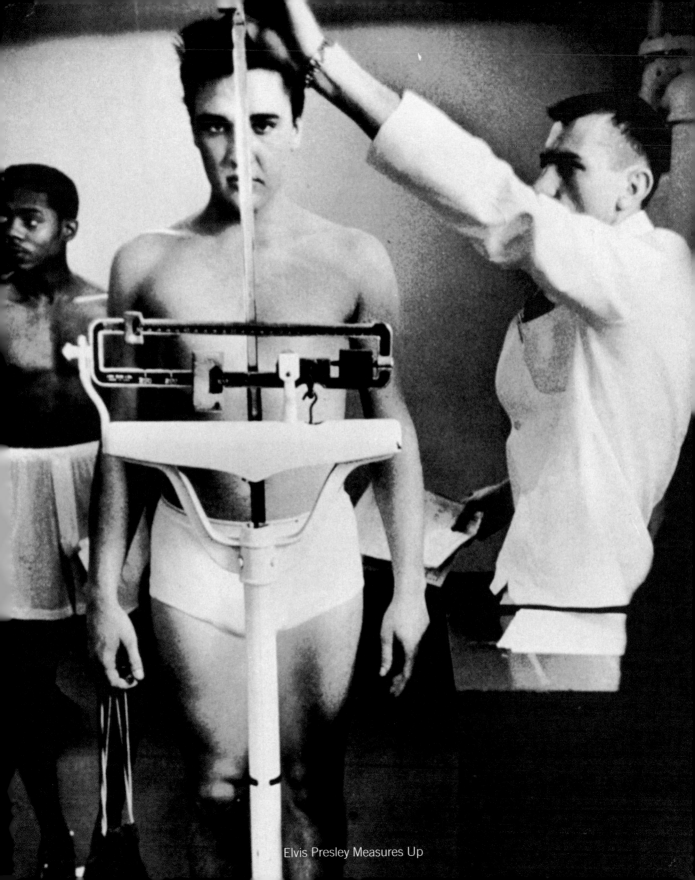

Elvis Presley Measures Up

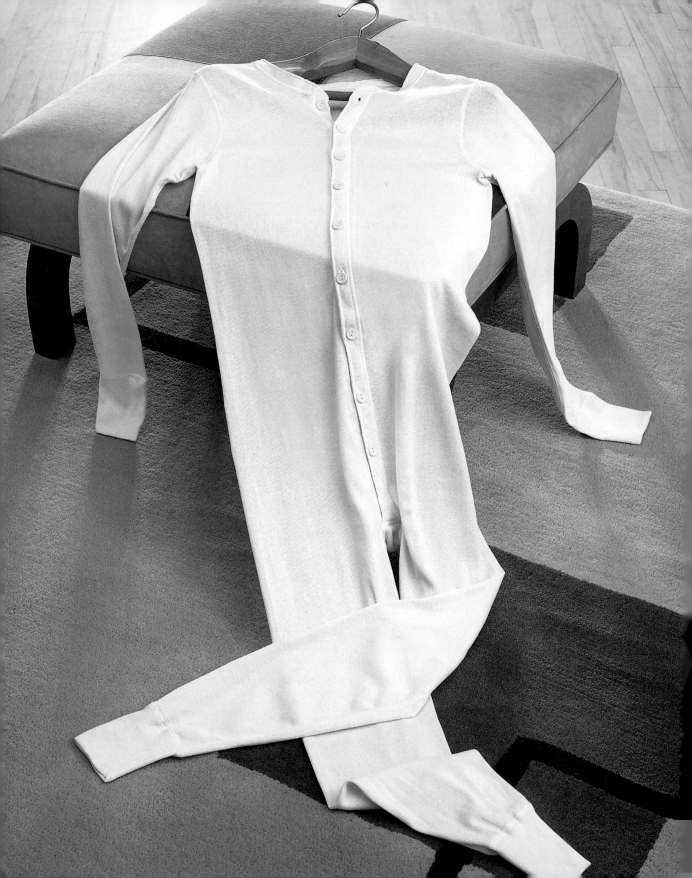

HIS UNDERWEAR 101

AH, *HIS* INTIMATES. UNDERWEAR IS THE LAYER OF CLOTHING THAT TOUCHES HIS SKIN IN the most private way and in the most private of places. More than any other piece of clothing he owns, your guy's underwear has to feel comfortable.

One of the hottest and most provocative men's underwear and sleepwear collections in stores today is by 2(x)ist. The company's strappy thongs—yes, thongs!—boxer briefs, and tight-ribbed tank tops have amassed a cult following stretching from the East Coast to the West. 2(x)ist's creative director and founder, Gregory Sovell, and Jeff Danzer, the company's vice president of marketing and licensing, believe that the best and most fashionable underwear is the result of marrying function with form. While impressing *you* is always important, Gregory and Jeff offer some advice on your guy and his underwear:

The biggest underwear mistake men make:

Women need to know how to dress their men in the newest options in underwear fabrics, shapes, and colors. Try something fresh other than the same old pair in the same old style. Black underwear can be very sexy, and it's quite easy to keep it looking brand-new. You can wash black underwear in cold water, and years from now they'll look as good as the day they were bought.

Another thing to consider: Avoid aluminum-based deodorant products, which can react with some men's body chemistry and causes yellowing stains on the armpits of his T-shirt.

On helping underwear last longer:

Most people think that to get your whites white, you have to use chlorine bleach, but what they don't realize is chlorine bleach disintegrates the Lycra© and makes the waistbands and leg binding weak. So if you want to make your underwear last longer, start using nonchlorine bleach. A simple switch in bleach is going to make his underwear last much longer. It will also make your whites whiter, logos won't fade, and the elastic will last.

Where to spend the most:

Loungewear. They're dressier than worn-out sweats and are more comfortable than stiff cotton pjs. They're not pajamas! We love loungewear because it's softer and more comfortable than old sweats or heavy flannels. Women should try purchasing something for their men that's contemporary and casual, as opposed to stiff men's pajamas. It's also sexy and unexpected. Oftentimes men will wear a T-shirt to bed, or worn-out underwear, and that's about it. Loungewear would be fun for both of you and comes in soft cotton, silks, and cashmere.

Items women should toss from their man's underwear drawer:

Underwear with the holes. There's no excuse. Remember: If a woman is purchasing her guy some underwear, keep in mind that she should select something that suits not only him, but she should also splurge on some underwear she likes as well. Underwear's a very intimate item.

The Basics

Toss away your visions of a muscle-clad Mr. Universe in his streamlined European skivvies, or the chiseled Chippendale dancer in his satin G-string. Most men won't go there. If there's anything in a man's wardrobe he probably thinks "ain't broke" and not in need of fixing, it is doubtless his underwear. Many men want underwear that's comfortable and reliable. Below is a rundown of some of the styles that most men like.

The Classic Brief

Affectionately known as "tighty whities," the classic brief is a "full rise" and covers a man from waist to thigh. This style is the best choice to wear under dress pants. Look for cotton-covered elastic leg bands for maximum comfort and durability.

The Mid-Thigh Brief

This is a comfortable alternative to the classic brief, which some men find constricting around the crotch. Many mid-thigh briefs are often made with a touch of Lycra©, which means this style is a good choice for an active man. Mid-thigh briefs wear well with dress pants as well as with loose-fitting khakis and jeans.

The Athletic Brief

Also a "full rise" style with an elongated leg that typically extends to just above the knee. Sometimes this style is "no-fly" and is considered the most athletic of these basic underwear styles, since it offers the fullest support in both 100 percent cotton and cotton/Lycra© blends. With this in mind, stay away from dress pants, or suits in soft fabrics—it could create a clingy nightmare.

The Boxer Brief

The boxers-vs.-briefs issue ends right here. This hybrid is fitted like a brief but is cut longer in the leg, like a boxer. This style is comfortable for most men and can be worn with almost any kind of pants. Europeans push the boxer brief a little further by offering "no-fly" fronts.

The Low-Rise Brief

This brief sits about two inches below the waist at the hip, and covers to the top of the thigh. Next to the bikini—first made infamous in the '70s—this is men's answer to high-fashion underwear. The low-rise brief is the perfect solution for guys who wear hip-huggers or baggy trousers. Some brands call this style the "hip brief," and it's not recommended for men with thick waists and hips.

The Boxer

Boxers allow a man total freedom and are great for men with larger thighs—but provide little support where it counts. Boxers are best for lounging. And whether they are 100 percent cotton or a cotton/polyester blend, boxers are the wrong choice for dress pants and suit trousers because they can add bulk and unsightly wrinkles.

The Mid-Thigh Brief

The Boxer Brief

Undershirts

The Tank Top

The tank provides classic, form-fitting comfort. A ribbed fabric is what makes the real difference, as it provides a very slight smoothing action over a belly. (The tank *smooths*, it doesn't minimize!) The tank's biggest drawback is that it is not the best choice for a man who sweats easily, because there's no absorption coverage for his underarm. The tank is the ideal undershirt for the warmer months, and works well under casual shirts because of its scooped collar.

The V-Neck

Invented for the popular V-neck sweaters of the late 1970s, the V-neck has come into its own and is considered both an undershirt and a T-shirt. Your man should be well stocked with these shirts if he either wears his shirts slightly unbuttoned or he is a larger man with a full neck and shoulders. Several companies have modified the V-neck to accommodate different V-neck sweater styles. Also look for a reinforced ribbed collar and double-stitched hems at the bottom and on the sleeves to help the shirt keep its shape after washing.

The Crew Neck

The crew neck is the most popular undershirt style for men. It's a classic that can be partnered with a guy's favorite jeans, and is the ideal match to any button-down dress shirt. This is the correct T-shirt style if your man wears a dress shirt and tie to work, because the neck does not interfere with the look of his shirt and tie. Your man should read the details on the package before grabbing that same old three-pack of white Ts. The narrow one-piece "collarette" with a smaller fine-gauge collar is more comfortable. And a taped "shoulder to shoulder" seam provides a stronger fit and lasts longer.

The Muscle T-Shirt

If your man doesn't have Schwarzenegger's biceps, this is not the undershirt for him. Muscle T-shirts open the wearer to total freedom of movement for athletic activities like weight lifting. Most men prefer an oversized muscle T for the basketball court. For the best quality, look for 100 percent cotton, or a nylon Lycra© blend finished with double-needle stitching on the hem and at the shoulder openings.

The Age Old Debate: Briefs vs. Boxers

Briefs	Boxers
• Almost useless, snug Y-front design	• Ultra-accessible, loose, U-shaped fly design
• Form-fitting	• Loose-fitting
• "Member supported"	• "Free membership"
• A "full rise"	• Rising not recommended
• Has tendency to trap heat	• Has tendency to welcome a breeze

Before

THE MAKEOVER

Brent Zachery and girlfriend, Tamara Spinner

Brent, a model, and Tamara, editor-in-chief of WinkMagazine, *a cross-cultural beauty and fashion magazine, have been dating for more than three years. They met after Brent traded the world of finance for fashion—a journey that's included trips to the runway for Hermès, Joseph Abboud, Romeo Gigli, and magazine layouts in* GQ *and* Maxim. *Dressing up for work, however, hasn't crushed Brent's love for comfortable well-worn underwear—just like any average guy.*

LLOYD: Tamara, some women say the first thing they notice is a man's shoes. Others say it's his fingernails. But then, many women, after they've gotten to know a guy, start to pay attention to his underwear. Tamara, tell me about Brent's underwear. The first pair you saw . . .

TAMARA: The first pair I saw were his favorite: Calvin Klein briefs.

LLOYD: Traditional briefs?

TAMARA: Just traditional briefs. When I was in college I was told guys who wore briefs were kind of corny, and that they should wear boxers instead. I had never seen a man look good in briefs until I saw Brent in them, and then I thought, "Oh, my God, wow!"

LLOYD: He looked good?

TAMARA: Yes, Brent looked very good in briefs, and they're still my favorite on him. I don't mind the boxer briefs, either. Regular boxers, however, don't work because of Brent's body type. If he wore boxers with slim pants, they would probably bunch up around his thighs. He needs to wear underwear that's more fitted.

LLOYD: Brent, how do you feel about underwear and style?

BRENT: Underwear is more or less utilitarian. I have certain kinds that I like, and within the past year I've tried to make more of an effort to be concerned about underwear, since it's important to Tamara. But there's still a pair or two you have to keep because they're way too comfortable to get rid of.

TAMARA: He has a pair of black Calvin Klein cotton briefs that have stretched out, so now they're baggy briefs. I mean, really baggy briefs.

BRENT: They're blown out—but I'm trying to change, and that's my only bad pair. I used to have about fifteen bad pairs.

TAMARA: There used to be a famous pair of white briefs—they had a hole right in the butt from a Rollerblading fall. But they were still good to work out in. The underwear you wear to work out in is different than the ones you wear when you go out.

LLOYD: How many pair of underwear do you own, do you think?

BRENT: About fifteen to twenty.

TAMARA: Not enough.

LLOYD: Now let me ask you, Tamara—thumbs up, or thumbs down. Would you want to see Brent in something like sheer Gucci underwear?

TAMARA: Maybe, yeah.

LLOYD: A thong or French-cut underwear?

TAMARA: That wouldn't bother me, but a thong? I don't know.

BRENT: It's not even "I don't know"; it's just a "no."

LLOYD: No thongs for Brent. But if one evening you wanted to impress Tamara, what would you wear?

BRENT: Hmmm, interesting. Have I ever tried to impress you with my underwear?

TAMARA: No.

LLOYD: So what would you go out and buy? A robe? Pajamas?

BRENT: I have a pair of pajamas that Tamara gave me that I like. They're flannel, pin-striped, with wide legs. I'd wear something like that.

TAMARA: I have to say this: I think Brent should wear more tank tops and luxurious underwear in silks and satins, because my favorite parts of his body are his chest, shoulders, and back. But he likes to cover up as much as possible. Some days we have four or five layers going—we have the T-shirt, the long-sleeved T-shirt, the sweater, and the jacket.

LLOYD: Kind of like a prepster.

TAMARA: Yes, that's *exactly* what he is—and a touch of luxe never hurt even the most conservative of guys!

The Make Over Prescription: *Tamara knocked her boyfriend, Brent's, socks off, and just about everything else, by saying goodbye to traditional, boring cotton underwear. Her advice on men's intimates is to imagine a Victoria's Secret man—and what he'd wear. For this, she chose a very rich platinum silk robe with a "money" green piping detail. After that, it's all about the midnight boxer briefs that fit him perfectly—and comfortably. The Result: She popped him into silk—he recently popped the question!*

After

His Grooming
The Routine Routine

SKIN CARE 101

IT'S A SHAME THAT MOST MEN PERPETUALLY CONVINCE THEMSELVES THAT THEIR SKIN CARE and grooming regimen is less complicated than that of their female counterparts.

The truth of the matter is if you're a living, breathing human with skin on your body, you have the same needs and maintenance requirements as anyone else, female or male.

Cleansing and Maintenance

New York dermatologist Dr. Deborah A. Simmons knows the importance of proper cleaning, and feels that it's the foundation for truly healthy, good-looking skin—whether you're a man or a woman. Trained at Brown University, Simmons practices in the heart of New York City, where millions of pores are in direct contact with some of the country's highest levels of dirt and germs. However, her "skin is skin" philosophy can be applied to any man, even those who think that the simple adolescent splash of soap and water to which they are accustomed will be enough to get them through the day.

Ever washed your man's face in hopes of showing him the correct way to cleanse? If your answer is no, then you're certainly not alone. Simmons says many people are surprised how much they don't know about good old soap and water.

On frequency:

He must wash his face twice a day. The majority of American men don't—they figure that they'll wash in the morning and not have to wash before bed. Twice a day means just that—morning and night. And wash again just after you've worked out. If you live in a big city like New York, Chicago, or Boston, it's especially important to wash often.

On choosing the right products:

I highly recommend that men use milder soaps regardless of their skin type. If your man has oily skin, he can certainly use cleansers specifically formulated for "normal to oily skin." If he's a dry-skin guy, clearly look for something that's created for men with dry skin. My personal favorite is the line of Cetaphil products because they're effective, inexpensive, and are usually found at local drugstores.

On the prep:

Men should wash their hands well, for three to four seconds, before washing their face. Follow with a good rinsing, making sure that he turns his hands down into the sink so that all the dirt and water runs down the drain, not back onto his wrists and forearms.

To get him all wet:

He should always put a little bit of water on his skin first. It helps to facilitate the lathering and to decrease friction. Warm water is best.

On lathering up:

Have him use a dime-size amount of cleanser and apply in circles with hands. Don't ignore that area where the nose meets the cheek, and the crevices around his mouth and neck.

On the rinse cycle:

Thorough rinsing with warm water is the best, which means rinsing until the skin feels "squeaky clean."

The pat-down:

Men should pat their faces with a clean, dry face towel. I always recommend he have a separate face towel. The body towel goes places that you ordinarily would not want near your face.

For the man on the run:

If your man is totally on the run and needs a quick cleaning trick, I sanction the occasional use of liquid hand sanitizers and certain antiseptic cleansers, like Sea Breeze. These are great for him to keep in his desk drawer or gym bag. For the busy new dad, a travel pack of baby wipes (without lanolin).

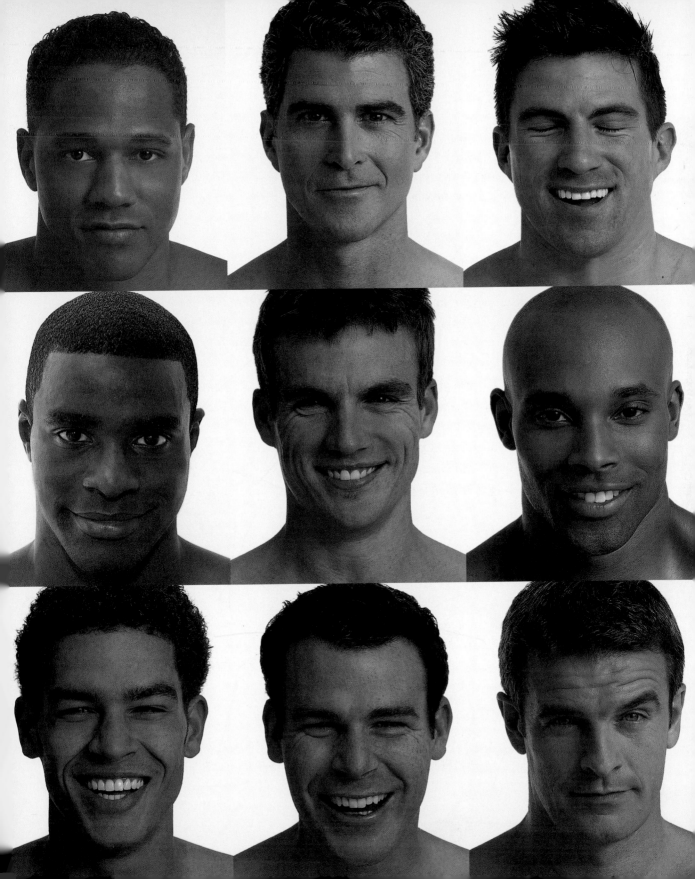

On toners and astringents:

For oily skin, your man should use a toner or a mild astringent. Ladies, since the inexpensive drugstore brands are just as effective as the designer lines, you do not have to go out and purchase an astringent that costs $50. Know that toners and astringents are best applied with a cotton pad.

Moisturizing:

Most people don't realize that the facial skin is a major barrier to infection for the entire body, so by moisturizing as part of the cleansing routine, he is also minimizing the dirt and bacteria that might build up on the skin later. And because shaving causes minor breaks and cuts in the skin, the chances of men getting infected are greater. So I combine the cleansing/moisturizing step, and recommend products that will take advantage of the water that's already in and on the skin, and help to seal that moisture in.

Certain men should also consider choosing a moisturizer with sunscreen year-round. No matter if you are fair, blond-haired, blue-eyed, red-haired, or even a light-skinned black or Latino. Men should get into the habit of protecting the skin from the sun's harmful rays. It can't hurt—and might just help.

Remember that his moisturizer should be applied on each quadrant of the face, using a dab not larger than the head of a Q-tip.

I recommend moisturizers that are noncomedogenic, which means they do not clog pores. If it's not labeled as such, regardless of whether it's from the cologne counter or the drugstore, he may be taking a chance. So be sure to check the label and avoid ingredients such as lanolin, mineral oil, petroleum, and squalene for men with oily and acne-prone skin. If your man has combination skin, he should follow these same tips. Men with average to dry skin should look for products with propylene glycol or a little touch of glycerin.

On man-handling blemishes:

Don't pop it! Don't squeeze it! The occasional adult male acne outbreak should be handled carefully. Squeezing a pimple can lead to more inflammation and discoloration. The sebum and bac-

teria that's enclosed actually helps create a new pimple when it plops on good skin and stimulates further production of oil, too. So we professionals prefer that you don't squeeze. Have him apply a warm compress until it comes to a head. Apply a little bit of Listerine to it—sounds crazy, but it helps because it is an antiseptic. The alcohol content helps to dry up the pimple. Some people use toothpaste—I don't recommend it, but a lot of people swear by it.

Doctor's final orders:

If you can get your man to stop doing one thing, it should be applying straight alcohol to the skin. Believe it or not, a lot of men do it, because they've seen barbers apply it to their tools to prevent the spread of germs from one customer to another. Actually it's very irritating, and over time can become excessively drying. The alcohols that are used in the astringents and some of the toners are really more appropriate for facial skin.

Scent of a Man

How to apply fragrance, or better still, how to tell a trigger-happy man "enough is enough":

Matthew Teri, vice president of Global Product Development, Estée Lauder and Aramis Designer Fragrances, has a few words for the man who loads on the cologne with wild abandon:

There's nothing worse on a well-dressed man than a burst of overpowering cologne. Many men make the mistake of putting the fragrance only on their outer clothing after getting dressed. To maximize your guy's scent potential, suggest that he spritz fragrance on skin first—neck, back, chest, even arms. Not only will it help him cool down, but skin and hair will hold fragrance. If he wants to spray his T-shirt, or even his sports jacket, go ahead, but the more layers he applies, the more concentrated and heavier the scent. Don't forget—deodorants, shampoos, even aftershaves will all contribute to his overall scent as he walks out the door.

The Scent-a-lizer test:

Knowing "when to say when" has to do with the makeup of a fragrance. Bolder, musky fragrances need less intensity. Lighter, citrus-y notes make layers in stronger hits without the potential for overkill. I don't think there's a set answer as to how much is enough. When your man puts on fragrance and he smells it around him as he gets dressed just short of overpowering his own nose—that's enough.

The Final De-scent:

When shopping for a fragrance for your man, you should learn his likes and dislikes before buying to avoid contributing to the graveyard of old gift scents in his bathroom. For the record, ladies, one year is the max shelf life of a fragrance.

SHAVING 101

THE PERFECT SHAVE

With the help of men's shaving expert Myriam Zaoui, co-owner of The Art of Shaving, a high-end and aromatherapy-based shaving and skin care line, and author of the book *The Art of Shaving*, your guy can learn everything there is know about the perfect shave.

The Art of Shaving—with store locations in Miami, on New York's tony Madison Avenue and Wall Street, and within select Neiman Marcus stores—is fast becoming one the country's elite manufacturers of shaving products and fine accessories. Myriam's mission and personal vision is to help all men to enjoy the intricacies of shaving. From woman to woman, she shares her advice for your man and his routine:

On preparing him to wet-shave:

The most important element of successful wet shaving is the steaming process, which he can achieve by shaving just after a hot, steamy shower, or by placing a hot face towel around his face for thirty seconds or so. This step prepares his skin by opening his pores and softening his beard.

Apply a preshave oil before shaving cream, because it protects the face and softens the beard. I recommend a noncomediogenic, lavender-essential moisturizing oil for normal to sensitive skin. Lemon- or lime-essential moisturizing oil is good for normal to oily skin types. Sandalwood-essential moisturizing oil is best for normal to dryer skin types.

The shaving cream:

Your man can use shaving cream or shaving soap, but make sure that it is a bar soap formulated for shaving and not bathing. Genuine shaving soap has added fat, which provides additional lubrication.

As for shaving cream, your man should look for products that have glycerin or fatty oils for additional lubrication, which over-the-counter shave creams don't have. Avoid products with cooling menthol that numbs the skin when he is shaving. When applying cream, your man should use a shaving brush made from badger hair that will not irritate his face. To lather, put some warm water on the shaving brush and some shaving cream on the brush tips and then lather directly on the face. By doing this, he will generate a very warm lather to open the pores and soften the beard. The shaving brush will also lift the beard and lightly exfoliate his skin in a way that can't be done with his hands. Applying a gel straight to the face with his fingers actually flattens the hair on his face, and he'll need to push on his razor to catch the hair.

Begin the Shave

Here are Myriam's basic steps:

- Choose a quality razor. I recommend the Gillette Mach III. This disposable razor has a swivel head and comes with three blades, which allows men to shave a lot faster along the natural contours of his face and avoid cuts.

- Pay attention to the direction. He should note the direction of the hair growth and shave with it in smooth, even, controlled strokes. The blade should be rinsed after each stroke. Most men's hair grows downward from the cheek to the chin through the top of the neck. From the chest to the top of the neck, the hair usually grows up. On the second round, it's okay for men with straight hair to shave against the grain. I would advise men with curly hair, especially men of color, to avoid this step to prevent in-grown hairs.

- Rinse with cold water after shaving to close the pores.

- Apply an alcohol-free aftershave balm or moisturizing gel.

For men with curly hair

Men with curly hair, especially men of color, are prone to a common shaving irritation called *pseudofolliculitis barbae,* commonly known as "razor bumps," which appear when sharp, closely shaven hairs curl back into the skin and cause a large pimple to form. Myriam has a few separate tips to prevent razor bumps that differ from some dermatologists' recommendations to "dry shave."

"I have several clients who have successfully transitioned from electric to wet shaving. It's a little-known fact that razor bumps are also caused by wrong shaving techniques and poor shaving products. If your man doesn't treat an ingrown hair right away, it can become a cyst that can last for years and require a dermatologist to remove it."

- Men who suffer from this condition need to first understand the importance of protecting existing "bumps" by using a preshave oil, which will allow the sharp razor to glide over the

A Good Rinse

Nick Fixes

bumps and keep them intact until the ingrown hair is properly tweezed out. If he shaves over them and nicks the surface, they could get reinfected and may never heal.

- Avoid products that contain alcohol when you have ingrown hairs—especially on the front of the neck and shaving areas—to prevent excessive dryness and further irritation.

Moisturize:

Even when using high-quality products, men often remove a small layer of skin when shaving and need to regenerate the skin by applying moisturizer all over the face, including the nonshaved areas. Moisturizers containing algae work best on damaged skin.

Nick fixes:

If your man should nick or cut himself, the first-aid method I suggest is the alum block, an all-natural stone similar to the styptic pencil. Place the stone in cold water first, then rub it against the cut for a few seconds to stop the bleeding.

THE PERFECT
MEDICINE CABINET

Skin-Clearing
Solution

His 7 A.M. Spa

It takes fifty-one minutes, on average, for a man to get showered, groomed, and dressed. The downside of going through this part of a makeover with your man is that you may soon have to sacrifice some of your space in the medicine cabinet. Sorry, ladies!

While a shave and a haircut are all the grooming most men require, there are those out there trying to sway male vanity. Companies like Nivea skin care, Neutrogena, and fragrance powerhouse Aramis have both launched grooming lines just for men. Actors, politicians, and pro athletes have dymystified macho attitudes about hair color, earrings, whitened teeth, and even plastic surgery. Today, men can't help but be bombarded with grooming details.

His bulging medicine cabinet is the evidence of this growing trend. But is it swelling with the right products to keep his grooming balanced and effective? Or is it packed with repetitious products that keep him stuck in a virtually ungroomed groove? He only *thinks* he's polishing up his act. Let's peek into the perfect medicine chest and see what's there.

Face Cleanser   Exfoliator

Shower Gel   Electric Pr

Pure Castile Soap   Facial Brush   Shaving Set

Shaving Bowl   Aftershave Balm   Preshave Oil   Quality Shaving   Cleansing Mask
                                                   Cream

Cotton Swabs   Glycerin Soap   Manicure Set

Before

THE MAKEOVER

Star Jones and friends Sean, Tre, and Charles

His first manicure. His first pedicure. Both courtesy of Star Jones, cohost of ABC daytime talk show The View, *and a woman who admits to loving a little pampering herself. She may be a lawyer by training, but make no mistake—Star's a lover, not a fighter. She made sure to use a little tenderness in the first manicure she lavished on her friends Sean (bottom left), a marketing director for Braver, James Sports Management; Tre (top right), a catering assistant with New York City–based Urban Staffing; and Charles (top left), a personal trainer.*

LLOYD: Before Star got ahold of you, Sean, had you ever had a manicure or pedicure before?

SEAN: No.

LLOYD: How did your first manicure feel?

SEAN: Having another person touching your hands and feet, being gentle, and detailing certain parts of the fingers is great. The fact that you have a beautiful woman doing it makes it even better.

LLOYD: Charles, you're working out and training for eight hours a day—that must take a lot of wear and tear on your hands and feet.

CHARLES: Weights create a lot of wear and tear on the hands. I have big-time calluses all over my hands. Gloves help to a point, but when you're lifting four hundred pounds on your hands, it tends to pull the skin off.

LLOYD: Tre, have you ever thought about the importance of nails and feet before today?

TRE: Nails are a big thing in the catering business, because the first thing people see are your hands carrying a cup or a plate. So it's important to keep your hands nice.

LLOYD: Would you do it again?

TRE: Yeah, certainly. It makes you feel a lot better knowing that your hands can feel this good. It's a great stress release.

LLOYD: What about the pedicure? That's something that kind of tickles me, literally, to this day, and I get them regularly. How did it feel for you?

SEAN: I loved it. Anything to do with my feet I love.

CHARLES: The pedicure was very good as well. It's very relaxing, and hopefully it will stop me from getting ingrown toenails.

LLOYD: Star, I see you smiling—you gave these men a real work over. Why are a man's well-kept hands and feet so important to women?

STAR: I think that a man's hands and feet are indicative of how a man grooms himself. Most gentlemen extend a hand when you meet them. I always notice his nails, his cuticles. I notice if the palm of his hand is rough or callused. And not for nothing, if he's not a construction worker, there's no excuse for that.

LLOYD: Sean said something about the stigma men feel when they go into a salon for a manicure. What's a good tip for guys so they can get in and feel comfortable?

STAR: Walk in with confidence. Whenever I'm sitting in a manicurist's chair and I see a man walk in, what usually impresses me is when he comes in after work in his beautiful tailored suit and gorgeous tie, with the knot just right, and sits down for the manicure. When he walks in with confidence, I know he's got it all together. Guys should walk in like the manicure is the finishing touch.

LLOYD: Any grooming nightmares with men that you care to talk about?

STAR: I have to tell you, there is nothing worse—other than probably bad teeth—than a man with bad feet walking around in sandals. I remember going out with a guy who refused to wear sandals in the summer. And I couldn't figure out why he refused to wear sandals. We're out in the Hamptons. He comes to my house with sandals, but with socks on. It was bad. I said, "Am I dating Mike Brady?" So I said he had to take the socks off. Then I discovered why. Bad, bad . . . get thee to a pedicure right away.

LLOYD: Today, a lot of women think, "I love my man, but I'm not kneeling at his feet to do his toenails." What do you say to those women?

STAR: Oh, it's all right to kneel at his feet. It's all right to be a little giving in that regard. Trust me, they'll give it back tenfold.

LLOYD: That's amazing. Do you have a preference—buffed nails on a man, polished with clear or just left naturally manicured?

STAR: I'm a buffed nails girl. I like a nice buff, not a high gloss. I like clean, neat, trimmed, buffed nails.

LLOYD: What should a woman do to get her man in the mood for a manicure or pedicure?

STAR: She should set the scene. Get him comfortable so he knows that it comes from a place of love. Don't criticize. Set the scene. Light a candle; put out the beautiful crisp, white towels and start with a nice warm soak. If a man knows that the nail makeover is coming, I say, put on a nice, warm robe and relax. You're about to have the time of your life.

After

THE STAR JONES PERFECT
MANICURE/PEDICURE FOR MEN

For His Hands

Step 1. Set the Mood

Create a relaxing atmosphere. Start with scented candles and soft music, and make him slip into something comfortable.

Step 2. Moisturize Hands

Massage his hands with an emollient hand cream and cover them with a warm, moist towel for five minutes to allow the moisturizer to sink in.

Step 3. Cuticle Care

Apply a few drops of cuticle oil to his cuticles. Give the oil about a minute to soak in. Take an orangewood cuticle stick and gently push cuticles back toward the wrists using soft strokes. Cuticles should never be cut or clipped, as this increases the chance of infection.

Step 4. A Clip and a Shape

With a standard fingernail clipper, snip the sides of each fingernail, followed by a clip to the center of each nail. Smooth out the rough edges with a cushioned emery board. File lightly with uniform strokes from the outside of the nail toward the center of the nail.

Step 5. Soak and Relax

Soak his hands in a small dish filled with a solution of warm water and a mild hand soap, or lightly scented bath gel, for two to three minutes per hand to cleanse off remaining moisturizer and nail filings. Wet a cotton pad with a bit of astringent, like Sea Breeze, and clean the surface of each nail.

Step 6. Polish vs. Buff

It's important to let him choose the finish he most prefers. Start from the side of the nail and apply a base coat of clear polish from the bottom of the nail upward. Repeat on the opposite side, and complete each fingernail with a center stroke. Allow clear polish to dry about five minutes and, in the same manner, apply a topcoat.

For the "buff" man, a three-way buffer, available at most drugstores and beauty supply shops, is the simplest way to achieve a salon-quality finish. First use the rough areas to smooth down the nail surface. For the second pass, take the slightly finer area and smooth—and buff—each nail. The smoothest area on the buffer gives the nails a shine. Buff evenly and be sure not to over shine.

For His Feet

Step 1. Set the Mood

Again, create a relaxing atmosphere. Some people (both male and female) aren't comfortable having others focus on their feet, so make him feel extra comfortable.

Step 2. A Good Soak

In a basin of warm water, soak his feet for about five to ten minutes, depending on the condition of his skin. The longer he soaks, the softer and more pliable his skin will be for the pedicure. To the footbath add a bath gel, or take a more natural route with wonderful essential oils like bergamot, tea tree, sandalwood, or jasmine.

Step 3. Soften His Soles

Using a natural pumice stone, gently buff the bottom of his wet feet to remove dead skin. A grainy body scrub—one with microbeads, or an apricot scrub—gives similar results. Then, pat his feet with a clean, dry towel.

Step 4. Clip and Shape His Toenails

Take a toenail clipper and first snip the toenail straight across. Then, in the same way you shaped his fingernails, take the clipper and snip the sides of each toenail. Smooth the edges by using an emery board, starting at the side of the nail, with strokes toward the center of his toenail.

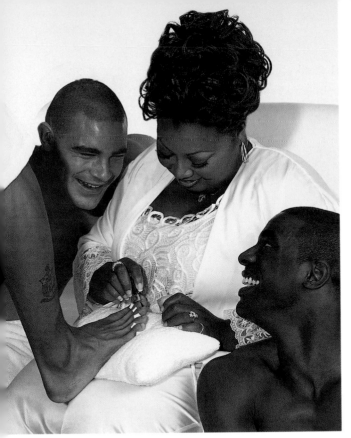

Step 5. Moisturize His Cuticles and Push Them Back

Just as you did with his hands, gently push back his cuticles by using a fresh orangewood cuticle stick. (Don't use the same orangewood stick you used for his hands; keep foot and hand tools separate.)

Step 6. Moisturize His Feet

Cover each foot entirely with a rich, intense moisturizer. Cover with a warm, moist towel and allow about five minutes to absorb.

Step 7. Buff

I'd avoid polishing your man's toes with clear polish, but if he insists—go for it. A gentle buffing, done with the same technique as that for the hands, will look just as fabulous on his newly pedicured feet.

Actress Jane Berkin and Pop Composer Gervase

His Closet
The Dumping Ground

FOR MOST MEN, THE CLOSET IS—AND WILL FOREVER BE—THE ARCHIVE OF EVERYDAY FAVORITES and a haphazard mix of crushed and folded clothing jammed between empty plastic dry cleaner bags.

This sad profile of closets wasn't always the case for the American male. His closet, stationary valet, dresser, and haberdashery furniture were once his pride and delight—not a fancy of fiction like the classic scene in F. Scott Fitzgerald's epic novel *The Great Gatsby,* in which Gatsby reveals the contents of his closet.

> *Recovering himself in a minute he [Gatsby] opened for us two bulking patent cabinets which held his massed suits and dressing gowns and ties, and his shirts piled like bricks in stacks a dozen high.*
>
> *He took out a pile of shirts and began throwing them one by one before us, shirts of sheer linen and thick silk and fine flannel which lost their folds as they fell and covered the table in many-colored disarray. While we admired he brought more and the soft rich heap mounted higher, shirts in stripes and scrolls and plaids in coral and apple green and lavender and faint orange with monograms of Indian blue.*

A bit over the top? Yes, in the 1920s and 1930s many men did care for their attire in an exemplary fashion. In fact, in previous decades men and women shared similar dressing regimens and attention to details regarding clothes—a woman wouldn't dare to leave her house without gloves, and a man couldn't step outside without a hat.

The Duke of Windsor is cited as the originator of several lasting menswear trends—the cuffing of trousers, the "Windsor" tie knot, and the mixing of sportswear with suits. So it's no surprise that the royal style arbiter had a closet that celebrated his love of style.

The duke is remembered to have had a private dressing room that led to a luxurious marble bathroom. His wife, the Duchess of Marlboro, always called her husband "impeccably dressed." *International Herald Tribune* fashion writer Suzy Menkes noted in her 1987 book *The*

The Duke of Windsor

Windsor Style that the duke was a man who "wore perfectly tailored suits and never [had] a hair out of place. His Royal Highness was so fussy about his suits . . . they had to be hung in the closet in order and rotated. And his valet would iron his shirts just the moment before he put them on."

No less discriminating men—and closets—have been captured in print—like the classic shot of Jane Berkin and Gervase in a perfectly mod wardrobe—and on the screen in films like 9½ *Weeks*, *The Family Man*, and *American Gigolo*. In the last, director Paul Schrader uses the closet to create tension and anticipation for both his male and female audience. Richard Gere, the film's escort-for-hire star, readying himself for a late-night appointment with a client, opens a closet full of Armani suit jackets hung up and organized loosely by color. He then pulls out four, lays them on the bed, and opens three drawers. The first is a drawer of neatly folded ties. The other two drawers contain button-down shirts, most of which are blue and black. Gere places a shirt on each of his four jackets, then one tie on each of the four shirts. He examines them, then switches two ties with each other and picks out one of the outfits to wear, leaving the others on the bed. He then takes his shoes out of his shoe trees, puts them on, laces them up, and he's ready to go.

You will find that modern, well-dressed men who appreciate style—and all the studied maintenance that comes along with it—see an ordered closet as a wellspring of possibilities. Helping your guy get rid of the unnecessary clutter can do a lot to improve his attitudes toward clothes. Think of it as a purifying ritual to get rid of the old and spruce the space—by choosing "good" hangers and adding cedar shoe trees.

So forget the heated image of bestselling author Terry McMillan's bitter character Bernadine, in *Waiting to Exhale*, who angrily raids her unfaithful husband John's closet, ultimately setting the majority of his well-crafted designer clothing ablaze inside his luxury BMW. The first step involves one simple question: "Honey, is it OK if I send just a few of your old things to the Goodwill along with mine?" And with "honey" being the operative word, let the games begin.

Mia Farrow and Robert Redford in *The Great Gatsby*

HIS CLOSET 101

No Wire Hangers. Ever.

Retooling his closet may involve only reorganizing his belongings and not necessarily throwing things away. The current chaos may simply be a result of not having a functional system for putting clothes away at the end of the day.

Elle Décor magazine special projects editor John Yunis, owner of interior design firm John Yunis Ltd., is an expert at helping his readers and clients maximize the space in their closets—regardless of size. Yunis is celebrated for solving space problems; his modest-size New York City apartment has graced *Elle Décor*'s cover, and he's offered his spacesaving tips on E! Entertainment Television and HGTV. Here he offers some simple organizational advice for any and all closets and then a few small-space solutions that you ladies can pass along to your guys—no saw and hammer required.

Organizing the Closet

The forgotten spaces:

One thing people need to realize is that having a well-designed closet isn't about money. It's about common sense and organization.

It's not like "starting over":

Don't create complicated storage solutions for a busy or careless man. Clothes and accessories should be easy to find and easy to put away. If your man wears a suit five days a week, he's going to want easy access not only to his suits but ties, belts, and dress shirts as well. When arranging a closet, think about the clothes he wears most frequently and then prioritize those items.

Assessing the closet:

When I'm redoing a client's closet, the first thing I look at is how much they have hanging and how much of it really needs to be hanging, because the hanging space must be mapped out. For instance, if a whole bunch of shirts is being stored, a single bar at about sixty inches high with two shelves is the most useless way you could organize such a closet space. What I would do is knock out the two top shelves, put the bar up high, then measure down thirty-six inches and install a second bar to create room for suits. So, within a space that's six to eight feet high, you can double your hanging space.

Usually at the bottom of the closet there's a shelf for shoes, which I consider another waste of space. At the bottom of a closet I recommend either shoe drawers or installing a series of little shelves that have about six inches between them. In the twenty-one inches or so that you have on the bottom of your closet, you can have three rows of shoes that are six or seven feet long. Suddenly, you have room for twenty-four pairs of shoes in a space that normally held eight pairs. And then, when you open the closet, you're seeing all your options—shirts, pants, suits, and shoes. You won't forget what you have.

Speaking of shoes:

In general, most people fail to store their shoes properly. They shouldn't be piled up on top of each other at the bottom of the closet, and they shouldn't be piled up in boxes. You need to be able to see them and get to them. Choose unvarnished cedar shoe trees, because they absorb moisture and keep the shoes from wrinkling. If shoe trees are used regularly and properly, his shoes will remain just as flat and as smooth as when they were first purchased.

Hanging up clothes:

The classic wooden hanger is the perfect choice for the well-maintained closet, but they're bulky and take up about three inches of space per garment. So if you don't have a lot of space, I recommend you use sturdy and nonbendable plastic hangers. A few wooden hangers are good here and there to hold things like suits and winter coats. But I actually just got rid of all my wooden hangers for white plastic ones, and I was able to increase the number of garments I hang by about 50 percent.

His pants, your hangers:

For his trousers, I love to use skirt hangers—if your closet can accommodate them, because they're a bit bulky. By hanging pants upside down, the weight of the waistband gives them a little bit of a pressing while they're in the closet. For the busy man, hanging trousers on skirt hangers can be a real timesaver.

On suit storage:

If your man doesn't want to use a "skirt" hanger for his trousers, suits should be stored with their pants folded over the hanger to save vertical space and avoid separating the pants from the jackets. Store suits on a sturdy hanger that can help the suit's shoulders retain their shape; wood hangers help the suit keep its form. And, most important, give your suits breathing room. Try not to cram them—they need about an inch of hanging space between them.

Knot finished yet:

I like the look of the circular tie racks, but the best tie storage is simply a basic tie rack attached to the back of a closet door. The tie rack is also a good place to keep belts and braces. You can certainly fold ties (like in department stores) and keep them in a drawer, but hanging them properly keeps them looking nicer. Necktie hangers are also a cool solution because they can hold about twenty ties staggered and he can still see each tie's pattern.

His head trip:

Casual hats, like baseball caps, should be folded and stacked. Dressier hats should sit freely on a shelf. I use clear shoe drawers with knit hats, cashmere hats, wool hats, and skullcaps. Each drawer is labeled, and the hats may be stacked on top of each other. The better the hat, the more care it needs. Fedoras and such should always be stuffed with the original paper or

Hanging Suits and Shirts

Shoe Storage

Underwear Storage

foam and board lining and stored in the box provided when the hat was purchased.

Look for the cedar lining:

A cedar closet is the ultimate because it keeps your clothes in a carfully controlled environment, but it's expensive. Many home stores now sell pieces of cedar that fit together and lie across closet shelves. Hardware stores sell long pieces of cedar that can be nailed to the wall of the closet. On a budget, or for a quick fix, cedar sachets can be placed on shelves or in drawers that store wool sweaters.

Tips for closets in small spaces

The value of editing:

To maximize space, get rid of old clothes. I constantly edit my wardrobe to create additional space.

Seasonal rotation:

There are many inexpensive off-season storage options out there, ranging from beautifully crafted wood to durable or transparent plastic. I recommend whatever works for your budget, taste, lifestyle, and clothes. Remember that natural-fiber clothes breathe better in storage containers made of natural, untreated wood. His sweaters and foldable knits hold their shape better if they're folded and put in plastic or wooden bins. I use clear plastic shoe drawers for underwear, belts, and socks so it's easy to see what's in them, especially when dressing in low light.

Hanging Pants

THE PERFECT CLOSET

IF THIS PHOTO MAKES YOU THINK "IF my man had a closet as big and beautiful as this, of course I could help him keep it in perfect condition," you're probably wrong.

This is the kind of thinking that keeps men with average closets—and the women who love them—perpetually digging through humps of ill-fitting sweaters, balled-up sweatpants, and lumpy mounds of shoes, because a well-organized man's closet has more to do with the contents, organization, and accessibility than the actual space and structure itself.

The much-celebrated California Closets company—known for their popular, much-sought-after, custom closet creations for both celebs and average folk who simply want to find their favorite shirt without a tussle—created this perfect man's closet specifically to guide you in making over the man that you love. Take a peek and hopefully glean a tip or two for his space to hold his new look: ➢

Sort

Set aside clothes that your guy doesn't wear anymore and decide what to do with them. If he insists on keeping something that evokes warm thoughts or memories, at least box it up and put it in storage. Remember, his closet should house the wardrobe that he actually uses. It's not a museum.

If he hasn't worn a garment for a year, out it goes! If he's dithering, ask him: Does it fit well? Does it flatter your frame? Is it truly timeless?

When he buys some new piece of clothing, encourage him to get rid of something old. Or you do it, with caution.

His Sweaters, Sweatshirts, and Casual Shirts

You should assist him in folding and displaying these items on a shelf in his closet, for two reasons: First, when clothing is buried inside dresser drawers, it's out of sight and he won't be as likely to wear it. And second, a hanger can distort a sweater's shape and necessitate more frequent dry cleaning to keep the garment looking good.

His Dress and Casual Pants

For the man on the go, hanging pants upside down by their cuffs is a practical way for him to save time pressing and ironing later. Purchasing uniform skirt hangers will often do the trick. If his challenge is finding space to hang pants, most standard closets will allow at least thirty-six inches of hanging space when cleared of extra shoes and boxes that eat up space at the bottom of the closet.

His Jewelry and Accessories

Help him to take special care of these items by keeping them in small, dedicated drawers where they can have breathing space and will not fall in between larger clothing items.

His Ties and Belts

Encourage him to hang them on space-saving racks, not bunched up on a single hanger, or worse yet, in a tangle inside a drawer.

His Shoes

The ultimate storage solution for a man's shoes, especially his new quality dress shoes, would be an eye-level shoe rack. The custom version shown here is certainly ideal, but a freestanding unit in stainless steel or cedar will work perfectly. Such shoe units hold more in less space once the boxes are eliminated, and he'll be able to easily view all his shoes.

The Positive/Negative

When helping your guy get rid of clothes, don't make the common mistake of keeping certain items of clothing and accessories just to keep the space looking full and complete. Edit freely and with brutal honesty on wearability, and embrace the negative space that comes with it.

Some helpful information:

    www.salvationarmy.org
    www.goodwill.org
    www.careergear.org

Before

THE MAKEOVER

Patti LaBelle and her son, Zuri Edwards

It takes more than just an ordinary diva to see the big, fabulous picture and still enjoy the smaller pleasures of life. After more than forty years as a recording artist and twenty albums, with hits like "Lady Marmalade" (with LaBelle) and "On My Own" and "New Attitude" (both solo efforts), Patti has earned two Grammy Awards, seven NAACP Image Awards, and a star on the Hollywood Boulevard Walk of Fame. She's also a mother of three sons—Zuri, Dodd, and Stanley—who loves nothing better than having a real life and real home in Philadelphia. Keeping it real is important to Patti. She's lived through a lot: She's lost three sisters and best friends to cancer, all before the age of forty-four; she parted with Armstead Edwards, Zuri's dad, after thirty years of marriage; and she has endured the death of her mother to diabetes and her own battle with the same disease. The lessons she's learned— like "You can't be a doormat if you don't lie down"—are the focus of her third book, Patti's Pearls: Lessons in Living Genuinely, Joyfully, Generously. *Zuri is a musician who's recently gone management and is now in business with his father at Edwards Entertainment Group, an entertainment management firm.*

LLOYD: The music business is certainly a social business. You can work and play all in one big happy evening. Zuri, tell me about how you maintain a balanced wardrobe.

ZURI: I really just concentrate on keeping my sneakers and my jeans in order.

PATTI: Every time I see him, there's a new pair of Timberlands or sneakers. He's got hundreds and hundreds of casual shoes. He won't wear sneakers once they get dirty. But he gives a lot of them away to people. Thank God he does that. He passes them on.

ZURI: I have a very neat closet, because I recycle everything. I have lots of jeans, but I alternate between three pairs during the week. The jeans are hung up on hangers and the sneakers and Timberlands are stacked in boxes, so everything looks really neat.

PATTI: He's changed. Back in the day, I would close the door to his room because I didn't want to see the stuff on the floor. It was a jungle. He would say, "Mom, I'm going to clean up tonight." And tonight never came. He loved living like that, sleeping on the clothes. I don't know, but there were probably people in there under all those clothes.

LLOYD: Patti, what should a guy like Zuri pack for a short trip?

PATTI: He could pack a gray suit and some casual pants. Two colorful shirts, dress shoes, and a pair of Timberlands. Men have it easier than women.

LLOYD: Zuri, who inspired your style growing up?

ZURI: I really like the way my dad dresses. He dresses much more corporate than I do, but he has a great sense of style and I really admire that. He'll usually wear a nice sweater, a nice pair of slacks and shoes—and sometimes a nice sport jacket.

PATTI: And real nice overcoats.

LLOYD: Does his closet look any better than yours? Do you like the way he maintains it?

ZURI: He's very organized. He has all of his pants on one side.

PATTI: And all the socks put together and color-coordinated.

ZURI: He has it all together. And he always keeps it pretty simple when he goes away. He'll take a nice suit, a pair of jeans, a T-shirt, and some nice shoes.

LLOYD: So he's a one-bag traveling man, and you're more of a ten-plus, Patti?

PATTI: Ten-plus. Plus! Then a whole trunk of my wigs. A girl's gotta carry her hair.

LLOYD: What should a woman keep in mind as she's helping her man find his sense of style?

PATTI: Don't force anyone into anything, or force anyone into a style that he's not accustomed to. Zuri always listened to his heart, which is very good. He followed his own heart, feelings, and his own way of wanting to look. It wasn't the way I said or the way his father said. Now when he puts on a suit, I swear to God, he's so handsome and he looks just like he's in *GQ* or *Esquire*. He's not even trying to look cute when he puts on a suit. You know, let them keep their own, but you try and frill it up a bit.

LLOYD: And, Zuri, if Patti starts reaching in your closet, how would you protect your territory?

ZURI: Put some jeans to the side just in case. And hide the valuable casual stuff.

The Make Over Prescription: *Patti has blessed her son, Zuri, with one of the greatest gifts of all: Style with a strategy! Her winning solution for her baby boy starts with a soft, brown cashmere sports coat and clay cashmere turtleneck. The look is polished off simply with Patti's celebrated eye for the right accessories: a contrasting camel pocket square in plaid, stately charcoal ribbed dress socks, and high-shined, chestnut brown perforated slip-ons. The Result: A young man with a believeable, sage take on style. Mama definitely knows best.*

After

A Hollywood take on the male/female shopping trip. James Mason and Joan Bennett in *The Reckless Moment*.

His Shopping
The Great Divide

MEN ARE HUNTERS; WOMEN ARE GATHERERS. IT MAY SOUND LIKE AN OVERSIMPLIFIED AND A politically incorrect cliché, but when it comes to shopping the adage holds a real kernel of truth. Men—to be fair, a lot of men, perhaps most men—do not enjoy shopping. At all.

How does shopping exactly equate with hunting? And isn't the hunter analogy better associated with bargain-seekers? Not really. Hunting, in this modernized case, means a quick-and-dirty purchase. Some men will go shopping on a whim, but most need a reason to get them into the mall. A job interview. A friend's wedding. Christmas. A hot date. That event turns into an imminent need, which turns into a quest that must be conquered quickly.

A hot date + a need for a new shirt = buying a new shirt. Retailers understand this oversimplified equation and use it to their best advantage. This is why men's departments always occupy the most convenient and best real estate at major store chains and department stores. Women, on the other hand, will travel by escalator, stairs, and elevator to get to the department they desire. For them, shopping is a gathering experience—it is slow, it is methodical, and most often, it is social.

Self-help guru John Gray, Ph.D.—bestselling author of the books *Men Are from Mars, Women Are from Venus* and *Mars and Venus Starting Over*—says:

> *Thirty minutes of unfocused shopping is the maximum a man can take before he begins to tire. For women, a few hours of unpressured shopping can be relaxing, centering, and rejuvenating. Acknowledgment of this difference is steadily growing; notice that in most women's stores there are now chairs strategically placed for the husband or boyfriend to sit in.*

Bud Light even made a funny reference to the "boyfriend couch" in a commercial starring Sean Hayes, in his pre–*Will & Grace* days, which aired in the late 1990s. The boyfriend, as played by Sean, was asked to hold his girlfriend's purse so she could try on an armful of clothes in the dressing room. A voice whispers from within a nearby circular round of clothes and motions Sean to dive in. Beneath all the clothes and hangers he's met by a group of other boyfriends, all holding purses, drinking a beer, watching a game on TV, and saying: "Isn't shopping great?"

Alan King resists Ali McGraw's shopping tips in *Just Tell Me What You Want*.

Men's distaste for shopping wasn't always the case. Before mass-produced apparel, generations of men of certain breeding and particular professions viewed shopping as a ritual. Months before temperatures would dip or rise, the "proper" man would order his clothing and accessories. He would be fitted for a classic suit, or two, and a fashionable one. This was followed by shirts, accessories, and formal wear, to get him through the approaching season.

For the most part, men's fashion still follows a pattern similar to what the well-heeled man once required. Even today, spring apparel reaches stores in February, soon followed by Father's Day goods. And summer is still blazing hot while tweedy fall clothes fill the mall, and at holiday time, menswear departments fill with sherbet-colored resort wear—all just begging to be taken to Palm Beach, Palm Springs, or by the shade of the first palm tree available.

Indeed. Most American men do not buy an entire wardrobe every season. Savvy men—or those associated with a pro "gatherer"—understand that playing the retail sales waiting game can have its rewards. For instance, when fall and winter apparel gets deeply reduced around New Year's Day or when retailers look to seriously unload beachy clothes around July Fourth. Add to that another pleasant shopping memory most men can relate to—back-to-school—and consider sale time as an opportunity to load up on basics. It's no small task to ask a man to shop when he's not under the gun. But, armed with a list, and an enticing sale, most men will at least understand the cost-saving logic.

The Bud Light commercial touches on an emotion men can relate to: fraternity. Hanging out and feeling like he belongs is important for a guy. An atmosphere that makes him feel as if he's visiting a favorite haunt where he belongs, like a golf-course pro shop or a paneled club hall, eases his shopping fears. This is why your man may relate to Brooks Brothers better than the *uber*-hip Barneys Coop in downtown Manhattan. A legion of better men's stores still thrive in this country—stores like Mitchell's of Westport, Connecticut, and James David in Memphis—because they rely on a mixture of the old-style wardrobing culture with a dash of the neighborhood club and a sales staff to individualize and satisfy each man's style needs. Now smart retailers create this sense of belonging by having VIP programs and in-store cocktail parties for men. The more comfortable they feel in their store, the better. For you, too.

Julia Roberts and Richard Gere in *Pretty Woman*'s memorable shopping scene.

SHOPPING 101

Shopping with Him

Most men prefer swift and focused shopping. They often see shopping as a clear and irrefutable mission that must be accomplished: Need a new suit—must go get a new suit. The taste part is where you enter the picture—infusing a bit of *your* likes to update *his* look, while still honoring his style and comfort zone. Like any difficult operation, its execution, on both your part and your guy's part, requires generous doses of patience and flexibility.

Dave Lackey, events and public relations manager for Harry Rosen, a Canadian institution since the 1940s and one of the country's well-heeled clothes retailers, has a few pointers on how you can mold your tone, manner, and preshop "setup" to break up those dark clouds that can hang over your guy's mood when you are shopping.

Mold and hold him:

Unlike women, most men don't go in with a lot of preconceived ideas when they shop, so encourage him to try on different styles to determine what he likes. Most men will be resistant at first, but when they put on something new and take a look in the mirror, they'll say, "Hey, you know this looks kind of good on me."

A vote of confidence:

At Harry Rosen, we find most men are afraid to show personality or originality when getting dressed and, instead, tend to dress like clones. They don't try out a bold-checked dress shirt, a pocket square, or a fine watch until a woman really gives it her nod of approval. Women should know that they are essential to retailers in that respect. So a woman should feel confident that helping her man to look good and her role in making his wardrobe choices is something we never take for granted.

The scouting report:

If time allows, the best way to shop with the man you love is to go into the store ahead of time and browse. Try to find some things your guy will be able to relate to, or talk to a knowledgeable sales-

man who may have some common interests or approaches to style as your guy—then come back to the shop when he's working. This way you begin to foster a relationship with someone who's well informed and trustworthy, and in the future your guy will be confident that he's already got someone who will take care of him.

Remember, this is his day, not yours:

Start shopping slowly. The worst thing a woman can do is to go through a man's closet and throw out everything in sight. Most men will get a little resentful of that bold action and a little anxious about the shopping that needs to be done to get it all replaced. Pay attention to his needs, not your own.

Start with investing in a good suit, or a great shirt-and-tie combo, or a nice cashmere sweater. And keep reinforcing how good he looks. As soon as he gets compliments from you and at work, it will be easier for him to move on and shop for something more.

Shopping for Him

Okay, now the situation is going to flip and you have the daunting task of picking up a "little something" for *him*.

Whether it's at his request or you're presenting him a gift from the heart, there are some dos and don'ts when buying something new for your guy.

Macy's is commonly known as the "largest department store in the world" in real bricks and

mortar and also online. The department store giant is a menswear institution, from basics like socks to fine tailored suits, shirts, and ties. Randy Heil, men's fashion director for Macy's West, said he rolls out the welcome mat for women shopping for—and with—the men in their lives. His advice on shopping for the man in your life:

No woman is an island:

> *Don't be afraid to ask for a salesperson's assistance. Within any department store, particularly Macy's, there are very specific "vendor shops" for designer brands like Tommy Hilfiger, Perry Ellis, and Nautica, where there are educated sales staff who are very familiar with the clothing and can help you find what works for your guy.*

On strategizing your plan:

> *It's important for a woman to sit down with the man in her life and truly understand who he is. This doesn't necessarily mean to ask him what kind of clothing he likes, because he may not know or be able to articulate what style he's looking for. But she needs to be aware of likes and dislikes, how he spends his time both professionally and personally. For instance:*

- *Where does he go?*
  On Saturday afternoons, would he like to go watch a football game, or is he a lunch-and-a-movie guy?
- *What does he naturally wear?*
  Does he need to "get dressed up" often? Does he wear a suit to work, or is his office "business casual"?
- *What is his taste?*
  I'm not sure if you know the old saying "Don't let your wife pick out your ties," which came about because women try to impose their own taste, their own likes, their own color preferences onto their men. Discover his likes and preferences.
- *What is his true size?*
  Take a soft measuring tape and take his measurements if he allows. Knowing measurements can take the guesswork out of shopping and reduce his frustration with having to return ill-fitting clothes.

The safe starter list:

> *Every man should own a certain grouping of American classics. If you ever need to surprise your guy with a gift, look at this list to help you find a piece that has a relaxed, elegant edge and a*

gentlemanly flair. These essentials will keep him comfortable and good-looking enough to keep you happy, too. Here are my picks:

- *The black cashmere turtleneck*
- *The traditional navy blazer*
- *The flat-front khaki*
- *The white dress shirt*
- *The basic Levis jeans*
- *The traditional loafer*
- *The navy wool pea coat*
- *The black leather blazer*

With these quality pieces, and your help, his outfit combinations become almost limitless.

Papa's got a brand new bag!:

Accessories are the easiest way to help a man update his style. Savvy men are starting to understand that a quick test of the well-dressed man is what kind of watch he is wearing, and how his belt and shoes look. When buying a gift, accessories are a nice and easy place to shop for your guy. I feel that there is nothing nicer than receiving a good-quality belt. A guy can never have too many belts, pairs of gloves, or scarves, depending on the climate. If it's a warmer area, buy a great pair of sunglasses or a great watch. And these stylish items don't discriminate by size.

Shoppers beware:

The foundation of any well-dressed man's wardrobe is the suit. Unfortunately, that is not something I recommend a woman go out by herself and purchase for a man. This is a large purchase your guy needs to be involved in, and he needs to be present for tailoring. If the man you're shopping for does not own a simple black or navy three-button suit, that should be his first purchase.

And because most women are shoe lovers, I don't recommend that you spend a lot of time in the men's dress shoe department without your man with you. Again, shoes are something that have to be tried on specifically, placing fit and comfort first.

Big & Tall Rescue

If men's style rules are bending and changing, so are the clothing choices for men of size. American designers and major clothing labels have finally caught on to the fact that 59 percent of American men have a body mass index that is above "normal" and are finally offering these men stylish clothing to suit their needs. Whether your man is a classic round frame who needs darker tones in the middle and a little lighter tones in his bottoms, or the endomorph who needs dark trousers and strong-shouldered jackets to balance his frame, modern options are available. Just look for pieces that fit and flatter, keeping these 10 rules in mind:

- *Buy for fit, not size. Clothing should enhance his body, not stroke his ego. If your man has a 50" waist and still believes that he's a 46", buy the 50" and snip out the tag.*

- *Go ahead and stripe! Unlike strict no-stripe style dictates of old, if the garment fits properly, and does not hug or swallow your man up, think of him as free to embrace stripes, plaids, and tasteful prints.*

- *Pleats, please. Flat fronts are for men with the same. Larger-sized men with waists over 48" need to stick to pleated pants. Flat fronts tend to visually squeeze a larger midsection and amplify the line of the leg. Pleats allow the pant to drape.*

- *On suits, his shoulder line should extend slightly beyond his hips. Avoid soft-shouldered suits that have no structure if your man is thick-waisted. Bold, shouldered jackets work best to balance his frame.*

- *Pant legs, cuffs, and shoes should be in proportion to his body. Trendy, narrow trousers work best on narrow men. When cuffing tailored and casual pants for a man of size, think 1¾" and up. Measly shoes never foot the bill on a larger man; go a bit chunkier in the shape if he is broad because his shoe should enhance his overall shape in proportion, not be a tightly squeezed finish.*

- *Accessorize with abandon. Go for cuff links, pocket squares, and quality belts that do not inhibit fit or proportion. But, avoid constraining haberdashery like tie bars on the man with a 22" neck.*

- *Stick to the classics. Trends that work in glossy magazines or on the silver screen do not always translate to big and tall men.*

- *If shopping without him, bring a garment or a list of his sizes to the store with you. Fit is critical, so come prepared.*

- *Trust the experts! Know that sales staff in stores dedicated to men of size are usually very sensitive to their customers' needs and concerns. This is a specialized business, so don't be afraid to ask questions. Most modern chains keep customer profiles with a man's sizes on hand to assist him with each visit.*

- *Men of size want style, too. Choices are available. Big and tall men may have gotten a bad style rap in the past because of the lack of stylish clothing offerings. Not anymore. Larger chains carry cool labels ranging from Tommy Hilfiger and Donna Karan to Versace!*

HOW TO BUY A QUALITY TIE

FOR MEN, A NECKTIE IS ONE OF THE FEW AREAS OF TRUE SELF-EXPRESSION, yet one of the most common clothing purchases made by women for men. It's the way your guy can separate himself from the sea of suits when he enters a room or rushes down a busy boulevard. At the end of the day, a dark suit is just a dark suit; it's the tie that creates opportunities for men to make a "me" statement.

With this in mind, buying a tie can be a challenge. Use the following pointers to ensure that you purchase the right tie for your man: ➢

A. Fabric   There are several choices out there, but silk is by far the best all-around tie material. Make sure the tie is made from 100 percent silk that is soft to the touch. Polyester ties look cheap and dated.

Gum twill, or foulard, is a featherweight silk/twill with a sophisticated hand that pairs best with suits and blazers with the same light feeling.

Crepe de chine is pure silk with a shinier surface than most ties, and a slightly scrunched surface. This silk holds pattern and print well and looks best with robust suiting fabrics such as cashmere, mohair, and flannel.

Poplin, a blend of silk and wool, is sometimes called "Irish poplin." This tie has a fuller hand than wool and little more rigidity. These ties are versatile and look great with almost any type of suit, blazer, and quality dress shirt.

Wool ties are easy to discern by their pronounced texture, unlike a traditional silk tie. From classic 100 percent wool to cashmere and even alpaca, wools are much more casual and look great with or without a tailored jacket.

The word *knits* may make you think of those square ties from the 1980s, but knit ties are available in the classic pointed shape and are quite natty and versatile. Some regard the silk knit tie as a man's "everyday" tie, taking him from casual to dressy when done in solids.

B. Lining   It's usually invisible, but a wool lining is a very important groundwork of a quality tie because it helps the tie maintain its shape. Be sure the wool is covered in silk, and that the entire lining is securely stitched inside the tie.

C. Cut and Construction   As with the lining, the outer shell of the tie fabric should also be cut on the bias, allowing maximum suppleness and flexibility when tying. Also, make sure the tie falls properly in line from end to end: Holding the tie at its center over your finger, make sure the tie folds exactly at the center. The silk or fabric of your choice should be soft and strong at the same time. Note that many high-quality ties have "hand-rolling" (slightly uneven sewing that appears to be done by hand) on the stitching from tie fabric to lining fabric.

D. Slip Stitch   This is not a loose thread. The slip stitch visible on the underside of the tie has an important function. When pulled, the stitch helps create a give that allows a quality tie to keep its shape.

E. Bar Tack   This is a simple, clean stitch that keeps the two back flaps of fabric from separating. Unless it's a signature of the designer or brand, the bar tack should be tonal, and should discreetly match the tie.

F. Length   The standard tie length can range from 54 to 58 inches, which can be difficult to gauge by sight. If your man is taller than six feet, or has a large midsection, select longer ties. If you are not sure, take one of his old ties that fits him properly along with you when shopping.

G. Style   This is the caveat. When in doubt, keep it simple, and keep the receipt. Your guy's tie should not speak before he has a chance to—it will inevitably say the wrong thing. Solid ties—and those that are in effect solid, but with a pronounced weave or bold texture—are great, for they work well with most suit-and-shirt pairings. Be mindful of patterns and prints that are printed onto the surface—the dye should never be raised to the touch. This is a sign of poor craftsmanship. Any decorations should be woven into the surface of the tie by the strands of the material.

H. Loop   The best ties have a loop that is made of the same fabric and pattern as the tie itself. Many superior-quality ties also have a button eyelet in the center of the tie loop that your man can fasten to a corresponding shirt button to avoid constant flyaways—and maybe a few dry-cleaning bills.

SHOPPING WITH KIMORA LEE SIMMONS

KIMORA LEE SIMMONS—WIFE OF RUSSELL SIMMONS, FOUNDER OF DEF JAM RECORDS AND Phat Farm and the creator of the collection's sexy sister line Baby Phat—is a well-practiced shopper. This quick tour with Kimora details where to find the best items for your favorite man.

Burberry: *A cashmere scarf in the classic Burberry check design is something every man will wear forever. Burberry is also the place to find the best trench coat, umbrella, or classic cashmere overcoat, a big-ticket item that will last for years and years and never go out of style.*

The Gap: *The best stop for clothing staples such as jeans, sweatshirts, T-shirts, and, believe it or not, leather. Their leather jackets and blazers are easy to wear and can take a man through several seasons.*

Phat Farm: *Phat Farm has great leather jackets. The collection's signature, however, is an argyle sweater and a pair of khakis that, when pulled together, is urban and hip-hop, but it's also yuppie and works everywhere in America.*

Tiffany & Co.: *Tiffany is renowned for its silver. My three suggestions for your guy: the thick-linked bracelet; the love knot cuff links; or if he's not into jewelry, a beautiful pen.*

Tommy Hilfiger: *His casual shirts in bright-colored gingham and stripes are perfect for the summertime, or for a more playful, all-American look, Tommy's shirts look great with a suit. Tommy's stuff has been in department stores for years, and he's just started opening his own stores around the country.*

Salvatore Ferragamo: *I love Salvatore Ferragamo's classic shoes for men. Good shoes and accessories, like a crocodile belt or a great tie, are wardrobe touches and investments that can last forever.*

Thomas Pink: *Every man should have a crisp, classic, and tailored white shirt, and Thomas Pink has it mastered. Or, try French blue and, if he's really confident, a well-fitting pink dress shirt looks very sexy on a man.*

Hickey-Freeman: *A navy blue pinstripe is one of the most fabulous—and versatile—items in men's fashion, and a suit from a classic maker like Hickey-Freeman is one of the best items to really splurge on. This suit can easily be dressed up, but you can also dress it down with a bright-colored sport shirt and sandals.*

Before

THE MAKEOVER

Businessman Don Weisberg and Colleagues Jennie and Lori

Don Weisberg is a COO of a major publishing house in New York. Born and raised in the Bronx and now a resident of Westchester, New York, Don has had twenty different jobs during his twenty-year tenure at the company known for it's superstar authors and bestsellers. Jennie Richie and Lori Zarahn are colleagues who offered to help Don make a style transition into his newest position.

LLOYD: Don, has your style changed much since you became COO?

DON: Not at all.

JENNIE: He's a very casual dresser, but publishing today is pretty casual.

LORI: His average outfit is basically what he's wearing today: slacks, shirt, usually a billowy shirt, tucked in. The sleeves always look a little too long like he's hiding in his shirt.

JENNIE: If you see him in a suit and a tie, which isn't very often, you know that there's a heavy-duty meeting. On Fridays during the summer he might wear a golf shirt.

LLOYD: So it seems like comfort is most important to Don when it comes to style. He gets dressed to be comfortable and to get his job done.

DON: Yep.

LLOYD: So ladies, what's it like shopping with a guy? Any man: husband, boyfriend, colleague, brother, Dad?

JENNIE: It's hard because they all have their own way of dressing, and you don't want to offend them. Either the clothes don't fit, they're a little dumpy, something's just not right, and they always buy things too big.

LLOYD: I've found that women shop strictly by sizes. If you're a six, you buy a six. If you're a twelve, you buy a twelve.

JENNIE: But with guys, if it fits in some way, they buy it. When you shop with a guy, you're constantly picking out things for them that you like and know are sophisticated, and they seem to want a different look entirely. The reason you're with them is to get something new, and they want to stay with the old. So . . . if it ain't broke don't fix it.

LORI: But it *is* broken, they just don't know it!

LLOYD: So how do you say: "This might work?"

LORI: I say, "Let's buy it. If you hate it, we'll return it."

JENNIE: I say, "Just take it home and try it later with a different piece of clothing." It usually works.

LLOYD: In the last several years most companies have gone corporate or business casual. Don, has that been a challenge for you?

DON: My wife says that I don't have bad taste; I have no taste. So when I have to match things, it's virtually impossible because I don't have a clue. So corporate casual is even more difficult because it's not white shirts and gray suits. With casual dress, a lot of different things come into play, and that's when it gets really tricky. I don't even shop for myself; my wife does.

LLOYD: So she knows your sensibility, and she'll pick out things that she knows you're comfortable with.

DON: She does a good job, but [laughs] I don't think she cares too much about my sensibilities!

LLOYD: So ladies, what's the ideal casual or business casual outfit for a man? What would you like to see him in?

JENNIE: Black pants and a good shirt tucked in with a nice belt or sweater. No turtlenecks. Just the basics. Two easy pieces.

LORI: I agree with Jennie. I like dark pants and a solid shirt. I'm not a plaid person.

LLOYD: Why not? A lot of men feel safe and kind of rugged and outdoorsy in plaid. We love plaids.

LORI: Plaids are too busy. A big plaid is fine; but a little plaid …Why not wear elephants on your shirt? I also like sports jackets.

LLOYD: Don, any advice for guys who are targeted for a makeover?

DON: Give in. His life will be simpler that way. In a relationship, you've got to decide where you want to make sacrifices, and everybody's got to make sacrifices. And depending on the woman you're with and what it means to her, being made over is, as far as I see it, a very simple sacrifice.

The Make Over Prescription: *Jennie and Lori chose a warm khaki suit with a fit that looks tailor-made and a black cashmere polo sweater, worn atop an unexpected peach spread-collar dress shirt. Don's spiffy, crisp white pocket square and casually elegant cocoa loafers create a finished touch of haberdashery that is rarely seen in the workplace in this day and age. The Result: Relaxed elegance that can take any executive straight to the top.*

After

Style Clinic

"Fashion is what you're offered. Style is what you choose."
—Lauren Hutton

WELL, LADIES, I HOPE THAT IF YOU'VE LEARNED ANYTHING FROM THIS BOOK SO FAR IT'S THIS: True style is about being confident, classic, and most important, resourceful! From here on is where the adage "knowledge is power" comes into play. Now is the time when you and your man put into action the lessons on the needs and functions of his wardrobe.

For this reason, I've composed a resource guide for you. Let's think of it as a clinic of sorts—a style clinic you can go to when you need a little fashion first aid as you make over your man. Some of the advice here goes beyond your initial makeover, and you may find it to be a resource you consult again and again.

Here you'll find answers to some of the most frequently asked questions I've received over the years from women who see me as a television style expert. I've also compiled some simple tips to help your man travel light and in style and quick fixes for his little stains and basic wardrobe care.

For the hands-on woman, I've also included original illustrated diagrams that show how to tie a tie–from a quick late-for-the-office knot to a flawless bow tie for formal black-tie occasions.

The glossary in this section gives easy-to-understand definitions for many of the words and terms in menswear, from "alpaca" to "zoot suit." I've also compiled a where-to-go list of the absolute best men's clothing and accessory stores, brands, and designers that offer you quality clothes for your money. Many of these resources have been my personal favorites for years, and not only do they provide quality goods, but they also have impeccable service—in shopping, that's half the battle.

And finally, check out the style credits I've provided for a head-to-toe roadmap of all the outfits celebrated on the men in this book. You can get style ideas from the real men, celebrities, models, and the still-life shots I've created and then take the information straight to the source to get a similar look for the man you love.

Hopefully, my style clinic will serve as a tool to help you reach your style goals for your man. And together you can create a new look he sticks with and looks fabulous wearing, for years and years!

FREQUENTLY ASKED QUESTIONS

What are some no-fail basics to start a business-casual wardrobe?

While it flits in and out of fashion, a suit-and tie-combination never falls flat in the office. However, for a workplace with a business-casual dress code, each man needs to start with seven neutral-colored apparel pieces: a sport coat, two pairs of trousers, a white dress shirt, a woven sport shirt, a cashmere V-neck sweater, and a fine polo sweater. Add a color-coordinated belt and oxford shoes for the essential building blocks of a fine and masculine wardrobe.

What's the difference between business casual and dressy casual?

Not much, but there are some nuances to be conscious of, so use this simple rule: Business casual should be worn to make or land a new business deal, dressy casual can be worn afterward to celebrate.

When executed correctly, business casual should look like a man just loosened his tie—not his killer instinct. Dressy casual should reflect more of a man's personality, his favorite colors and clothing pieces. The key phrase here is "dress to impress" without a suit or tie. So, think of what could be worn to lunch with the in-laws for daytime and cocktails with the boss for nighttime. Leave the jeans and club wear for some other time.

How do you tell the difference between khakis and chinos?

These days, the words have become almost interchangeable since both terms describe light-colored, simply styled cotton pants. Think of it this way—khakis are fashioned from sturdy cotton twill, chinos are made of a lighter fabric. Khakis come from the Hindi word meaning "dust-colored" and are now considered year-round wear; chinos, of polished cotton or poplin, can be worn on summer days.

Is a suit still needed for a job interview?

Let's just put it this way, wearing a suit won't *hurt* your chances of getting the job. For men interviewing for a white-collar job—financial and legal services, insurance, politics, and other administrative positions—a suit is still a must regardless of the company's current dress code. It's best to select a dark suit with an equally conservative shirt and tie.

In advertising, media, and high-tech circles, the rules are a bit different. Your creative talents are onstage here, not your sartorial abilities. A guy should dress at *least* at the same level as the person or persons interviewing him. If you don't wear a suit, play it safe with an elegant pair of trousers, a woven sport shirt opened slightly at the collar, and a sport coat.

Remember this: It's okay if your guy is a bit confused and doesn't know what to wear to an interview. There are so many dress codes these days. To eliminate the "what-ifs," suggest that he call the company's human resources department and ask about the company's dress code and what constitutes appropriate interview attire.

What is preppy?

Preppy used to refer only to those in the moneyed, well-bred, prep-school circles. The word gained popular usage in the 1970 movie *Love Story* when Ali McGraw's Jennifer Cavalieri used it as a nickname for Ryan O'Neal's character, Oliver Bartlett IV. When referring to style, it means a strong-willed affinity for well-made Brit-American classics. For men, that means cashmere, khakis, polo shirts, and a navy suit or blazer. The preppy style is all about quality, consistency, and color, and isn't influenced by what's currently in fashion, so the clothes have a timeless feel. What Brooks Brothers started in 1818 has become the hallmark for American designers like Tommy Hilfiger and Ralph Lauren.

What's the difference between a sport coat and a blazer?

The terms are not interchangeable. Blazers come mainly in navy, camel, or black and can be equipped with brass buttons; they go with just about everything from jeans to khakis to gray flannel trousers. Sport coats are usually plaid or a bold textured pattern. Paired with a fine pair of trousers, a sport coat can just about match the effect of a suit.

Why are there so many different styles of dress shirt collars? How do you know which is the right one?

It depends on the man. The correct collar can give balance and proportion to a man's face. While the regular straight-point collar is widely considered the universal dress shirt, subtle nuances can enhance a man's appearance. If he has a round or oval face, select a longer-point collar. Longer- or narrow-faced men should select a spread or a Windsor collar for balance. Consider custom-made shirts for men who are hard to fit. You'll find that the personal attention to collar size, height, and shape is an excellent investment. Also, large- and full-faced men should stay away from button-down collars, which can make the face appear bigger.

How much of a dress shirt's cuff should show when wearing a suit?

Just a bit, about a quarter-inch. Suit jacket sleeves should be tailored to the wrist to allow some shirt cuff to show through.

When should pants have a cuff?

For the most part, cuffs are widely accepted for all kinds of casual pants and trousers and are considered a matter of a man's personal taste. Cuffs, however, are a must for trousers in double-breasted suits.

Cuffs seem dressy, but they're not considered acceptable when it comes to formal suits, tuxedos, or military uniforms. Cuffs should not be worn with flat-front pants. Shorter men should stay away from them, as they shorten the leg. And a final note, cuffs should be at least 1½" deep, no less.

What's a dimple?

When a necktie is tied it should have a single or double dimpled crease just below the knot. This dimple forces the tie—which is always a focal point when wearing a suit and tie—to appear fuller and drape gracefully.

What should men know about undershirts?

The undershirt is becoming less common among well-dressed men. There are three important advantages to wearing an undershirt—in the winter, it becomes an extra layer of warmth, it absorbs sweat in the summertime, and it can serve as a camouflage when wearing light-colored dress or sport shirts.

What looks better: flat-front or pleated trousers?

Fashion's whims have favored both flat fronts and pleats in recent years. A flat-front silhouette looks best on trim, fit men—it can also hide a few extra pounds for men with a slightly heavier frame. Pleats, obviously, tend to be a bit more forgiving for full-bodied men and give them extra room to sit down comfortably. When buying both casual and formal pleated pants, be sure the pleats sit flat.

Why buy a cashmere sweater?

Cashmere is the best year-round sweater money can buy. And it is a smart investment piece for both men and women. Cashmere has a soft luster that can be either dressed up with a sport coat or worn with relaxed jeans or trousers. It adds warmth to winter layers, despite being light and fine. Since it's feather light, the cashmere sweater can also be worn on cool spring and summer nights. Avoid single-ply cashmere for long wear. The higher the ply, the longer the life of the garment—and the better the look.

What's a 10-month suit?

Thank high-tech fabrics—and global warming—for broadening a category of suits that can be worn virtually year-round. A cornerstone for work attire, the suit should be made of resilient 12- to 14-ounce wool in a dark neutral color and should be able to handle all but the coldest and hottest weather.

What's a summer suit?

When the mercury rises, a regular suit can feel like a suit of armor. So that's when linen, feather-light tropical wool, ultra-fine cashmere, cotton khaki, poplin, seersucker, and sometimes silk become as welcome as a summer breeze. Casual and comfortable fabrics take on a dressed-up attitude in a suit. Mix up all its elements and a summer suit is the best—and one of the most sartorial style statements—in all of menswear.

What is microfiber?

Microfiber is a newfangled word for polyester, and there are three reasons to love the wonder fabric: (1) It's as smooth as silk. (2) It's cool when it needs to be and warm when it needs to be. (3) It's durable. Scientists created microfiber but fashion is better for it.

Can my guy wear regular clothes on the golf course?

Of course, as long his attire is welcome on a club's fairways. However, there's a reason why golf wear exists—the purpose of golf wear is to withstand a golf course's 18 holes and its clubhouse rules. If your guy wants to wear a polo shirt and khakis to play golf, make sure he can move in them. Golf wear polo shirts have a longer shirttail to make sure it stays tucked in. The shirt has large armholes and inside seams that have been taped to prevent chafing that sometimes occurs when a man vigorously swings a club. So, have him take a swing. Ask him to bend over and down. There has to be room to move in the shoulder and in the knees; typical golf trousers are straight and roomy through the leg.

Are belts and shoes supposed to match?

When pairing a belt with shoes, match the color of the leather and quality with the clothes and style of dress. A weathered braided belt just won't go properly with a pair of wing tips.

ON THE ROAD

BEFORE YOUR MAN PACKS HIS BAGS, HAVE HIM WRITE DOWN A LIST OF WHERE HE'S GOING and what he's doing while away to help him focus on what to bring and to avoid dreaded over-packing. Meeting with clients, a barbecue with old friends, and a quick workout in the hotel's gym? Include it all. Checklists are key and prevent you from overlooking the most basic, everyday things like underwear and a toothbrush. Always take a pair or two more underwear and socks than you think you need, for a trip can always drag out a day longer than planned. Check weather reports for where you are headed. With all this in mind and once you get your list ready, here are some other notes to consider:

- Pack lightweight, breathable, and wrinkle-resistant clothes. This will save wrinkles and time.

- Pack as light as possible by selecting one family of neutrals to wear on your trip. Some pieces can do double duty if you need them to.

- Curb wrinkling by folding your clothes around a piece of tissue paper or a plastic dry clean-ing bag before you put them in your suitcase. Do the same with ties, but roll them and secure with a rubber band and put in a suit jacket pocket.

- Checked and patterned shirts hide wrinkles.

- Carry a toothbrush and a pair of underwear with you in your carry-on bag. One lost bag or cancelled flight and you'll be thankful.

- Turn suit jackets inside out, but not the sleeves, if using a traditional suitcase. Fold it into itself and then in half and place in a plastic bag.

- Empty pants pockets and put them in your suitcase first. Just lay them in there with the legs hanging over the side. Pack everything on top of them and fold the legs over to prevent a stubborn crease.

- Fold shirts at a point that will hit below the belt. Figure out where your waist is on the shirt and put it on a flat surface to fold. Doing so will prevent a wrinkle across your stomach cut-ting the shirt in half. Sleeves should be folded back straight at the shoulder seam.

- Hold on to the bags that come with your good shoes. If you don't use them for storage, at least use them for packing. Another alternative is a plastic bag for short trips. Don't lay shoes flat on the bottom of your suitcase and pack on top of them. Arrange them around the sides, they stabilize the bag you are packing.

- Wear your heaviest shoes and hardest-to-pack clothing pieces, like a suede blazer, when traveling.

- Be sure to gather all your dirty laundry together and put in a hotel laundry bag for your return trip home. Keep all the worn clothes together and have it ready to throw right in your laundry basket at home.

THE TLCs

IT MAY SOUND SIMPLE, BUT IF YOU TAKE CARE OF YOUR CLOTHES, THEY WILL LAST. AND that means that sometimes just soap and water may be part of what is required. Here are some quick tips to keep your man's clothes looking their best.

- Tell your man to give his suit one day's rest for every day he's worn it that week. One day on, one day off. After he undresses and before he hangs up the suit, have him give it a good brushing with a soft, natural-bristle clothes brush. Yes, a brushing. It helps to clear the dust and will save time between dry cleans.

- Rest shoes, too. Dust shoes off at the end of the day and give them two days rest (in a row) for every day worn. It allows sweat to dry and the shoe to regain its shape.

- Separate whites from darks when doing laundry. Wash dark apparel inside out to help it retain color longer. When in doubt, leave the red sock or fuchsia polo shirt out of the whites and give it its own wash cycle. Washing one red turtleneck may seem extravagant—until you wash it with whites and suddenly everything you own is pink.

- Remove clothing from the dryer immediately and fold it properly. Mom was right.

- Starch dress shirts—lightly. Either have it done at the dry cleaners, or do it at home. It helps shirts keep their shape.

- Don't ignore stains. They don't go away magically. First look at a garment's label to see how to treat a stain. Prewash stain removers work best on cotton garments. Always read the label on all cleansers and stain removers. Always point stains out when dropping clothes off at the dry cleaners—and if it's a difficult stain ask them how it will be treated and what is the likelihood it will look like new. Here are some other tips:

  - Don't try to remove a stain yourself on a garment that's labeled dry clean only.

  - Remove chewing gum and tape from apparel by scraping off as much as you can, then applying ice. Wait until the sticky stuff hardens and peel it off. Then take the garment to the dry cleaners.

  - Mop up grease stains—like butter, salad dressing, and mayonnaise—by dusting them with talc. Then pretreat before you wash cottons or bring synthetics to the dry cleaners.

  - Apply a combination cleaning solvent to multicategory stains like gravy and chocolate milk; dab and rinse washables in cold water. For nonwashables, dab the area with cold water and dry.

  - Soak protein stains—such as egg or blood—in cold water. Then wash.

  - Rub out ballpoint pen with a cotton pad soaked in alcohol. In a pinch, hairspray also works.

SIZING CHART

Suits and Sport Jackets

	34R	36R	38R	40R	42R	44R	46R	48R
US	34R	36R	38R	40R	42R	44R	46R	48R
European	44	46	48	50	52	54	56	58
Actual Waist	28	30	31½	33½	35½	37	39	40

			38T	40T	42T	44T	46T	48T
US			38T	40T	42T	44T	46T	48T
European			94	98	102	106	110	114
Actual Waist			31	33	35½	37	39	40

			38S	40S	42S	44S		
US			38S	40S	42S	44S		
European			24	25	26	27		
Actual Waist			33	35	37	39		

Trousers

	S	S	M	M	L	L	XL	XL
US	28	30	31½	33½	35½	37½	39	40
European	44	46	48	50	52	54	56	58

Dress Shirt (neck)

	S	S	M	M	L	L	XL	XL
US (inches)	14	15	15½	15¾	16	16½	17	17½
Eurpoean (ml)	37	38	39	40	41	42	43	44

Sweaters

	XS	S	M	M/L	L	XL
US	XS	S	M	M/L	L	XL
European	46	48	50	52	54	56

Knits

	S	M	L	XL
US	S	M	L	XL
European	5	6	7	8

Belts

	30	32	34	36	38	40	42
US (inches)	30	32	34	36	38	40	42
European (ml)	80	85	90	95	100	105	110

Shoes

	7½	8	8½	9	9½	10	10½	11	11½	12
US	7½	8	8½	9	9½	10	10½	11	11½	12
European	40½	41	41½	42	42½	43	43½	44	44½	45

Sleeve length for most European dress shirts is standardized per size; traditionally, European sleeve lengths run slightly long.

R = Regular   S = Short   T = Tall   M = Medium   L = Large   XL = Extra Large

HOW TO PROPERLY TIE HIS TIE

The Four-in-Hand Knot

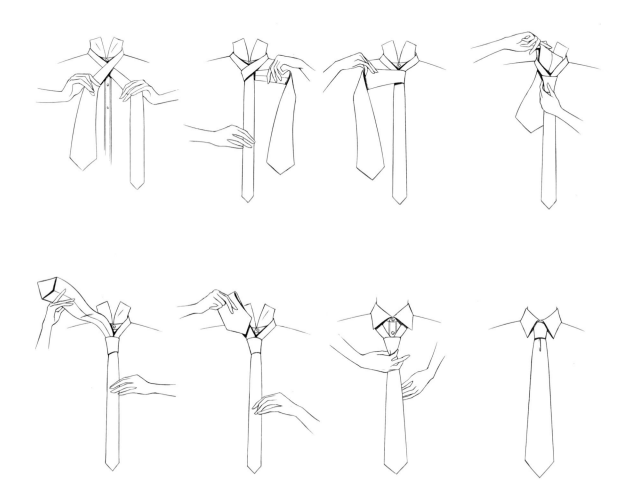

The Windsor Knot

The Half-Windsor Knot

The Bow Tie Knot

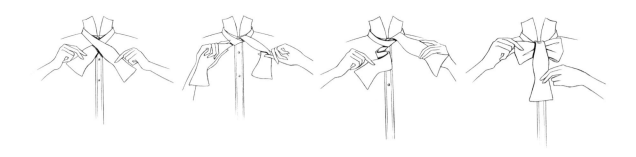

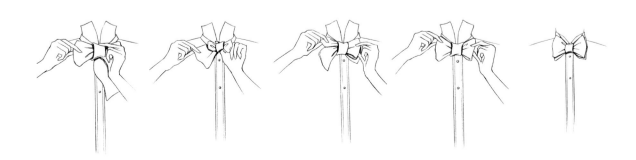

Glossary
From A to Zoot Suit

A pocketful of helpful terms

Alpaca   A fine, long-hair yarn that comes from a species of llama living high in the mountains of Peru. The yarn is soft, light, resilient, and extremely warm.

Anorak   A waist-length, hooded outerwear jacket usually cinched at the waist with a drawstring. The jacket is often lined with fur.

Balmacaan   A loose-fitting, knee-length raincoat with raglan shoulders and a narrow collar. Named in honor of the Balmacaan estate near Inverness, Scotland.

Banded collar   A short stand-up collar that drifts in and out of fashion. The shirt—which can either be a casual sport shirt or a tuxedo shirt—resembles what a dress shirt used to look like when collars were removable. Banded-collar tuxedo shirts are often worn with a decorative button or pin at the throat.

Barrel cuff   A single cuff attached to a dress shirt with a simple button closure. Most dress shirts come equipped with a barrel cuff.

Bellow's pleat   A deep fold of fabric along the side of a pocket, allowing more room to move.

Besom pocket   A slim jacket pocket with edges that are folded over and hemmed on both the upper and lower edges.

Bespoke   A British term for custom made.

Bird's eye   A woven or knitted two-tone pattern with a small dot that looks like a bird's eye. The pattern is used for suits, neckwear, and sweaters.

Bi-swing jacket   A sport or golf jacket with a bellow of extra fabric from the shoulder to the waistline to allow better movement.

Blazer   Single or double-breasted sport coat in navy blue, black, or camel matte fabric. Often equipped with brass buttons. (See sport coat.)

Bomber jacket   Leather jacket with a sturdy zipper, sheepskin lining, and elasticized waistband and cuffs, which was modeled after those worn by fighter pilots during WW II.

Braces   A British term for suspenders.

Break   The point where a pant's cuff hits the shoe. A break is best when pants are long enough to sit slightly over the instep of the shoe.

Buck   Casual lace-up shoe with no ornamental stitching and a rubber sole.

Camp shirt   A relaxed and roomy shortsleeve shirt with a soft collar; bottom of shirt is squared off. Add flowers and the shirt instantly becomes Hawaiian.

Car coat   A three-quarter-length wool coat. The style became popular with the station-wagon set during the post–WW II suburban boom.

Chalk stripe   A pin-striped suit with thick stripes that resemble chalk lines.

Chevron   A decorative pattern that looks like stacked inverted letter Vs.

Convertible collar   A jacket collar with small lapels. Keep the lapels open and it looks like a jacket; close at the neck and it looks like a typical shirt collar.

Cuff link: An object shaped to fit a French cuff buttonhole and keep it fastened with a bar, chain, or cord. Can be buttonlike, jeweled, or a tightly bound knot of silk rope.

Crew neck   A simple ribbed neckline for a pullover sweater, knit jersey, or T-shirt.

Donegal tweed   Woolen tweed identified by colorful nubs originating in county Donegal in Ireland.

Convertible cuffs   Dress-shirt cuffs that can be buttoned or worn with cuff links.

Double-breasted   A suit jacket or overcoat with a dramatic overlapping closure.

Drape   The way to describe how a garment's fabric hangs when on a man's body.

Drop   The difference between a suit's jacket size and its trousers. If a suit jacket is a 42 regular and the trousers have a 34-inch waist, the drop is 8.

Eisenhower jacket   Or an "Ike." A waist-length jacket with a lapel collar and banded bottom.

End on end   A shirt weave alternating white with colored yarn forming fine and delicate checks.

Eton collar   A dress-shirt collar with slightly rounded edges requiring a tiepin. The collar is named for the formal shirt worn at Eton College, the secondary school near Windsor, England.

Fly front   A plaquet hiding a zipper or buttons.

French cuff   An extra stiff, turned-back dress-shirt cuff requiring cuff links.

Furnishings   A retailing term for basic items every man cannot live without—underwear, socks, dress shirts, and ties.

Gauge   The number of loops per inch of knitted fabric. The number varies according to how heavy a yarn is, how big the knit loops are, and the size of knitting needles used. The higher the gauge, the finer and more lightweight the knit will be.

Gorge   The seam line where a collar and a lapel meet.

Guayabera   A lightweight and relaxed shortsleeved shirt with a convertible collar, patch pockets, and an even, squared bottom hem. The classic Cuban shirt also has embroidered stitching or a pintuck design running vertically from the shoulder to the shirt bottom on both the front and back.

Haberdasher   A retailer who specializes in men's furnishings, apparel, and accessories.

Hand   Term used to describe how a fabric feels.

Henley   A collarless casual shirt with a buttoned placket at the neckline.

In seam   The distance along a pant leg from the crotch to the pant cuff.

Jacquard   Fabric with a design woven or knit into it.

Khaki   A Hindu term meaning "tan," or "dusty-colored." British soldiers first dyed their white uniforms in tea to better camouflage themselves while in India. The hearty tan cotton fabric has evolved from being used as a staple for military clothes to a favorite for everyday casual pants.

Loafer   Slip-on shoe with either tassels or a half-moon cut out on the upper.

Loden   Heavy wool twill fabric used for overcoats. Also a term to describe a deep olive green.

Madras   A brightly dyed plaid in lightweight cotton that fades with continued wash and wear. From Madras, India, this fabric is a summertime preppy standard.

Mandarin collar   This standing band collar—also called a Chinese collar or a Nehru collar—wraps around a man's jacket and is open just a bit to expose the front of the neck. Named after Jawaharlal Nehru, the first prime minister of independent India and made famous in 1967 by the electric-colored uniforms worn by the Beatles on the cover of their *Sgt. Pepper's Lonely Hearts Club Band* album.

Mercerized cotton   A process—named for John Mercer in 1844—which makes cotton appear shiny when knit. Often used for golf shirts.

Microfiber   Fine, wrinkle-free polyester. The fabric usually has a silky feel, wears well, and is considered a performance fabric because of its durability. Used for casual trousers and golf wear.

Motorcycle jacket   An armorlike, thick, heavy, leather jacket that sits at the waist and is characterized by either a wide belt, or a metal zipper on the pockets or along the arms from wrist to elbow.

Nail head   A small, two-toned dotted pattern resembling the head of a nail. Used to decorate knits, suits, and ties.

Nap   Word that describes the surface of soft fabrics, like flannel or velvet.

Natural shoulder   A suit or sport-jacket design using little or no padding in the shoulder.

Notched lapel   Identified by a wide, V-shaped cutout between the jacket's lapel and its collar.

Ombre   A fabric that's dyed from the lightest shade to a darker shade of one color. Often used to create a masculine plaid shirt of two-toned plaid squares.

Oxford   A plain weave cotton/polyester shirt fabric, or a low-heeled lace-up shoe.

Peacoat   The double-breasted woolen coat with oversize buttons was once standard issue for the U.S. Navy. The coat is thick and warm and can range in length from waist to ankle-length.

Peaked lapel   A lapel that comes to a sweeping point close to the shoulder.

Pinstripe   A fine dotted or beaded line decorating suits or trousers.

Pintuck   A decorative detail, often used in womens wear, created by a series of very small pleats.

Placket   A strip of fabric sewn over a garment's buttons, zipper, or snaps, which keeps the closures hidden.

Point collar   A dress-shirt collar that is elongated and comes to a point.

Polo shirt   A shortsleeved cotton pique shirt made popular in the 1920s by French tennis star René Lacoste. While the lightweight shirt was originally designed to help Lacoste improve his tennis game, it's now become a weekend wardrobe staple.

Poplin   Lightweight cotton with a soft sheen used for summertime apparel.

Raglan   Identified by a diagonal seam or contrast color separating the arms from the body of a T-shirt, sweater, jacket, or coat. Named for Baron Raglan, who commanded the British troops during the Crimean War (1853–56).

Regimental stripe   A tie striped diagonally with colors meant to distinguish different British military regiments.

Rep   A hearty, corded silk tie with bold diagonal stripes.

Rise   Measures the distance from a pant's crotch to the waistband.

Sartorial   Dressed up like a fine gentleman.

Savile Row   A sweeping term to describe good men's tailoring stemming from the heart, soul, and home of bespoke tailors in London's West End.

Seersucker   Light, striped cotton fabric usually blended with silk or polyester to give a puckered effect. Used for summertime shirts, suits, chinos, and shorts.

Sharkskin   A smooth-finished wool or acetate-blend fabric, used for suits or ties, that gives off a slight shine.

Shawl collar   A rolled collar and lapel. Typically used in tuxedos.

Spectator   A two-toned shoe.

Sport jacket   A single-breasted jacket that is not a part of a suit. Often plaid or tweed and should not be confused with a blazer, which is made from a flat matte fabric and comes with brass buttons.

Sport shirt   Any shirt that is not a T-shirt or a formal dress shirt, a huge category of shirts ranging from knit polos to plaid button-downs to bowling shirts.

Spread collar   A dress-shirt collar with shortened tips spread far apart and often comes with a secondary tab to support a tie. Also known as a cutaway collar.

Straight collar   The most common collar for dress and sport shirts. The collar measures about three inches in length.

Super   As in "Super 100," "Super 120," "Super 180," which measures how fine the yarn is in a suit or trousers. The higher the number, the finer, more resilient, and more luxurious the fiber and the fabric.

Tartan   Plaid design often designating a specific Scottish clan. Official familial and corporate designs (i.e., Burberry and Dewar's) are filed with the Scottish Tartans World Register.

Tattersall   A pattern of colored horizontal and vertical lines (which creates simple squares) on a solid background. First used for horse blankets and waistcoats worn at auctioneer Richard Tattersall's horse market in the late 1700s.

Ticket pocket   A small pocket outside the coat that's located on the right side of a jacket (or an overcoat) directly above the coat's regular pocket. Created to hold a train ticket.

Tropical wool   Lightweight, softly woven wool used for summertime suits.

Twill   Sturdy cotton or wool fabric woven into a subtle diagonal stripe. Khakis are typically made from this cloth.

Unconstructed suit   A casual suit made without padding or a lining.

Vent   Slit found at the center or sides of a jacket or coat. A double-breasted suit jacket should always have side vents.

Weight   A measure of a linear yard of fabric used for a suit signaling its season of wear. Winter suits range from 14 to 16 ounces; summer suits are from 8 to 11 ounces.

Windsor collar   A dress-shirt collar that's slightly shorter and spread far apart with a forward tilt to accommodate a wide Windsor knot. Both the Windsor knot and Windsor collar are named in honor of the late Duke of Windsor, a trendsetter, whose signature style was popular in the early to mid-1900s.

Wing tip   A shoe with a decorative tip in the shape of a bird's wing. A classic shoe to wear with a suit.

Zoot suit   Suit popularized between 1939–42 with a knee-length jacket identified by heavily padded shoulders, tapered waist, and full-cut trousers.

Retail Source Listing

THE BEST STORES FOR SHOPPING WITH OR FOR YOUR MAN, SELLING EVERYTHING FROM luxury goods and clothing to light-on-the-wallet gear, services, and accessories. This selective listing encompasses all that he'll ever need from head to toe—nationwide, and globally on the World Wide Web.

The Suit

Alan Flusser
611 Fifth Avenue, 6th Floor
New York, NY
(212) 888-7100

Alfred Dunhill
450 Park Avenue
New York, NY
(212) 753-9292
www.dunhill.com

Agnès b.
79 Greene Street
New York, NY
(212) 219-6000

Bally
628 Madison Avenue
New York, NY
(212) 751-9082
www.bally.com

Barneys New York
Madison Avenue and 61st
  Street
New York, NY
(212) 826-8900

Beau Brummel
421 West Broadway
New York, NY
(212) 219-2666
www.beaubrummel.com

Bergdorf Goodman Men
745 Fifth Avenue
New York, NY
(212) 758-7300
(800) 964-8619

Bigsby & Kruthers
1750 North Clark Street
Chicago, IL
(312) 440-1750

Bloomingdale's
1000 Third Avenue
New York, NY
(212) 705-2000
(800) 232-1854
www.blommingdales.com

Britches of Georgetown
1247 Wisconsin Avenue NW
Washington, DC
(202) 338-3330
www.roberttalbott.com

Brooks Brothers
346 Madison Avenue
New York, NY
(212) 682-8800
(800) 556-7039
www.brooksbrothers.com

Bullock & Jones
340 Post Street
San Francisco, CA
(415) 392-4243

Burberry
www.burberry.com
(800) 284-8480

Cable Car Clothiers
246 Sutter Street
San Francisco, CA
(415) 397-4740

Calvin Klein
595 Madison Avenue
New York, NY
751-0040
(800) 294-7978
www.calvinklein.com

Canali
(212) 767-0205
www.canali.it

Casual Male Big & Tall
949 W. Addison Street
Addison Mall
Chicago, Il 60618
(773) 463-8071
www.casualmale.com

Cheo Tailors
30 East 60th Street
New York, NY
(212) 980-9838

Corneliani
(800) 222-9477
www.corneliani.com

Daffy's
111 Fifth Avenue
New York, NY
(212) 529-4477
www.daffys.com

Davide Cenci
801 Madison Ave.
New York, NY
(212) 628-5910
www.davidecenci.com

Despos
500 Crescent Court
Suite 152
Dallas, TX
(214) 871-3707

**Dion Scott Custom
Wardrobe Designer**
343 South Robertson Blvd.
Beverly Hills, CA
(310) 659-8497
(by appointment)

Dolce & Gabanna
825 Madison Avenue
New York, NY
(212) 249-4100
www.dolcegabbana.com

Donna Karan Collection
819 Madison Avenue
New York, NY
(212) 861-1001

Douglass Fir
8317 West Third Street
Los Angeles, CA
(323) 651-5445

Duah Brothers
41 W. 35 Street
New York, NY
(212) 947-4444

Duende
(made to measure)
328 Flatbush Avenue
Suite 321
Brooklyn, NY
(718) 230-5201

Ermenegildo Zegna
745 Fifth Avenue
New York, NY
(212) 751-3468

Etro
720 Madison Avenue
New York, NY
(212) 317-9096

Everett Hall
5345 Wisconsin Avenue
Washington, DC
(202) 362-5345

Francis Hendy
(212) 354-4764
www.francishendy.com

Georges' Place Limited
(Big & Tall)
1001 H Street NE
Washington, DC
(202) 391-4113

Giacomo
732 North La Cienega
   Boulevard
Los Angeles, CA
(310) 652-6393

Giorgio Armani
760 Madison Avenue
New York, NY
(212) 988-9191
www.giorgioarmani.com

Gianfranco Ferre´
845 Madison Avenue
New York, NY
(212) 717-5430
www.gianfrancoferre.com

Harry Rothman's
200 Park Avenue South
New York, NY
(212) 777-7400

Hart, Schaffner and
Marx
Marshall Fields
111 North State Street 382
Chicago, IL
(312) 781-1000
www.hartschaffnermarx.com

Hickey-Freeman
666 Fifth Avenue
New York, NY
(212) 585-6481
(800) 603-8968
www.hickeyfreeman.com

Hugo Boss
132 Greene Street
New York, NY
(212) 965-1300
www.hugo.com

J. Lindeberg
126 Spring Street
New York, NY
(212) 625-9403
www.jlindeberg.com

J. Press
7 East 44th Street
New York, NY
(212) 687-7642

Jack Silver Formal Wear
1780 Broadway, 3rd Floor
New York, NY
(212) 582-0202
www.jacksilverformal.com

Jeffrey New York
449 West 14th Street
New York, NY
(212) 206-1272

John Varvatos
149 Mercer Street
New York, NY 10012
(212) 965-0700

Jos. A. Banks
366 Madison Avenue
New York, NY
(212) 370-0600
(800) 285-2265

Kiton
(hand-made suits)
www.kiton.com

Leonard Logsdail
510 Madison Avenue
New York, NY
(212) 752-5030
(by appointment on select days)

Lord & Taylor
424 Fifth Avenue
New York, NY
(212) 391-3344
(800) 223-7440

Louis, Boston
234 Berkeley Street
Boston, MA
(800) 224-5135

Macy's
Broadway at Herald Square
New York, NY
(212) 695-4400
(800) 431-9644
www.macys.com

Moe Ginsberg
162 Fifth Avenue
New York, NY
(212) 242-3482

Nordstrom
865 Market Street
San Francisco, CA
(415) 243-8500

Oxxford Clothes
36 East 57th Street
New York, NY
(212) 593-0205

Paul Smith
108 Fifth Avenue
New York, NY
(212) 627-9770

Paul Stuart
Madison Avenue at 45th
   Street
New York, NY
(212) 682-0320

Polo Ralph Lauren
867 Madison Avenue
New York, NY
(212) 606-2100

Pucci
333 North Michigan Avenue
Chicago, IL
(312) 332-3759

Randolph Williamson
(custom, made-to-measure)
(615) 333-3484

Rochester Big & Tall
1301 Sixth Avenue
New York, NY
(212) 247-7500
(800) 282-8200

ron + ron
(212) 625-9387
www.ron-n-ron.com

Saks Fifth Avenue
611 Fifth Avenue
New York, NY
(212) 753-4000

Salvatore Ferragamo
725 Fifth Avenue
New York, NY
(212) 759-7990
(800) 445-1874
www.salvatoreferragamo.com

Shaka King New York
825 Upshur Street NW
Washington, DC
(202) 291-8700

Stanley Korshak
500 Crescent Court
Suite 100
Dallas, TX
(214) 871-3600

Syd Jerome
2 North LaSalle Street
Chicago, IL
(312) 346-0333

Syms
111 North Wabash Ave.
Chicago, IL
(312) 419-8100
www.syms.com

Today's Man
529 Fifth Avenue
New York, NY
(212) 557-3111
(800) 950-7848
www.todaysman.com

Tommy Hilfiger
372 West Broadway
New York, NY
(800) 888-8802
www.tommy.com

Turnbull & Asser
42 East 57th Street
New York, NY
(212) 319-8100
(877) 887-6284
www.turnbullandasser.com

Ultimo
114 East Oak Street
Chicago, IL
(312) 787-0906

Valentino
747 Madison Avenue
New York, NY
(212) 772-6969
(877) 360-0864
www.valentino.it

Weathervane for Men
1132 Montana Avenue
Santa Monica, CA
(310) 395-0397
www.weathervaneformen.com

Wilkes Bashford
375 Sutter Street
San Francisco, CA
(415) 986-4380

William Fioravanti
45 West 57th Street
New York, NY
(212) 355-1540
(by appointment on select days)

Yohji Yamamoto
103 Grand Street
New York, NY
(212) 966-9066

Yves Saint Laurent Rive
Gauche Hommes
88 Wooster Street
New York, NY
(212) 274-0522
(800) 424-8600

Zeller Tuxedo
1010 Third Avenue
2nd Floor
(212) 688-0100
www.zellertuxedo.com

The Shirt

Addison On Madison
698 Madison Avenue
New York, NY
(212) 308-2660

Alpana Bawa
(212) 965-0559
www.alpanabawa.com

Arthur Gluck Shirtmakers
47 West 57th Street
New York, NY
(212) 755-8165
www.shirtcreations.com

Ascot Chang
(custom-made shirts)
7 West 57th Street
New York, NY
(212) 759-3333
www.ascotchang.com

Banana Republic
(Flagship)
17 West 34th Street
New York, NY
(212) 244-3060
www.bananarepublic.com

Barneys Coop
236 W.18th Street
New York, NY
(212) 593-7800
www.barneys.com

Bergdorf Goodman Men
745 Fifth Avenue
New York, NY
(212) 758-7300
(800) 964-8619

Best of Class by Robert
Talbott
(800) 747-8778
www.roberttalbott.com

Bloomingdale's
1000 Third Avenue
New York, NY
(212) 705-2000
(800) 232-1854
www.bloomingdales.com

Brioni
55 East 57th Street
New York, NY
(212) 376-5777
www.brioni.it
(800) 444-1613

Britches of Georgetown
1247 Wisconsin Avenue NW
Washington, DC
(202) 338-3330
roberttalbott.com

Brooks Brothers
346 Madison Avenue
New York, NY
(212) 682-8800
(800) 556-7039
www.brooksbrothers.com

Bullock & Jones
340 Post Street
San Francisco, CA
(415) 392-4243

Burberry
(800) 284-8480
www.burberry.com

Buttondown
3415 Sacramento Street
San Francisco, CA
(415) 563-1311

Canali
(212) 767-0205
www.canali.it

Corneliani
(800) 222-9477
www.corneliani.com

Davide Cenci
801 Madison Ave.
New York, NY
(212) 628-5910
www.davidecenci.com

Ermenegildo Zegna
745 Fifth Avenue
New York, NY
(212) 751-3468

Etro
720 Madison Avenue
New York, NY
(212) 317-9096

Geoffrey Beene
(800) 632-5843
www.randacorp.com

Harry Rothman's
200 Park Avenue South
New York, NY
(212) 777-7400

Ike Behar
(212) 315-2626
www.ikebehar.com

J. Lindeberg
126 Spring Street
New York, NY
(212) 625-9403
www.jlindeberg.com

John Varvatos
149 Mercer Street
New York, NY
(212) 965-0700

Jos. A. Banks
366 Madison Avenue
New York, NY
(212) 370-0600
(800) 285-2265

Lands' End
(800) 963-4816
www.landsend.com

Leslie & Co.
1749 South Post Oak Road
Post Oak Plaza
Houston, TX
(713) 960-9113

Loehmann's
101 Seventh Avenue
New York, NY
(212) 352-0856

Lord & Taylor
424 Fifth Avenue
New York, NY
(212) 391-3344
(800) 223-7440

Loro Piana
821 Madison Avenue
New York, NY
(212) 980-7961

Macy's
Broadway at Herald Square
New York, NY
(212) 695-4400
(800) 431-9644
www.macys.com

Nautica
50 Rockefeller Center
New York, NY
(212) 664-9594
www.nautica.com

Nordstrom
865 Market Street
San Francisco, CA
(415) 243-8500

Oxxford Clothes
36 East 57th Street
New York, NY
(212) 593-0205

Paul Smith
108 Fifth Avenue
New York, NY
(212) 627-9770

Polo Ralph Lauren
(888) 475-7674
www.polo.com

Polo Ralph Lauren
867 Madison Avenue
New York, NY
(212) 606-2100

Robert Talbott
680 Madison Avenue
New York, NY
(212) 751-1200

Rochester Big & Tall
1301 Sixth Avenue
New York, NY
(212) 247-7500
(800) 282-8200

Saks Fifth Avenue
611 Fifth Avenue
New York, NY
(212) 753-4000
www.saksfifthavenue.com
(800) 345-3454

Sean
132 Thompson Street
New York, NY
(212) 598-5980

The Shirt Store
51 East 44th Street
New York, NY
(212) 557-8040
(800) buy.a.shirt
www.shirtstore.com

Sulka
301 Park Avenue
New York, NY
(212) 980-5226

Ted Baker London
107 Grand Street
New York, NY
(212) 343-8989

Theory
(Company Store)
520 Fifth Avenue
3rd Floor
New York
(212) 398-2777

Tommy Hilfiger
372 West Broadway
New York, NY
(800) 888-8802
www.tommy.com

Thomas Pink
520 Madison Avenue
New York, NY
(212) 838-1928
(888) 336-1192
www.thomaspink.co.uk

Turnbull & Asser
42 East 57th Street
New York, NY
(212) 752-5700
(custom and pre-sized shirtings)

Valentino
747 Madison Avenue
New York, NY
(212) 772-6969
(877) 360-0864
www.valentino.it

Wilkes Bashford
375 Sutter Street
San Francisco, CA
(415) 986-4380

Yves Saint Laurent Rive
Gauche Hommes
88 Wooster Street
New York, NY
(212) 274-0522
(800) 424-8600

The Pant

Agnès b.
79 Greene Street
New York, NY
(212) 219-6000

Banana Republic
(Flagship)
17 West 34th Street
New York, NY
(212) 244-3060
www.bananarepublic.com

Barneys New York
Madison Avenue and 61st
    Street
New York, NY
(212) 826-8900

Barneys Coop
236 W.18th Street
New York, NY
(212) 593-7800
www.barneys.com

Bloomingdale's
1000 Third Avenue
New York, NY
(212) 705-2000
(800) 232-1854
www.bloomingdales.com

Brooks Brothers
346 Madison Avenue
New York, NY
(212) 682-8800
(800) 556-7039
www.brooksbrothers.com

Brioni
55 East 57th Street
New York, NY
(212) 376-5777
www.brioni.it
(call (800) 444-1613 for local
    listings)

Bullock & Jones
340 Post Street
San Francisco, CA
(415) 392-4243

Burberry
www.burberry.com
(800) 284-8480

Calvin Klein
595 Madison Avenue
New York, NY
751-0040
(800) 294 7978
www.calvinklein.com

Canali
(212) 767 0205
www.canali.it

Corneliani
(800) 222-9477
www.corneliani.com

Davide Cenci
801 Madison Ave.
New York, NY
(212) 628-5910
www.davidecenci.com

Giorgio Armani
760 Madison Avenue
New York, NY
(212) 988-9191
www.giorgioarmani.com

Harry Rothman's
200 Park Avenue South
New York, NY
(212) 777-7400

J. Lindeberg
126 Spring Street
New York, NY
(212) 625-9403
www.jlindeberg.com

Jack Taylor
341 North Camden Drive
Beverly Hills, CA
(310) 274-7276

John Varvatos
149 Mercer Street
New York, NY
(212) 965-0700

Lands' End
(800) 963-4816
www.landsend.com

Loehmann's
101 Seventh Avenue
New York, NY
(212) 352-0856

Lord & Taylor
424 Fifth Avenue
New York, NY
(212) 391-3344
(800) 223-7440

Loro Piana
821 Madison Avenue
New York, NY
(212) 980-7961

Macy's
Broadway at Herald Square
New York, NY
(212) 695-4400
(800) 431-9644
www.macys.com

Nautica
50 Rockefeller Center
New York, NY
(212) 664-9594
www.nautica.com

Nordstrom
865 Market Street
San Francisco, CA
(415) 243-8500

Paul Smith
108 Fifth Avenue
New York, NY
(212) 627-9770

Paul Stuart
Madison Avenue at 45th
   Street
New York, NY
(212) 682 0320

M. Penner
2950 Kirby Drive
Houston, TX
(713) 527-8200

Polo Ralph Lauren
(888) 475-7674
www.polo.com

Randolph Williamson
(custom, made-to-measure)
(615) 333-3484

Rochester Big & Tall
1301 Sixth Avenue
New York, NY
(212) 247-7500
(800) 282-8200

Sean
132 Thompson Street
New York, NY
(212) 598-5980

Ted Baker London
107 Grand Street
New York, NY
(212) 343-8989

Today's Man
529 Fifth Avenue
New York, NY
(212) 557-3111
(800) 950-7848
www.todaysman.com

Wilkes Bashford
375 Sutter Street
San Francisco, CA
(415) 986-4380

Yves Saint Laurent Rive
Gauche Hommes
88 Wooster Street
New York, NY
(212) 274-0522
(800) 424-8600

The Shoe

a. Testoni
665 Fifth Avenue
New York, NY
(212) 223-0909
(call 877-testoni for the
   location nearest you)
a.testoni (877) 837-8664
   www.atestoni.com

Adidas
www.adidas.com

Alan Flusser
611 Fifth Avenue, 6th Floor
New York, NY
(212) 888-7100

Aldo
579 Broadway
New York, NY
(212) 226-7974
www.aldoshoes.com

Allen-Edmonds
551 Madison Avenue
New York, NY
(212) 308-8305
www.allenedmonds.com

American Rag Cie
150 South La Brea Avenue
Los Angeles, CA
(323) 935-3154

Athlete's Foot
1568 Broadway
New York, NY
(212) 768-3195
www.theathletesfoot.com

Bally
628 Madison Avenue
New York, NY
(212) 751-9082
www.bally.com

Banana Republic
626 Fifth Avenue
New York, NY
(212) 277-8953
www.bananarepublic.com

Barneys New York
Madison Avenue and 61st
   Street
New York, NY
(212) 826-8900

Barneys Coop
236 W.18th Street
New York, NY
(212) 593-7800
www.barneys.com

Best of Class by Robert
Talbott
(800) 747-8778
www.roberttalbott.com

Bloomingdale's
1000 Third Avenue
New York, NY
(212) 705-2000
(800) 232-1854
www.bloomingdales.com

Bostonian
515 Madison Avenue
(212) 758-7551
www.bostonian.com

Brooks Brothers
346 Madison Avenue
New York, NY
(212) 682-8800
(800) 556-7039
www.brooksbrothers.com

Bullock & Jones
340 Post Street
San Francisco, CA
(415) 392-4243

Bruno Magli
677 Fifth Avenue
New York, NY
(212) 752-7900
www.brunomagli.com

Canali
Bloomingdale1s
1000 Third Avenue
(212) 705-2000
www.canali.it

Church's
428 Madison Avenue
New York, NY
(212) 755-4313
(800) 221-4540
www.churchsshoes.com

Clark's
www.clarks.co.uk

Cole Haan
667 Madison Avenue
New York, NY
(212) 421-8440
(800) 488-2000
www.colehaan.com

Converse
(800) 428 2667
www.converse.com

Daffy's
125 East 57th Street
New York, NY
(212) 376-4477
www.daffys.com

Diego Della Valle
595 Madison Avenue
New York, NY
(212) 588-5945

Donald J. Pliner
106 East Oak Street
Chicago, Illinois 60611
(312) 202-9600
www.donaldplinerchicago.com

E. Vogel
19 Howard Street
New York, NY
(212) 925-2460
(*specializing in custom
footwear*)

Emporio Armani
110 Fifth Avenue
New York, NY
(212) 727-3240
www.emporioarmani.com

Ermenegildo Zegna
743 Fifth Avenue
New York, NY
(212) 421-4488
www.ezegna.com

Etro
720 Madison Avenue
New York, NY
(212) 317-9096

Foot Locker
94 Delancey Street
New York, NY
(212) 533-8608

Fratelli Rossetti
625 Madison Avenue
New York, NY
(212) 888-5107
www.rosetti.it

Frye boots
www.fryeboots.com

Georges' Place Limited
(Big & Tall)
1001 H Street NE
Washington, DC
(202) 391-4113

Giraudon
152 Eighth Avenue
New York, NY
(800) 278-1552
www.giraudonnewyork.com

Gucci
(201) 867-8800
(*call for store listings*)

H
8622 Sunset Boulevard
West Hollywood, CA
(310) 659-5785

Hogan
134 Spring Street
New York, NY
(212) 343-7905

J.M. Weston New York,
Inc.
42 East 57th Street
New York, NY
(212) 308-5655
(*specializing in custom
footwear*)

Jeffrey New York
449 West 14th Street
New York, NY
(212) 206-1272

Jill Kohl
9566 Dayton Way
Beverly Hills, CA
(310) 858-7182

John Lobb
680 Madison Avenue
New York, NY
(212) 888-9797
www.johnlobb.com

Johnston & Murphy
345 Madison Avenue
New York, NY
(800) 424-2854
www.johnstonandmurphy.com

Jos. A. Banks
366 Madison Avenue
New York, NY
(212) 370-0600
(800) 285-2265

Jutta Neumann
(custom)
(212) 982-7948
www.juttaneumann-
newyork.com

Kenneth Cole New York
353 Columbus Avenue
New York, NY
(212) 873-2061
(800) 487-4389
www.kencole.com

K-swiss
(800) 297-1919
www.kswiss.com

Lands' End
(800) 963-4816
www.landsend.com

Men's Wearhouse
380 Madison Avenue
New York, NY
(212) 856-9008
(800) 776-7848
www.menswearhouse.com

Mezlan
mezlanshoes.com

New Balance
51 West 42nd Street
New York, NY
(212) 997-9112
www.newbalancenewyork.com

Nicole Farhi
10 East 60th Street
New York, NY
(212) 223-8811

Niketown
6 East 57th Street
New York, NY
(212) 891-6453
www.niketown.com

Nordstrom
865 Market Street
San Francisco, CA
(415) 243-8500

Paul Smith
108 Fifth
New York, NY
(212) 627-9771
www.paulsmith.co.uk

Prada
45 East 57th Street
New York, NY
(212) 308-2332

Rochester Big & Tall
1301 Avenue of the Americas
New York, NY
(212) 247-7500

Rockport
160 Columbus Avenue
New York, NY
(212) 579-1301
(800) 762-5767
www.rockport.com

Ron Donovan
www.rondonfoot.com
(by appointment only)

Saks Fifth Avenue
611 Fifth Avenue
New York, NY
(212) 753-4000
Saks Fifth Avenue
www.saksfifthavenue.com
(800) 345-3454

Salvatore Ferragamo
725 Fifth Avenue
New York, NY
(212) 759-7990
(800) 445-1874
www.salvatoreferragamo.com

Steve Madden
540 Broadway
New York, NY
(212) 343-1800
(800) 747-6233
www.stevemadden.com

To Boot NY
603 Washington Street
New York, NY
(212) 463-0437
(call for store listings)

Tod's
650 Madison Avenue
New York, NY
(800) 457-TODS
www.tods.com

Tommy Hilfiger
372 West Broadway
New York, NY
(800) 888-8802

Tootsi Plohound
273 Lafayette Street
New York, NY
(212) 431-7299

Vincent & Edgar
972 Lexington Avenue
New York, NY
(212) 753-3461
(specializing in custom
footwear)

Outerwear

Andrew Marc
(800) 424-MARC
www.andrewmarc.com

Barbour
(800) 338-3474
www.barbour.com

Barneys New York
Madison Avenue and 61st
Street
New York, NY
(212) 826-8900

Barneys Coop
236 W.18th Street
New York, NY
(212) 593-7800
www.barneys.com

Beau Brummel
421 West Broadway
New York, NY
(212) 219-2666
www.beaubrummel.com

Bergdorf Goodman Men
745 Fifth Avenue
New York, NY
(212) 758-7300
(call (800) 964-8619 for
listings)

Best of Class by Robert
Talbott
(800) 747-8778
www.roberttalbott.com

Bloomingdale's
1000 Third Avenue
New York, NY
(212) 705-2000
(800) 232-1854
www.bloomingdales.com

Brooks Brothers
346 Madison Avenue
New York, NY
(212) 682.8800
(800) 556-7039
www.brooksbrothers.com

Brioni
55 East 57th Street
New York, NY
(212) 376-5777
www.brioni.it
(call (800) 444-1613 for local
listings)

Burlington Coat Factory
707 Sixth Avenue
New York, NY
(212) 229-1300

Burberry
www.burberry.com
(800) 284-8480

Calvin Klein
595 Madison Avenue
New York, NY
751-0040

Cole Haan
667 Madison Avenue
New York, NY
(212) 421-8440
(800) 488-2000
www.colehaan.com

Daffy's
125 East 57th Street
New York, NY
(212) 376-4477
www.daffys.com

Davide Cenci
801 Madison Ave.
New York, NY
(212) 628-5910
www.davidecenci.com

Donna Karan Collection
819 Madison Avenue
New York, NY
(212) 861-1001

Dunhill
711 Fifth Avenue
New York, NY
(212) 753-9292
www.dunhill.com

Eddie Bauer
711 Third Avenue
New York, NY
(212) 808-0820
www.eddiebauer.com

Ermenegildo Zegna
743 Fifth Avenue
New York, NY
(212) 421-4488
www.ezegna.com

Etro
720 Madison Avenue
New York, NY
(212) 317-9096

Harry Rothman's
200 Park Avenue South
New York, NY
(212) 777-7400

Herno
www.herno.It

Hermès
11 East 57th Street
New York, NY
(212) 751-3181
(800) 441-4488

Holland & Holland
50 East 57th Street
New York, NY
(212) 752-7755
www.hollandandholland.com

J. Crew
99 Prince Street
New York, NY
(212) 966-2739
(800) 562-0258
www.jcrew.com

J. Press
7 East 44th Street
New York, NY
(212) 687-7642

Jeffrey New York
449 West 14th Street
New York, NY
(212) 206-1272

John Varvatos
149 Mercer Street
New York, NY
(212) 965-0700

Lands' End
(800) 963-4816
www.landsend.com

Loehmann's
101 Seventh Avenue
New York, NY
(212) 352-0856

Lord & Taylor
424 Fifth Avenue
New York, NY
(212) 391-3344
(800) 223-7440

Loro Piana
821 Madison Avenue
New York, NY
(212) 980-7961

Macy's
Broadway at Herald Square
New York, NY
(212) 695-4400
(800) 431-9644
www.macys.com

Nautica
50 Rockefeller Center
New York, NY
(212) 664-9594
www.nautica.com

Nicole Farhi
10 East 60th Street
New York, NY
(212) 223-8811

Orvis
522 Fifth Avenue
New York, NY
(212) 697-3133
www.orvis.com

Paul Stuart
Madison Avenue at 45th
  Street
New York, NY
(212) 682 0320

Polo Ralph Lauren
867 Madison Avenue
New York, NY
(212) 606-2100

Randolph Williamson
(custom, made-to-measure)
(615) 333-3484

Rochester Big & Tall
1301 Sixth Avenue
New York, NY
(212) 247-7500
(800) 282-8200

Salvatore Ferragamo
725 Fifth Avenue
New York, NY
(212) 759-7990
(800) 445-1874
www.salvatoreferragamo.com

Swiss Army
(212) 965-5714
www.swissarmy.com

Today's Man
529 Fifth Avenue
New York, NY
(212) 557-3111
(800) 950-7848
www.todaysman.com

Tommy Hilfiger
372 West Broadway
New York, NY
(800) 888-8802
www.tommy.com

Turnbull & Asser
42 East 57th Street
New York, NY
(212) 319-8100
(877) 887-6284
www.turnbullandasser.com

Yves Saint Laurent Rive
Gauche Hommes
88 Wooster Street
New York, NY
(212) 274-0522
(800) 424-8600

Accessories

a. Testoni
665 Fifth Avenue
New York, NY
(212) 223-0909
(call 877-testoni for the
  location nearest you)
(877) 837-8664
www.atestoni.com

Addison On Madison
698 Madison Avenue
New York, NY
(212) 308-2660

Alan Flusser
611 Fifth Avenue, 6th Floor
New York, NY
(212) 888-7100

Alexander Kabbaz
903 Madison Avenue
New York, NY
(212) 861-7700
(closed during the month of
  August)

Alfred Dunhill
450 Park Avenue
New York, NY
(212) 753-9292
www.dunhill.com

Anthony T. Dress
Furnishings
(718) 783-2570

Arnold Hatters, Inc.
620 8th Avenue
New York, NY
(212) 768-3781

Bally
628 Madison Avenue
New York, NY
(212) 751-9082
www.bally.com

Banana Republic
(Flagship)
17 West 34th Street
New York, NY
(212) 244-3060
www.bananarepublic.com

Barneys New York
Madison Avenue and 61st
  Street
New York, NY
(212) 826-8900

Barneys Coop
236 W.18th Street
New York, NY
(212) 593-7800
www.barneys.com

Beau Brummel
421 West Broadway
New York, NY
(212) 219-2666
www.beaubrummel.com

Bergdorf Goodman Men
745 Fifth Avenue
New York, NY
(212) 758-7300
(call (800) 964-8619 for
  listings)

Bloomingdale's
1000 Third Avenue
New York, NY
(212) 705-2000
(800) 232-1854
www.bloomingdales.com

Brioni
55 East 57th Street
New York, NY
(212) 376-5777
www.brioni.it
(call (800) 444-1613 for local
  listings)

Brooks Brothers
346 Madison Avenue
New York, NY
(212) 682-8800
(800) 556-7039
www.brooksbrothers.com

Bullock & Jones
340 Post Street
San Francisco, CA
(415) 392-4243

Burberry
(800) 284-8480
www.burberry.com

Cable Car Clothiers
246 Sutter Street
San Francisco, CA
(415) 397-4740

Calvin Klein
595 Madison Avenue
New York, NY
751-0040
(800) 294 7978
www.calvinklein.com

Cartier
www.cartier.com

Coach
(800) 444-3611
(call for store listings)
www.coach.com

Cole Haan
667 Madison Avenue
New York, NY
(212) 421-8440
(800) 488-2000
www.colehaan.com

Corneliani
(800) 222-9477
www.corneliani.com

Daffy's
125 East 57th Street
New York, NY
(212) 376-4477
www.daffys.com

Davide Cenci
801 Madison Ave.
New York, NY
(212) 628-5910
www.davidecenci.com

Dunhill
711 Fifth Avenue
New York, NY
(212) 753-9292
www.dunhill.com

Emporio Armani
110 Fifth Avenue
New York, NY
(212) 727-3240
www.emporioarmani.com

Ermenegildo Zegna
743 Fifth Avenue
New York, NY
(212) 421-4488
www.ezegna.com

Etro
720 Madison Avenue
New York, NY
(212) 317-9096

Fratelli Rossetti
625 Madison Avenue
New York, NY
(212) 888-5107
www.rosetti.it

Ghurka
41 East 57th Street
New York, NY
(212) 826-8300
(800) 587-1584
www.ghurka.com

Harry Rothman's
200 Park Avenue South
New York, NY
(212) 777-7400

Hermès
11 East 57th Street
New York, NY
(212) 751-3181
(800) 441-4488

Hickey-Freeman
666 Fifth Avenue
New York, NY
(212) 585-6481
(800) 603-8968
www.hickeyfreeman.com

Holland & Holland
50 East 57th Street
New York, NY
(212) 752-7755
www.hollandandholland.com

Hugo Boss
717 Fifth Avenue
New York, NY
(212) 485-1800
www.hugo.com

J. Crew
99 Prince Street
New York, NY
(212) 966-2739
(800) 562-0258
www.jcrew.com

J. Press
7 East 44th Street
New York, NY
(212) 687-7642

Jack Spade
56 Greene Street
New York, NY
(212) 625-1820

James Robinson
480 Park Avenue
New York, NY
(212) 752-6166

Jeffrey New York
449 West 14th Street
New York, NY
(212) 206-1272

JJ Hat Center
310 Fifth Avenue
New York, NY
(800) 622-1911
www.jjhatcenter.com

Jos. A. Banks
366 Madison Avenue
New York, NY
(212) 370-0600
(800) 285-2265

Kangol
www.kangol.com

Kenneth Cole New York
353 Columbus Avenue
New York, NY
(212) 873-2061
(800) 487-4389
www.kencole.com

L.A. Eyeworks
7407 Melrose Avenue
Los Angeles, CA
(213) 653-8255

Lands' End
(800) 963-4816
www.landsend.com

Links of London
(877) 79-LINKS
www.linksoflondon.com

Loehmann's
101 Seventh Avenue
New York, NY
(212) 352-0856

Lord & Taylor
424 Fifth Avenue
New York, NY
(212) 391-3344
(800) 223-7440

Louis Vuitton
703 Fifth Avenue
New York, NY
(212) 758-8877
(800) 847-2956
www.vuitton.com

Luxury Accessories
International
(877) 778-4355
www.luxuryaccessories.com

Malchijah Hats
225 De Kalb Avenue
Brooklyn, NY
(718) 643-3269

Massimo Bizzocchi
(212) 702-0136

Men's Warehouse
380 Madison Avenue
New York, NY
(212) 856-9008
(800) 776-7848
www.menswearhouse.com

Michael Newell
161 East Erie Street
Suite 306
Chicago, Il
(312) 951-9595

Michele Watches
(800) 522-TIME

Morgenthal-Frederics
685 Madison Avenue
New York, NY
(212) 838-3090

Movado Tourneau
635 Madison Avenue
New York, NY
(212) 758-6688
www.movado.com

Nicole Farhi
10 East 60th Street
New York, NY
(212) 223-8811

Nordstrom
865 Market Street
San Francisco, CA
(415) 243-8500

Norton Ditto
2019 Post Oak Boulevard
Houston, TX
(713) 688-9800

Oliver Peoples
(310) 657-5475
(nontraditional eyewear)
(call for store listings)

Oxxford Clothes
36 East 57th Street
New York, NY
(212) 593-0205

Paul Smith
108 Fifth Avenue
New York, NY
(212) 627-9770

Paul Stuart
Madison Avenue at 45th
    Street
New York, NY
(212) 682-0320

Pockets
9669 North Central
    Expressway
Suite 100
Dallas, TX
(214) 368-1167

Polo Ralph Lauren
867 Madison Avenue
New York, NY
(212) 606-2100

Robert Talbott
680 Madison Avenue
New York, NY
(212) 751-1200

Rochester Big & Tall
1301 Sixth Avenue
New York, NY
(212) 247-7500
(800) 282-8200

Rod Keenan
www.rodkeenannewyork.com

Saks Fifth Avenue
611 Fifth Avenue
New York, NY
(212) 753-4000
Saks Fifth Avenue
www.saksfifthavenue.com
(800) 345-3454

Salvatore Ferragamo
725 Fifth Avenue
New York, NY
(212) 759-7990
(800) 445-1874
www.salvatoreferragamo.com

Today's Man
529 Fifth Avenue
New York, NY
(212) 557-3111
(800) 950-7848
www.todaysman.com

Tommy Hilfiger
372 West Broadway
New York, NY
(800) 888-8802
www.tommy.com

Turnbull & Asser
42 East 57th Street
New York, NY
(212) 319-8100
(877) 887-6284
www.turnbullandasser.com

Valentino
747 Madison Avenue
New York, NY
(212) 772-6969
(877) 360-0864
www.valentino.it

Weathervane for Men
1132 Montana Avenue
Santa Monica, CA
(310) 395-0397
www.weathervaneformen.com

Wilkes Bashford
375 Sutter Street
San Francisco, CA
(415) 986-4380

Worth and Worth
331 Madison Avenue
New York, NY
(212) 867-6058

Young's Hat Center
139 Nassau Street
New York, NY
(212) 964-5693

Casual

A.Mandella Africa-USA
365 West 34th Street
2nd Floor
New York, NY
(212) 244-2306

A/X Armani Exchange
645 Fifth Avenue
New York, NY
(212) 980-3037
www.armaniexchange.com

Abercrombie & Fitch
199 Water Street
New York, NY
www.abercrombie.com

Agnès b.
79 Greene Street
New York, NY
(212) 219-6000

African Color Scheme
4341 Degnan Blvd.
Leimert Park Village, CA
(213) 298-9837

Ahneva Ahneva
3419B W. 43 Place
Leimert Park Village, CA
(213) 291-2535

American Eagle
Outfitters
89 South Street
New York, NY
(212) 571-5354
www.ae.com

American Rag
150 South La Brea Avenue
Los Angeles, CA
(213) 935-3154

Anyiam's Creations
1401 University Blvd.
Langley Park, MD
(301) 439-1110
(by appointment)

Bally
628 Madison Avenue
New York, NY
(212) 751-9082
www.bally.com

Banana Republic
(Flagship)
17 West 34th Street
New York, NY
(212) 244-3060
www.bananarepublic.com

Barneys Coop
236 W.18th Street
New York, NY
(212) 593-7800
www.barneys.com

Beads of Paradise
16 E. 17th Street
New York, NY
(212) 620-0642

Beau Brummel
421 West Broadway
New York, NY
(212) 219-2666
www.beaubrummel.com

Ben Sherman
www.benshermanusa.com

Benetton
597 Fifth Avenue
New York, NY
(212) 317-2501
www.benetton.com

Bergdorf Goodman Men
745 Fifth Avenue
New York, NY
(212) 758-7300

Berkley Cashmere
cocopari.com
(866) 4-Berkley

Bill's Khakis
(800) 43-KHAKIS
www.billskhakis.com

Bloomingdale's
1000 Third Avenue
New York, NY
(212) 705-2000
(800) 232-1854
www.bloomingdales.com

Brenda Bunson Bey
at 4W Circle of Art and
  Enterprise
704 Fulton Street
Brooklyn, NY
(718) 875-6500

Brian McKinney
9223 Fifth Avenue
Englewood, CA
(800) 222-9128
(800) 242-1499

Brooks Brothers
346 Madison Avenue
New York, NY
(212) 682-8800
(800) 556-7039
www.brooksbrothers.com

Bullock & Jones
340 Post Street
San Francisco, CA
(415) 392-4243

Burberry
(800) 284-8480
www.burberry.com

Burberry Ltd.
(800) 284-8480
(call for store listings)

Buttondown
3415 Sacramento Street
San Francisco, CA
(415) 563-1311

Calvin Klein
595 Madison Avenue
New York, NY
(212) 751-0040
(800) 294-7978
www.calvinklein.com

Camouflage
141 Eighth Avenue
New York, NY
(212) 741-9118

Carroll & Company
425 North Canyon Drive
Beverly Hills, CA
(310) 273-9060

Charivari
18 West 57th Street
New York, NY
(212) 333-4040

Claiborne
(800) 581-7272

Club Monaco
121 Prince Street
New York, NY
(212) 533-8930
www.clubmonaco.com
(888) 580-5084

Courtney Washington
674 Fulton Street
Brooklyn, NY
(718) 852-6899

D&G
434 West Broadway
New York, NY
(212) 965-8000
www.dolcegabbana.it

Daffy's
125 East 57th Street
New York, NY
(212) 376-4477
www.daffys.com

Davide Cenci
801 Madison Ave.
New York, NY
(212) 628-5910
www.davidecenci.com

Diesel
770 Lexington Ave.
New York, NY
(212) 308-0055
www.diesel.com

Diesel Style Lab
416 West Broadway
New York, NY
(212) 343-3863
www.dieselstylelab.com

DKNY
655 Madison Avenue
New York, NY
(212) 223-3569
www.dkny.com

Dolce & Gabbana
825 Madison Avenue
New York, NY
(212) 249-4100
www.dolcegabbana.com

Donna Karan Collection
819 Madison Avenue
New York, NY
(212) 861-1001

Douglass Fir
8317 West Third Street
Los Angeles, CA
(323) 651-5445

Eastern Mountain Sports
20 West 61st Street
New York, NY
(212) 397-4860
www.emsonline.com

Eddie Bauer
711 Third Avenue
New York, NY
(212) 808-0820
www.eddiebauer.com

Emporio Armani
110 Fifth Avenue
New York, NY
(212) 727-3240
www.emporioarmani.com

Epperson Studio
25 Thompson Street
New York, NY
(212) 226-3181

Ermenegildo Zegna
743 Fifth Avenue
New York, NY
(212) 421-4488
www.ezegna.com

Ethnic of Ybor City
428 E. Sample Road
Pompano Beach, FL
(305) 781-1145

Etro
720 Madison Avenue
New York, NY
(212) 317-9096

Everett Hall
5345 Wisconsin Avenue
Washington, DC
(202) 362-0191
(202) 362-5987

Exodus
(718) 246-0321

Fred Segal
8100 Melrose Avenue
Los Angeles, CA
(213) 651-4129

Fred Segal Melrose
8100 Melrose Avenue
Los Angeles, CA
(323) 651-4129

Freedom
29 S. Vincennes Avenue
Chicago, IL
(773) 488-3733

Gap
1212 Sixth Avenue
New York, NY
(212) 768-2987
(800) 427-7895
www.gap.com

Georges' Place Limited
(Big & Tall)
1001 H Street NE
Washington, DC
(202) 391-4113

Gianfranco Ferré
845 Madison Avenue
New York, NY
(212) 717-5430
www.gianfrancoferre.com

Giorgio Armani
760 Madison Avenue
New York, NY
(212) 988-9191
www.giorgioarmani.com

Giorgio Armani
815 Madison Avenue
New York, NY
(212) 988-9191

Gucci
(201) 867-8800
(call for store listings)

Guess?
537 Broadway
New York, NY
(212) 226-9545
www.guess.com

H.D.'s Clothing Company
3018 Greenville Avenue
Dallas, TX
(214) 821-5255

H&M (Hennes & Mauritz)
1328 Broadway
New York, NY
(646) 473-1164
www.hm.com

Harry Rothman's
200 Park Avenue South
New York, NY
(212) 777-7400

Hickey-Freeman
666 Fifth Avenue
New York, NY
(212) 585-6481
(800) 603-8968
www.hickeyfreeman.com

Holland & Holland
50 East 57th Street
New York, NY
(212) 752-7755
www.hollandandholland.com

Hugo Boss
717 Fifth Avenue
New York, NY
(212) 485-1800
www.hugo.com

Island Outpost
1332 Ocean Drive
Miami, FL
(305) 673-6300

J. Crew
99 Prince Street
New York, NY
(212) 966-2739
(800) 562-0258
www.jcrew.com

J. Lindeberg
126 Spring Street
New York, NY
(212) 625-9403
www.jlindeberg.com

Jeffrey New York
449 West 14th Street
New York, NY
(212) 206-1272

John Bartlett
Bloomingdale1s
1000 Third Avenue
(212) 705-2000

John Varvatos
149 Mercer Street
New York, NY
(212) 965-0700

Jos. A. Banks
366 Madison Avenue
New York, NY
(212) 370-0600
(800) 285-2265

Joseph Abboud
37 Newbury Street
Boston, MA
(617) 266-4200

KBOND
7257 Beverly Boulevard
Los Angeles, CA
(323) 939-8866
www.kbondla.com

Kenneth Cole New York
New York
353 Columbus Avenue
New York, NY
(212) 873-2061
(800) 487-4389
www.kencole.com

Keyi Ko Afrikan Arts
9765 S. Wood Street
Chicago, IL
(800) 295-0248

Kors
153 Mercer Street
New York, NY
(212) 966-5880
www.michaelkors.com

Lacoste
543 Madison Avenue
New York, NY
(212) 750-8115
www.lacoste.com
(800) 4-Lacoste

Lands' End
(800) 963-4816
www.landsend.com

The Leather Man
111 Christopher Street
New York, NY
(212) 243-5339

Levi Strauss
3 East 57th Street
New York, NY
(212) 838-2188
(800) 872-5384
www.levi.com

Loehmann's
101 Seventh Avenue
New York, NY
(212) 352-0856

Lord & Taylor
424 Fifth Avenue
New York, NY
(212) 391-3344
(800) 223-7440

Loro Piana
821 Madison Avenue
New York, NY
(212) 980-7961

Loro Piana
46 East 61st Street
New York, NY
(212) 980-7961

Lucky Brand Dungarees
38 Greene Street
New York, NY
(212) 625-0707
www.luckybrandjeans.com

Macy's
Broadway at Herald Square
New York, NY
(212) 695-4400
(800) 431-9644
www.macys.com

Maxfield
8825 Melrose Avenue
Los Angeles, CA
(310) 274-8800

Men's Warehouse
380 Madison Avenue
New York, NY
(212) 856-9008
(800) 776-7848
www.menswearhouse.com

Modell's
1535 Third Avenue
New York, NY
(212) 996-3800
(800) 275-6633
www.modells.com

Moshood (New York)
698 Fulton Street
Brooklyn, NY
(718) 2423-9433

Moshood (Atlanta)
217 Mitchell Street
Atlanta, GA
(404) 523-9430
(404) 523-9433
www.moshood.com

Nautica
50 Rockefeller Center
New York, NY
(212) 664-9594
www.nautica.com

Neiman Marcus
400 NorthPark Center
Dallas, TX
(214) 363-8311

Nicole Farhi
10 East 60th Street
New York, NY
(212) 223-8811

Nordstrom
865 Market Street
San Francisco, CA
(415) 243-8500

Old Navy Clothing
Company
150 West 34th Street
New York, NY
(212) 594-0049
(800) 653-6289
www.oldnavy.com

Oxxford Clothes
36 East 57th Street
New York, NY
(212) 593-0205

Pan-African Connection
612 E. Jefferson Blvd.
Dallas, TX
(214) 946-4798

Paragon Sporting Goods
867 Broadway
New York, NY
(212) 255-8036
(800) 443-9120
www.paragon.com

Paul Smith
108 Fifth Avenue
New York, NY
(212) 627-9770

Phat Farm
129 Prince Street
New York, NY
(212) 533-7428
www.phatfarmstore.com

Polo Sport
888 Madison Avenue
New York, NY
(212) 434-8000

Raif Atelier
887 Fulton Street
Brooklyn, NY
(718) 622-2377

Roberto Cavalli
711 Madison Avenue
New York, NY
(212) 755-7222
www.robertocavalli.com

Rochester Big & Tall
1301 Sixth Avenue
New York, NY
(212) 247-7500
(800) 282-8200

Saks Fifth Avenue
www.saksfifthavenue.com
(800) 345-3454

Saks Fifth Avenue
611 Fifth Avenue
New York, NY
(212) 753-4000

Salvatore Ferragamo
725 Fifth Avenue
New York, NY
(212) 759-7990
(800) 445-1874
www.salvatoreferragamo.com

Scott Hill
100 South Robertson Blvd.
Los Angeles, CA
(310) 777-1190

Sean John
Bloomingdale's
1000 Third Avenue
(212) 705-2000
www.seanjohn.com

Shaka King Menswear
207 Street James Place #3L
Brooklyn, NY
(718) 638-2933

shapes by anton
(212) 279-8111
www.shapesbyanton.com

Sports Authority
636 Sixth Avenue
New York, NY
(212) 929-8971
www.sportsauthoriy.com

Stranger Clothing
Company
110 E. Ninth Street
Los Angeles, CA
(213) 892-0706

Studio of Ptah
155 Canal Street
New York, NY
(212) 226-8487

Sulka & Company
840 Madison Avenue
New York, NY
(212) 452-1900

Swiss Army
(212) 965-5714
www.swissarmy.com

TJ Maxx
620 Sixth Avenue
New York, NY
(212) 229-0875
www.tjmaxx.com

TSE
(cashmere clothing)
(212) 472-7790

Today's Man
529 Fifth Avenue
New York, NY
(212) 557-3111
(800) 950-7848
www.todaysman.com

Tommy Hilfiger
468 North Rodeo Drive
Beverly Hills, CA
(310) 880-0132
www.tommy.com

Tommy Hilfiger
372 West Broadway
New York, NY
(800) 888-8802
www.tommy.com

Urban Outfitters
374 Sixth Avenue
New York, NY
(212) 677-9350
www.urbn.com

Valentino
747 Madison Avenue
New York, NY
(212) 772-6969
(877) 360-0864
www.valentino.it

Versace
(888) 383-7722
www.versace.com

Versace
815 Madison Avenue
New York, NY
(212) 744-6868
www.versace.com

Weathervane for Men
1132 Montana Avenue
Santa Monica, CA
(310) 395-0397
www.weathervaneformen.com

Wet Seal
901 Sixth Avenue
3rd Floor
New York, NY
(212) 216-0602

Wilkes Bashford
375 Sutter Street
San Francisco, CA
(415) 986-4380

Yves Saint Laurent Rive
Gauche Hommes
88 Wooster Street
New York, NY
(212) 274-0522
(800) 424-8600

Zara International
750 Lexington Avenue
New York, NY
(212) 754-1120
www.zara.com

Underwear

2xist
www.2xiStreetcom

Bloomingdale's
1000 Third Avenue
New York, NY
(212) 705-2000
(800) 232-1854
www.bloomingdales.com

c.cashmere atelier
(215) 232-1875

Calvin Klein
654 Madison Avenue
New York, NY
(212) 292-9000

Fruit of the Loom
www.fruitoftheloom.com

Hanes
www.hanes.com

Harry Rothman's
200 Park Avenue South
New York, NY
(212) 777-7400

International Male
www.internationalmale.com

Jockey
(866) 256-2539
www.jockey.com

Joe Boxer
www.joeboxer.com

Jos. A. Banks
366 Madison Avenue
New York, NY
(212) 370-0600
(800) 285-2265

Loehmann's
101 Seventh Avenue
New York, NY
(212) 352-0856

Lord & Taylor
424 Fifth Avenue
New York, NY
(212) 391-3344
(800) 223-7440

Macy's
Broadway at Herald Square
New York, NY
(212) 695-4400
(800) 431-9644
www.macys.com

Men's Warehouse
380 Madison Avenue
New York, NY
(212) 856-9008
(800) 776-7848
www.menswearhouse.com

Rochester Big & Tall
1301 Sixth Avenue
New York, NY
(212) 247-7500
(800) 282-8200

Saks Fifth Avenue
www.saksfifthavenue.com
(800) 345-3454

Sean John
Bloomingdale1s
1000 Third Avenue
(212) 705-2000
www.seanjohn.com

Sulka & Company
840 Madison Avenue
New York, NY
(212) 452-1900

Today's Man
529 Fifth Avenue
New York, NY
(212) 557-3111
(800) 950-7848
www.todaysman.com

Tommy Hilfiger
372 West Broadway
New York, NY
(800) 888-8802

His Spa

Acqua Beauty Bar
7 E. 14th Street
New York, NY
(212) 620-4329

Allure Day Spa and Hair
Design
139 E. 55th Street
New York, NY
(212) 644-5500

Anne Sémonin at the
Plaza Spa
768 Fifth Avenue
New York, NY
(212) 546-5772

Anthony Logistics For
Men
(866) ANTHONY

Aroma Pharmacy
(877) 533-7847
www.aromapharmacy.com

Art of Shaving
(800) 696-9999
www.theartofshaving.com

Ashe, Walden Skin and
Body Spa, Inc.
930 W. Washington Street
San Diego, CA
(619) 295-7302
(800) 943-2242
www.waldenashe.com

Bark
369 Atlantic Avenue
Brooklyn, NY
(718) 625-8997

Barneys Coop
236 W.18th Street
New York, NY
(212) 593-7800
www.barneys.com

Bliss Spa
(877) To.Bliss
www.blissworld.com

Bloomingdale's
1000 Third Avenue
New York, NY
(212) 705-2000
www.bloomingdales.com or
call (800) 777-0000 for your
nearest store

The Body Clinic
8820 S. Sepulveda Blvd.
Ste.104
Los Angeles, CA
www.the-body-clinic.com

Bodyjoys
3423 St. Charles Avenue
New Orleans, LA
(504) 895-4400
(800) 331-7812
www.bodyjoys.com

Breukelen
369 Atlantic Avenue
Brooklyn, NY
(718) 246-0024

Carol's Daughter
1 South Elliot Place
Brooklyn, NY

Creations by Alan Stuart
(800) 866-4424
www.creationsbyalanstuart.com

Elizabeth Arden Red
Door & Spa
Westin La Paloma
3660 E. Sunrise Dr.
Tuscon, AZ
(520) 742-7866, ext. 7890
reddoorsalons.com

Esteé Lauder
www.esteelauder.com

Ettia Holistic Day Spa
239 W. 72nd Street
New York, NY
(212) 362-7109

Giuliano, The Spa for
Beauty and Wellness
338 Newbury Street
Boston, MA
(617) 262-2220
www.giulianodayspa.com

HomeSpa
300 Court Street
Brooklyn, NY
(718) 596-8668

Inspirations
1395 Lexington Avenue
New York, NY
(212) 415-5795

Just Calm Down
32 W. 22nd Street
New York, NY
(212) 337-0032

Kiehl's
(800) Kiehls-1

La Prairie
www.laprarie.com

Lia Schorr Day Spa
686 Lexington Avenue
New York, NY
(212) 486-9670

Look Great European
Day Spa
771 E. Palmetto Park Rd.
Boca Raton, FL
(561) 391-2030
www.lookgreatdayspa.com

Macy's
Broadway at Herald Square
New York, NY
(212) 695-4400
(800) 431-9644
www.macys.com

Michael Anthony
Aveda Lifestyle Salon Spa
1637 W. Belmont
Chicago, IL
(773) 935-0707

Nickel
77 Eighth Avenue
New York, NY
(212) 242-3203

Origins
www.origins.com

Oscar Bond Salon and
Spa
42 Wooster Street
New York, NY
(212) 334-3777

Saks Fifth Avenue
www.saksfifthavenue.com
(800) 345-3454

Sephora
www.sephora.com

Spa Seven
2358 Pine Street
San Francisco, CA
(415) 775-6546
www.spaseven.com

Susan Ciminelli Day Spa
Bergdorf Goodman
754 Fifth Avenue
Ninth floor
New York, NY
(212) 872-2650

Tommy Hilfiger
372 West Broadway
New York, NY
(800) 888-8802

Tweezerman
www.tweezerman.com

Unique Salon and Day
Spa
1624 I Street N.W.
Washington, D.C.
(202) 331-7771
www.auniquesalon@msn.com

Warm Spirit
(888) 296-9854
www.warmspirirt.com

Woodstock Spa and
Wellness Center
The Benjamin Hotel
125 E. 50th Street
Third Floor
New York, NY
(212) 715-2517

Zirh
www.zirh.com

Zuri Boutique
3150 E. 3rd Avenue
Denver, CO
(303) 377-3377
www.zurisalonspa.com

Closet

Bed Bath and Beyond
www.bedbathandbeyond.com

Blue Light
www.bluelight.com

California Closets
www.californiaclosets.com

Closet Made www.closetmade.com	**Container Store** www.containerstore.com	**IKEA** www.ikea.com	**Organizes It** www.organizes-it.com
Closetry www.closetry.com	**Easy Closets** www.easyclosets.com	**Martha Stewart** www.marthastewart.com	**Stacks and Stacks** www.stacksandstacks.com
Coleman Closets www.colemanclosets.com	**Hold Everything** www.holdeverything.com	**Organize Everything** www.organize-everything.com	**Target** www.target.com

Photo Credits

Book Cover

Suit, Tommy Hilfiger; blue dress shirt, Davide Cenci; pocket square, Paul Stuart; alligator belt, Luxury Accessories International; woman's platinum wedding band, Fortunoff.

Women's Roundtable

Page 7. Clothing courtesy of Lord & Taylor.

His Suit

Page 22. Tan herringbone three-button bespoke suit, Corneliani; gray antique-stripe spread-collar shirt, Hickey-Freeman Collection; pocket square, Paul Stuart.

Pages 24, 27 (bottom) and 28. Gray with soft blue pin-striped double-breasted, double-vented, peak-lapel suit, Ermenegildo Zegna; white twill French-cuff shirt, Thomas Pink; basketweave pocket square, Paul Stuart.

Pages 25 (top) and 27 (top). Gray two-button worsted wool suit with center vent, Hart Schaffner & Marx; white twill French-cuff shirt, Thomas Pink; sterling cuff links and watch, Tiffany & Co.

Pages 26 (top) and 27 (bottom). Gray three-button worsted wool ventless suit, Hart Schaffner & Marx; white twill French-cuff shirt, Thomas Pink.

Page 26 (bottom). Grey single-button suit, Armani Collezioni; white twill French-cuff shirt, Thomas Pink; sterling cuff links, Tiffany & Co.

Page 30. Navy super 100's with light blue pin-striped suit, Corneliani; white pinpoint cotton, spread-collar dress shirt, Thomas Pink; blue silk tone-on-tone tie, Canali; camel three-button wool/angora/cashmere topcoat, Canali; hand-rolled, hand-stitched cotton pocket square, Paul Stuart; caramel eyewear, OP; black leather lace-up shoes, a. testoni.

Pages 32–33 (left to right)

Navy: Wool "Boardroom" single-breasted two-button suit, Hickey-Freeman Collection; midnight merino turtleneck, Davide Cenci.

Gray Flannel: Single-breasted two-button suit and pink gingham French-cuff shirt, Davide Cenci.

Navy Chalk-Stripe: Super 110's extra-fine wool single-breasted three-button suit, Davide Cenci; white high-collared, pin-stitched button-down shirt, Canali; silver satin hand-made tie, Anthony T. Dress Furnishings; blue woven foulard tie, Canali; yellow oxford stripe tie, Thomas Pink.

Khaki: Single-breasted three-button suit, Canali; white button-down, knit oxford shirt, Kiton.

Black: Super 100's worsted wool, single-breasted three-button "Jesse" suit, Today's Man; fuchsia superfine two-fold cotton, spread-collar shirt, Thomas Pink.

Plaid: Autumnal glen-plaid, single-breasted two-button suit and multicolored gingham button-down shirt, Paul Stuart.

Gray Pin-stripe: Super 120's wool single-breasted two-button suit, Davide Cenci; lavender herringbone spread-collar shirt, Thomas Pink; lavender and silver basketweave tie, Corneliani; white linen/cotton hand-rolled pocket square, Paul Stuart.

Page 39. Tiki after: Soft blue double-breasted pin-striped suit, Ermenegildo Zegna; pale blue shirt with French blue windowpane, spread-collar shirt, Thomas Pink; striped silk tie, and yellow hand-rolled pocket square with white edging, Ermenegildo Zegna; sterling knot cuff links, Tiffany & Co.; gray silk and cotton socks; brown wing-perforated derby shoes, a. testoni.

His Shirt

Page 44. Stack of shirts, Tommy Hilfiger.

Pages 46–47. Yellow and white check shirt, Ike Behar.

Page 49. Modified-spread-collar shirt, The Shirt Store; white, silver, and black patterned tie, Canali; sterling and black enamel "waffle" cuff links, Links of London.

Page 50. Straight-point-collar shirt, The Shirt Store; taupe tone-on-tone striped silk tie, Michael Newell.

Page 49. Tab collar shirt, The Shirt Store; black and blue, houndstooth, hand-made tie, Anthony T. Dress Furnishings; black silk-knot cuff links, Paul Stuart.

Page 49. Button-down-collar shirt, The Shirt Store; striped hand-made bow tie, Anthony T. Dress Furnishings.

Page 50. Full-spread-collar shirt with double-barrel cuffs, Thomas Pink; green blind-stripe, pin-dotted, silk tie, Michael Newell.

Page 49. "A" collar shirt, The Shirt Store; Silver gray repp tie, Paul Stuart.

Page 52. Superfine two-fold cotton straight-point-collar shirt, Thomas Pink; stone D-ring trousers, Zegna Sport; chronograph, Michele Watches.

Page 54. 1) Green linen, Ike Behar. 2) Yellow end-on-end, Thomas Pink; 3) pink end-on-end, Thomas Pink;4) tangerine twill, Today's Man; 5) gray twill, Hickey-Freeman Collection; 6) champagne small herringbone, Today's Man; 7) lavender large herringbone, Thomas Pink; 8) green pique, Lacoste; 9) pale lavender with brown top-stitching, Corneliani; 10) white with blue top-stitching, Canali; 11) peach basketweave, Thomas Pink; 12) blue and white basketweave, Club Monaco; 13) gray antique-stripe broadcloth, Hickey-Freeman Collection; 14) burgundy mille-raie stripe, Today's Man; 15) white pinstripe on lavender end-on-end, Today's Man; 16) fuchsia double-stripe on pink ground, Canali; 17) two-tone double-track pencil-stripe, Dunhill.

Page 55. 1) Two-tone chalk-stripe broadcloth, Corneliani; 2) blue candy-stripe oxford, Tommy Hilfiger; 3) navy candy-stripe broadcloth, Britches of Georgetowne; 4) variegated blue stripes, Today's Man; 5) blue and white hairline stripes on yellow end-on-end, Today's Man; 6) white stripe on blue broadcloth, The Shirt Store; 7) blue with white stripe, Corneliani; 8) blue and coral awning stripe, Kiton; 9) coral and peach two-tone stripe on pale blue ground, Canali; 10) peach small gingham, Today's Man; 11) pink medium gingham, Davide Cenci; 12) blue large gingham, Thomas Pink; 13) pink and blue tattersall, Thomas Pink; 14) beige button-down tattersall, Canali; 15) red windowpane button-down, Canali; 16) pale mini-check with brown tattersall overplaid, Corneliani; 17) pale blue windowpane on dusty pink ground, Lacoste; 18) subtle windowpane on blue end-on-end, Hickey-Freeman Collection.

Page 61. Pink check spread-collar shirt, Thomas Pink; flat-front chinos, Tommy Hilfiger.

His Pants

Page 66. Navy pin-striped trousers, Duah Brothers; Silver faille braces, Paul Stuart.

Page 69. Left to right: brown wool-and-cotton twill single-pleat cuffed dress trousers, Corneliani; tan merino wool sweater, Metropolitan at Lord & Taylor. Charcoal twill double-pleat D-ring trousers, Paul Stuart; blue pima cotton V-neck sweater, Canali. Cream wool crepe inverted-box-pleat trousers, Canali; yellow pima cotton polo, Canali; cognac hand-stained calfskin belt, Canali.

Page 70. Left to right: black wool gabardine flat-front trousers, Brooks Brothers; muscle T-shirt, Joe Boxer; black loafer mule, Hugo Boss. Natural wool reverse single-pleat trousers, Canali; ecru silk three-button polo, Canali; chestnut cap-toe oxford, a. testoni. Charcoal wool western-pocket pants, DKNY at Lord & Taylor; dark gray silk/wool blend T-shirt, Axis at Lord & Taylor; black matte alligator reversible military belt, Luxury Accessories International; black boots, Kenneth Cole.

Page 73. Tan moleskin flat-front, relaxed-fit, "Hudson" pant, Brooks Brothers; white "Jeremy" shirt, Ike Behar; penny-loafer driving moccasins, Cole Haan.

Pages 74–75. Left to right: Navy gabardine trousers, Hickey-Freeman Collection; tan worsted wool trousers, Dunhill; chocolate crepe chalk-stripe trousers, Duah Brothers; stone cavalry-twill trousers, Canali; grey flannel trousers, Duah Brothers; lemon linen trousers, Ike Behar; cognac herringbone tweed trousers, Duah Brothers.

Page 81. Brown silk striped jacket, yellow and white bias-striped shirt, white knit vest, and white cuffed flat-front trousers, Cynthia Rowley.

His Shoes

Page 84. Shoes, a. testoni and John Lobb.

Page 86. Brown suede "Pierson" hand-made oxfords, John Lobb.

Pages 88–89. Left to right: Black blucher, Canali; black trousers, Claiborne; French-cuff shirt, Thomas Pink; shoe polish, Kiwi. Black leather cap-toe oxfords, Cole Haan; silk and cotton socks, a.testoni; navy cuffed trousers with gray chalk-stripe, Canali; double-barrel-cuff shirt, Thomas Pink. Cognac wing-tip brogues, Canali; beige bead-stripe trousers, Shaka King New York. Chelsea boots, Fryc Boots; socks, Lord & Taylor; stretch trousers, Kenneth Cole at Lord & Taylor; blue shirt, Tommy Hilfiger; wedding band, Fortunoff.

Pages 90–91. Left to right: Black calf "Newland" hand-made monk-strap shoe, John Lobb; twill cuffed trousers, Claiborne. Driving moccasins, Tod's; khakis, Bill's Khakis. Black calf opera pumps, Ermenegildo Zegna; silk and cotton socks, a. testoni; satin stripe tuxedo trousers, Canali; bib-front shirt with pique-cuffs, Thomas Pink; vintage cuff links.

Page 92. Black "Alder" loafers, Banana Republic; "Brigade" plain-front chinos, Tommy Hilfiger.

Page 94. On Elizabeth: cashmere shirt dress, Berkley Cashmere; in her hand: shoe, Canali; in background: monk-strap "Matta" shoe, John Lobb.

Page 97. Camel shawl-collar cardigan, ecru silk-twill shirt and tan Hollywood trousers, Ralph Lauren Purple Label; natural ribbed-cotton lisle socks, Paul Stuart; tan cap-toe oxford shoes with brown piping and top-stitching, a. testoni.

His Outerwear

Pages 103, 106, 107 and 113. Flannel-lined jacket, Barbour.

Page 109. Trench coat with detachable wool collar and lining, Burberry; black crew neck sweater, Club Monaco; white shirt, Ike Behar; black flat-front trousers, Claiborne; black oxford shoes, Canali.

Pages 110–111. Left to right: Weatherproof cotton trench coat, Herno; Gray polar-fleece-lined anorak, Canali; Khaki canvas jacket with zippered cuffs, Dunhill; Bendingo lamb raw-edged blazer, Andrew Marc; Black cashmere/wool "Howleson" coat with gray shearling detachable notched collar, Andrew Marc; hangers, Hold Everything.

Page 117. White parka, Davide Cenci; oatmeal zip-front sweater, Dunhill; tattersall shirt, Corneliani; stone brushed-cotton, flat-front trousers, Davide Cenci; herringbone driving cap, Kangol; tan socks, Jockey; sand desert boots, Clark's; sunglasses, Tommy Hilfiger.

His Accessories

Page 122. Ivory silk-paisley evening scarf and sterling knot cuff links and studs, Paul Stuart.

Page 124. Top: Sterling knot cuff links, Tiffany & Co.; silk-knot cuff links, Britches of Georgetowne; glass, Apartment 48. Bottom: Gold woven braces, Britches of Georgetowne; leather diary, Holland and Holland.

Page 126. Belts, from top: smooth black with silver buckle, Ralph Lauren; dark brown grain leather with brass buckle, Paul Stuart; brown pebble-grain leather with silver buckle, Canali; black grain leather with silver buckle, Tommy Hilfiger; chocolate crocodile leather with silver military buckle, Luxury Accessories International.

Page 127. Top: Sterling collar stays, Dunhill; sterling money clip, Tiffany & Co. Bottom: Ribbed-cotton lisle socks, Paul Stuart.

Page 128. Navy super 120's wool/cashmere bead stripe two-button "Edward" suit, Paul Stuart; white pinpoint oxford full-spread, French-cuff shirt, The Shirt Store; white square-patterned tie, Canali; white rolled, hand-stitched pocket square, Paul Stuart; tortoise shell spectacles, vintage; black deerskin driving gloves, Paul Stuart; sterling and burl-patterned pen, Tateossian London; chronograph, Breitling; sterling knot cuff links, Paul Stuart; black matte alligator belt with nickel buckle, Luxury Accessories International.

Pages 132–133. Ties:

Woolens: Brown/blue plaid tie, Paul Stuart; muted plaid cashmere tie, Davide Cenci; dark muted color-block tie, Paul Stuart; cashmere Donegal tweed tie, Davide Cenci; brown/blue/yellow striped tie, Davide Cenci.

Knits: Bright bar-stripe, square-apron tie, Anthony T. Dress Furnishings; red square-apron lambswool tie, Davide Cenci; brown tie with red pin-dots, Davide Cenci; dark bar-stripe, square-apron tie Anthony T. Dress Furnishings.

Solids: Olive satin tie, Anthony T. Dress Furnishings; green basketweave tie, Massimo Bizzocchi; pumpkin vertical-ribbed faille tie, Davide Cenci; brown herringbone tie, Paul Stuart; black grenadine tie, Paul Stuart.

Stripes: Blue/brown/tan horizontal-stripe tie, Davide Cenci; blue/plum ribbon-stripe tie, Massimo Bizzocchi; pink/blue repp tie, Thomas Pink; cream/blue repp tie, Corneliani.

Prints: Yellow logo tie, Dunhill; coral tie with pineapple print, Anthony T. Dress Furnishings; red links print, Tommy Hilfiger; blue repeat-pattern tie, Hermès.

Club: Yellow heraldic tie, Tommy Hilfiger; whimsical lilac tie with white seagull motif, Paul Stuart; navy tie with red logo, Burberry; blue tie with wine mustang motif, Paul Stuart.

Paisley: Wool challis paisley tie, Anthony T. Dress Furnishings; burgundy/hunter silk twill paisley tie, Anthony T. Dress Furnishings; yellow tone-on-tone jacquard paisley tie, Thomas Pink; yellow/black paisley tie, Paul Stuart.

Dots: Wine tie with large cream-printed dots, Paul Stuart; olive herringbone tie with woven orange dots, Anthony T. Dress Furnishings; white and yellow dotted-jacquard tie, Canali; yellow tie with small printed burgundy dots, Anthony T. Dress Furnishings.

Plaid: Yellow/green/blue preppy tie, Canali; red/yellow/blue tartan tie, Paul Stuart; camel tie with navy and white windowpane plaid, Corneliani; purple and gold houndstooth tie, Anthony T. Dress Furnishings.

Foulards: Rust woven foulard tie, Dunhill; burnt orange printed twill foulard tie, Anthony T. Dress Furnishings; blue basketweave printed-foulard tie, Davide Cenci; purple/blue/red grenadine foulard tie, Anthony T. Dress Furnishings.

Woven: Navy tie with woven French blue squares, Canali; multi-green neat-pattern tie, Massimo Bizzocchi; green/gold woven optical-patterned tie, Michael Newell; green/tan/white basketweave tie, Ike Behar.

Page 134. Tyra and Donald: beaver hat on sofa, George's Place; all others, JJ Hat Center. Gray Borsalino fedora, JJ Hat Center.

Page 137. Gray velvet pin-striped three-button suit and white dress shirt, George's Place; silver/gray basketweave tie and magenta silk pocket square, Rochester Big & Tall; cuff links, vintage; gray Borsalino fedora, JJ Hat Center; black leather gloves, Davide Cenci; sterling-tipped walking stick, Paul Stuart; socks, George's Place; shoes, Mezlan at Rochester Big & Tall.

Casual

Page 142. Khakis: Club Monaco, Banana Republic, Tommy Hilfiger, Bill's Khakis, and Lands' End.

Page 144. Top: Braided leather belt, Britches of Georgetowne; Grosgrain ribbon belts, Tommy Hilfiger. Bottom: Long and shortsleeved polo shirts, Lacoste; cargo shorts, Abercrombie & Fitch.

Page 145. Top: Classic white sneakers, K-Swiss; leather thong sandals with rubber-tread soles, Abercrombie & Fitch. Bottom: Navy linen unconstructed blazer, Hugo Boss; hanger, Hold Everything.

Page 146. Linen newsboy cap, JJ Hat Center; straw porkpie hat, JJ Hat Center; corduroy "lobster" crusher, J. Crew.

Page 148. Tan satin goat-suede shirt, Cole Haan; camel V-neck pullover, Kenneth Cole at Lord & Taylor; tan moleskin pants, Brooks Brothers; gunmetal aviator sunglasses, Izod; silver dial watch with braided leather strap, Paul Stuart; chocolate rebel-cow jacket with shearling shirt collar, Cole Haan; cognac alligator cell-phone case, Luxury Accessories International; sterling key fob, Tiffany & Co.; canvas and pebble-grain weekender, Edward Green for Bergdorf Goodman; reddish-brown motorcycle boots, vintage.

Page 151. Black cotton shirt, Banana Republic; platinum wedding band, Fortunoff.

Page 155. Chocolate leather blazer, Andrew Marc; white T-shirt, Gap; jeans, his own; watch, his own Rolex; black leather moccasins, Cole Haan.

His Underwear

Page 160. Union suit, Dave's Army Navy; hanger, Hold Everything.

Page 163. Left: Classic cotton briefs, Jockey. Right: Cotton boxer briefs, Jockey.

Page 165. Left: Lo-rise cotton briefs, Jockey. Right: Classic cotton boxers, Jockey.

Page 166. His shirt, on her, Tommy Hilfiger; his own boxers.

Page 167. Charcoal silk robe with green piping, Sean John; black tactel boxer briefs, Jockey.

His Grooming

Page 176. Silver Mach III razor, Anthony Logistics for Men.

Page 179. Left: Cream, Anthony Logistics for Men. Right: Alum block, Art of Shaving.

Pages 180–181.

Top shelf: Cellular Refining Lotion, LaPrairie; Skin Clearing Solution, Lab Series for Men; Lip Balm for All Skin Types in Citrus, Anthony Logistics for Men; juice glass, Bark; in glass, horn comb, Art of Shaving; facial brush, Creations by Alan Stuart, faux tortoise shell toothbrush, Creations by Alan Stuart; shaving set with pure badger brush, Anthony Logistics for Men; Klaus Heidegger All-Sport Everday Shampoo, Kiehl's; candle, Votivo at Yù.

Middle shelf: Essential Exfoliator, LaPrairie; Close Call Shave Solution, Lab Series for Men; enamel and palladium shaving bowl, Art of Shaving; in bowl: cotton squares and tweezers for ingrown hairs or splinters, Tweezerman; After-Shave Balm, Pre-Shave Oil and travel-size Shaving Cream and chrome mustache razor, Art of Shaving; Alcohol-free, Fragrance-free Toner for Normal to Dry Skin and Deep Pore Cleansing Clay, Anthony Logistics for Men; Ultra Facial Moisturizer—SPF 15, Kiehl's.

Bottom shelf: Geranium Leaf Hydrating Body Treatment, Aesop; Electric Shave Solution, Lab Series for Men; Body Cleansing Gel for All Skin Types in Coriander Blend, Anthony Logistics for Men; Cellular Hydrating Serum and Cellular Eye Contour Cream LaPrairie; Instant Correcting Stick, Aramis Surface; white Japanese teacup, Breukelen; in cup: glycerin soap, Anthony Logistics for Men; Just Won't Quit Antiperspirant-Deodorant, Lab Series for Men; brushed metal manicure set, Kenneth Cole.

Page 182. Shower wraps, pedicure slippers, and bath towels, Creations by Alan Stuart, Star's own clothes.

Page 186. Nail clipper, Tweezerman.

Page 185. Crew-neck T-shirt, athletic tank, and V-neck T-shirt, Jockey; chinos, Lands' End. Star's gown, The Star Jones Collection at starjones.com; her own Dennis Basso coat.

Page 189. Left: Hypoallergenic nail polish, Firozé. Right: Lotion, Anthony Logistics for Men.

His Closet

Page 194. Deluxe cedar suit hangers, Britches of Georgetowne.

Page 197. Top photo, left to right: sport coat, Canali; khaki suit, Hickey-Freeman; ivory sport coat, Holland & Holland; canvas jacket, Dunhill; plaid linen shirt, Kiton; knit shirt, Dunhill; shirt, Canali; sweaters, Canali, Dunhill; shoes, Lands' End. Bottom: Classic white sneakers, K-Swiss; white bucks, Allen-Edmonds; sand suede shoes, a. testoni; shoe with shoe tree, John Lobb.

Page 198. Closet organizers, Hold Everything; braces, courtesy of Duah Brothers.

Page 199. Pant hangers, Hold Everything.

Pages 200–201. Closet Credits: California Closet. Closet organizers and hangers, Hold Everything; clothing: Bill's Khakis, Britches of Georgetowne, Canali, Corneliani, Dunhill, Kiton, Lands' End, Victorinox for Swiss Army; eyewear, Izod; braces, courtesy of Duah Brothers; footwear, a. testoni, Allen Edmonds, Clark's, John Lobb, K-Swiss, Lands' End, Old Navy, Tommy Hilfiger; hats, JJ Hat Center and Kangol; robe, Lands' End; Socks and Underwear, Jockey; Ties, Michael Newell; Tote, Lands' End; watches, Dunhill and Swiss Army.

Page 204. Patti holds red check shirt, vintage; peach windowpane shirt, Kenneth Cole. Zuri holds reversible blue bucket hat, Kangol; yellow striped shorts, Abercrombie & Fitch.

Page 207. Brown soft plaid sportcoat, Canali; soft gray turtleneck, Club Monaco; gray flannel trousers, Davide Cenci; tan plaid pocket square, Paul Stuart; charcoal ribbed socks, Lord & Taylor; chestnut perforated slip-on, a. testoni.

His Shopping

Page 213. Gift box, Links of London.

Page 214. Top: On model, white point collar shirt, Tommy Hilfiger. Left option: Yellow end on end shirt, Thomas Pink. Right option: White-and-blue awning stripes, Kiton. Bottom: White point collar shirt, Tommy Hilfiger; watch, Swiss Army; her "flap" handbag, Kenneth Cole.

Pages 218–219. Well-crafted tie with bar tack, slip stitch, and buttonhole, Massimo Bizzocchi.

Page 222. Kimora Lee Simmons in Baby Phat; shoes, Manolo Blahnik.

Page 224. On Don, peach French-cuff shirt, Thomas Pink; shirts in foreground, Polo at Lord & Taylor, The Shirt Store and Thomas Pink; shoes in background, Lord & Taylor. Jennie and Lori's own clothes.

Page 227. Khaki suit, Canali; black sweater, Tommy Hilfiger; peach spread-collar shirt, Thomas Pink; pocket square and socks, Paul Stuart; brown perforated tassel loafers, Donald J. Pliner at Lord & Taylor. Jennie and Lori's own clothes.

Page 228. Shirt and flat-front trousers, Tommy Hilfiger; Pen, Tatetossian London.

Archival Photo Credits

Every effort has been made to account for and credit the copyright owners of the archival photographs included in this book. Any inadvertent omissions should be brought to the attetntion of the author, care of the publisher.

AP Photo: p. 190. Everett Collection: p. 18; p. 20; p. 40; pp. 42–43; p. 62; p. 65; p. 82; p. 100, top right; p. 118; p. 121; p. 138; pp. 140–141; p. 158; p. 208; pp. 210–211. Getty Images: p. 98. Globe Photos: p. 21; p. 100, top left; p 100, bottom right. Kobal Collection: p. 100, bottom left; p. 193. MPTV: p. 156. TimePix: p. 159; p. 192.

Bibliography

Allen, James. *As a Man Thinketh*. New York: Barnes & Noble Books, 1992.

Andrews, Robert. *The Columbia Dictionary of Quotations*. New York: Columbia University Press, 1993.

Angeli, Giuliano, and Richardo Villarosa. *The Elegant Man: How to Construct the Ideal Wardrobe*. New York: Random House, 1990.

Angeloni, Umberto. *The Boutonniere: Style in One's Lapel*. New York: Universe Publishing, 2000.

Barron, James Douglas. *She Wants a Ring and I Don't Want to Change a Thing*. New York: Quill, 2001.

Berkowitz, Bob, and Roger Gittines. *What Men Won't Tell You but Women Need to Know*. New York: Avon, 1990.

Brody, Louise, and Julie Welch. *Leading Men*. New York: Crescent Books, 1985.

Calasibetta, Charlotte Mankey, Ph.D. *Fairchild's Dictionary of Fashion*. New York: Fairchild Books, 1998.

Campione, Adele. *Men's Hats*. San Francisco: Chronicle Books, 1988.

Chenoune, Farid. *A History of Men's Fashion*. Paris: Flammarion, 1993.

Chichester, Brian, and Perry Garfinkel. *Maximum Style: Look Sharp and Feel Confident in Every Situation*. Emmaus, Pa.: Rodale Press, Inc., 1997.

Close, Barbara. *The Spa Deck: 50 Recipes for Relaxation and Rejuvenation*. San Francisco: Chronicle Books, 2001.

Cramer, Richard Ben. *Joe DiMaggio: The Hero's Life*. New York: Simon & Schuster, 2000.

Dolce, Donald, with Jean-Paul DeVellard. *The Consumer's Guide to Menswear*. New York: Dodd, Mead & Company, 1983.

Flusser, Alan. *Making the Man: The Insider's Guide to Buying and Wearing Men's Clothes*. New York: Wallaby Books, 1981.

Flusser, Alan. *Style and the Man: How and Where to Buy Fine Men's Clothes*. New York: HarperCollins, 1996.

Foster, D. Glenn, and Mary Marshall. *How Can I Get Through to You?* New York: MJF, 1994.

Fox, Patty. *Star Style*. Santa Monica, Ca: Angel City Press, 1995.

Friedman, Steve. *The Gentleman's Guide to Life*. New York: Three Rivers Press, 1997.

Gray, John, Ph.D. *Mars and Venus Starting Over*. New York: HarperCollins Publishers, 1998.

———. *Men, Women and Relationships: Making Peace with the Opposite Sex*. New York: MJF, 1993.

Greenleaf, Clinton T. III. *A Gentleman's Guide to Appearance*. Holbrook, Mass.: Adams Media Corporation, 2000.

Gross, Kim Johnson, Jeff Stone, and Christa Worthington. *Chic Simple. Shirt and Tie*. New York: Alfred A. Knopf, Inc., 1993.

———. *Chic Simple. Clothes*. New York: Alfred A. Knopf, Inc., 1995.

Gross, Kim Johnson, Jeff Stone, and J. Scott Omelianuk. *Chic Simple. Work Clothes: Casual Dress for Serious Work*. New York: Alfred A. Knopf, Inc., 1996.

Gross, Kim Johnson, Jeff Stone, and Woody Hochswender. *Chic Simple. Men's Wardrobe*. New York: Alfred A. Knopf, Inc., 1998.

Hall, Lee. *Common Threads: A Parade of American Clothing*. Canada: Bulfinch Press, 1992.

Hochswender, Woody, and Kim Johnson Gross. *Men in Style: The Golden Age of Fashion from Esquire*. New York: Rizzoli International Publications, Inc., 1993.

Karpinski, Kenneth J. *Red Socks Don't Work: Messages from the Real World About Men's Clothing*. Manassas Park: Impact Publications, 1994.

Kinsel, Brenda. *In the Dressing Room with Brenda*. Berkley, Ca: Wildcat Canyon Press, 2001.

Lenius, Oscar. *A Well-Dressed Gentleman's Pocket Guide*. Great Britain: Prion Books, 1998.

Levene, Malcolm, and Kate Mayfield. *10 Steps to Fashion Freedom: Discover Your Personal Style from the Inside Out*. New York: Crown Publishers, 2001.

Luciano, Lynne. *Looking Good: Male Body Image in Modern America*. New York: Hill and Wang, 2001.

Marquand, Ed. *Beyond Soap, Water, and Comb: A Man's Guide to Good Grooming and Fitness*. New York: Abbeville Press Publications, 1998.

Martin, Richard, and Harold Koda. *Jocks and Nerds: Men's Style in the Twentieth Century*. New York: Rizzoli International Publications Inc., 1989.

McDowell, Colin. *The Man of Fashion: Peacock Males and Perfect Gentlemen*. New York: Thames and Hudson, 1997.

Meehan, Tim. *Suit Yourself: A Practical Guide to Men's Attire*. J. T. Meehan Publishing, 1999.

Moloney, Kathleen, and Glenn Waggoner. Esquire *Etiquette: The Modern Man's Guide to Good Form*. New York: Collier Books, 1987.

Newell, Waller R. *What Is a Man? : 3,000 Years of Wisdom on the Art of Manly Virtue*. New York: HarperCollins, 2000.

O'Hara Callan, Georgina. *The Thames and Hudson Dictionary of Fashion and Fashion Designers*. New York: Thames and Hudson Ltd., 1998.

Pinfold, Wallace G. *A Closer Shave: Man's Daily Search for Perfection*. New York: Artisan, 1999.

Prather, Hugh and Gayle. *A Book for Couples*. New York: MJF Books, 1988.

Rampersad, Arnold, and Rachel Robinson. *Jackie Robinson: A Biography*. New York: Alfred A. Knopf, Inc., 1997.

Reuter, Donald F. *Heartthrob: A Hundred Years of Beautiful Men*. New York: Universe Publishing, 1998.

Roetzel, Bernhard. *Gentleman: A Timeless Fashion*. Cologne: Könemann, 1999.

Salley, Columbus. *The Black 100: A Ranking of the Most Influential African-Americans, Past and Present*. New York: Citadel Press Books, 1993.

Schnurnberger, Lynn. *40,000 Years of Fashion: Let There Be Clothes*. New York: Workman Publishing, 1991.

Seitz, Victoria A. *Your Executive Image: How to Look Your Best & Project Success—For Men and Women*. Holbrook, Mass.: Adams Media Corporation, 1992.

Thourlby, William. *You Are What You Wear*. New York: Forbes/Wittenburg & Brown, 2001.

Tymorek, Stan. *Clotheslines: A Collection of Poetry and Art*. New York: Harry N. Abrams, Inc., Publishers, 2001.

Weber, Mark. *Dress Casually for Success for Men*. New York: McGraw-Hill, 1997.

Production Staff Credits

Creative Team

CREATIVE DIRECTOR: Lloyd Boston; PHOTOGRAPHER: Len Prince; PROJECT DIRECTOR: Craig Rose; CONTRIBUTING STYLIST: Sharon Pendana; SET DESIGN AND PROPPING: Westin Hill; MEN'S GROOMING DIRECTOR: Barry White; PHOTOGRAPHER'S 1ST. ASSISTANT: Robert Bean; PHOTOGRAPHER'S 2ND ASSISTANT: Scott Slater; VIDEOGRAPHER: Daryl Pendana; STYLIST ASSISTANTS: Naima Turner, Capree Feliciano, EJ Akbar, Lois Barret, Danny Suggs, Kwame Muhammed, Sean Allison; PHOTO RESEARCH EDITOR: Margarita Corporan; ILLUSTRATOR: Beth L. White; SENIOR RESEARCHER: Naima Turner; MODELS: Sean James-Ford, Damon Weeks-Next, Will Lamay-NY Models, James Magee-Click, Brian Lee Allen-Click,Chris Comfort-Ford, Todd Reigler- Ford, Rob O'Brien-TLG, Tre Bratt-TLG, Charles Deraczunas-TLG, Mike Dale-Click, Peter Hurley-Wilhelmina, Christina Ambers-Parts, Kevin Bulla-Click, Daryl Pendana, Craig Rose, Lloyd Boston, Brian Wince-NY Models; RESEARCHERS: G. Boyd Caldwell, Anthony Q. Bell, Stephanie Scott, Sean Allison, Calvin Moore, Nicole Brewer, EJ Akbar, Jennifer Griffin

Hair and Makeup Credits

Women's Roundtable: MAKEUP: Kim Weinstein; Shanon Grey Williams; HAIR: Brian Magallones for Oscar Blandi; Oscar James. *Tommy Hilfiger (foreword):* MAKEUP: Kim Weinstein; HAIR: Anthony Sorensen. *Lloyd Boston (foreword):* MAKEUP: Kim Weinstein; HAIR: Terence "T-Nice" Payne. *Lloyd Boston (author shot):* MAKEUP: Barry White; HAIR: Terence "T-Nice" Payne. *Cynthia Rowley:* MAKEUP: Jared for Timothy Priano Artists; HAIR: Anthony Sorensen. *Alan Cumming:* MAKEUP: Jared for Timothy Priano Artists; HAIR: Anthony Sorensen. *Elisabeth Filarski:* MAKEUP: Matin Maulawizada; HAIR: Anthony Sorensen. *Tim Hasselbeck:* MAKEUP: Matin Maulawizada; HAIR: Anthony Sorensen. *Elisabeth Parkinson:* MAKEUP: Matin Maulawizada; HAIR: Anthony Sorensen. *Scott Wise:* MAKEUP: Matin Maulawizada; HAIR: Anthony Sorensen. *Lisa Ling:* MAKEUP: Kim Weinstein; HAIR: Gina Picone for Oscar Blandi. *Doug Ling:* HAIR: Barry White. *Kimora Lee-Simmons:* MAKEUP: Christopher Michael; HAIR: Oscar James. *Tiki Barber:* GROOMING: Kim Weinstein. *Ginny Barber:* MAKEUP: Kim Weinstein; HAIR: Gina Picone for Oscar Blandi. *Bobbi Brown:* HAIR: Brian Magallones for Oscar Blandi; MAKEUP: Bobbi Brown. *Steven Plofker:* HAIR: Brian Magallones for Oscar Blandi; GROOMING: Bobbi Brown. *Tyra Banks:* MAKEUP: Jay Manuel; HAIR: Oscar James. *Donald Banks:* GROOMING: Barry White. *Patti Labelle:* MAKEUP: Jay Manuel; HAIR: Johnny Gentry. *Zuri Edwards:* GROOMING: Barry White. *Star Jones:* MAKEUP: Jay Manuel; HAIR: Elena George. *Sean James, Tre Bratt & Charles Deraczunas:* GROOMING: Loretta Alston for Barry White. *Tamara Spinner:* MAKEUP: Christopher Michael; HAIR: Oscar James. *Brent Zachary:* GROOMING: Christopher Michael

Additional Credits

Kim Weinstein—makeup/grooming for Outerwear and Shirt Diagrams; Barry White—grooming for Suit, Pant, Spa, and Underwear Diagrams; Gina Picone for Oscar Blandi—hair for Outerwear and Shirt Diagrams

Furniture and accessories supplied by Property and Salon Moderne

Sabrina Schilcher

DATE			